Crossing Religious Boundaries

C000065071

Religious pluralism, as encountered in multi-faith settings such as Nigeria's biggest city Lagos, challenges much of what we have long taken for granted about religion, including the ready-made binaries of Christianity versus Islam, religion versus secularism, religious monism versus polytheism, and tradition versus modernity. In this book, Marloes Janson offers a rich ethnography of religions, religious pluralism and practice in Lagos, analysing how so-called 'religious shoppers' cross religious boundaries, and the coexistence of different religious traditions where practitioners engage with these simultaneously. Prompted to develop a broader conception of religion that shifts from a narrow analysis of religious traditions as mutually exclusive, Janson instead offers a perspective that focuses on the complex dynamics of their actual entanglements. Including real-life examples to illustrate religion in Lagos through religious practice and lived experiences, this study takes account of the ambivalence, inconsistency and unpredictability of lived religion, proposing assemblage as an analytical frame for exploring the conceptual and methodological possibilities that may open as a result.

Marloes Janson is Professor of West African Anthropology and Associate Director of Research at SOAS University of London, and Senior Fellow of the Higher Education Academy. Her work lies at the intersection of anthropology and religion, focusing on Nigeria and the Gambia. She is the author of *Islam, Youth, and Modernity in the Gambia: The Tablighi Jama'at* (2013) which received the Amaury Talbot Prize for African Anthropology in 2014.

THE INTERNATIONAL AFRICAN LIBRARY

The International African Library is a major monograph series from the International African Institute. Theoretically informed ethnographies, and studies of social relations 'on the ground' which are sensitive to local cultural forms, have long been central to the Institute's publications programme. The IAL maintains this strength and extends it into new areas of contemporary concern, both practical and intellectual. It includes works focused on the linkages between local, national and global levels of society; writings on political economy and power; studies at the interface of the socio-cultural and the environmental; analyses of the roles of religion, cosmology and ritual in social organization; and historical studies, especially those of a social, cultural or interdisciplinary character.

For a list of titles published in the series, please see the end of the book.

Crossing Religious Boundaries

Islam, Christianity, and 'Yoruba Religion' in Lagos, Nigeria

Marloes Janson

SOAS University of London

International African Institute, London

and

 CAMBRIDGE
UNIVERSITY PRESS

Shaftesbury Road, Cambridge CB2 8EA, United Kingdom

One Liberty Plaza, 20th Floor, New York, NY 10006, USA

477 Williamstown Road, Port Melbourne, VIC 3207, Australia

314–321, 3rd Floor, Plot 3, Splendor Forum, Jasola District Centre, New Delhi – 110025, India

103 Penang Road, #05–06/07, Visioncrest Commercial, Singapore 238467

Cambridge University Press is part of Cambridge University Press & Assessment, a department of the University of Cambridge.

We share the University's mission to contribute to society through the pursuit of education, learning and research at the highest international levels of excellence.

www.cambridge.org
Information on this title: www.cambridge.org/9781108969079

DOI: 10.1017/9781108979160

First published 2021
First paperback edition 2022

A catalogue record for this publication is available from the British Library

Library of Congress Cataloging-in-Publication data
Names: Janson, Marloes, author.
Title: Crossing religious boundaries : Islam, Christianity, and 'Yoruba religion'
    in Lagos, Nigeria / Marloes Janson, SOAS University of London.
Description: Cambridge ; New York : Cambridge University Press, 2021. |
    Series: The international African library | Includes bibliographical references
    and index.
Identifiers: LCCN 2020055275 (print) | LCCN 2020055276 (ebook) |
    ISBN 9781108838917 (hardback) | ISBN 9781108969079 (paperback) |
    ISBN 9781108979160 (epub)
Subjects: LCSH: Religious pluralism–Nigeria–Lagos. | Lagos (Nigeria)–
    Religion.
Classification: LCC BL2470.N5 J36 2021 (print) | LCC BL2470.N5 (ebook) |
    DDC 200.9669/1–dc23
LC record available at https://lccn.loc.gov/2020055275
LC ebook record available at https://lccn.loc.gov/2020055276

ISBN   978-1-108-83891-7   Hardback
ISBN   978-1-108-96907-9   Paperback

For my angels:
Martie Janson
Wil Pieëte
For my guardian angel:
Kees Janson

In loving memory of J. D. Y. Peel

What practical options are opened up or closed by the notion that the world has no significant binary features, that it is, on the contrary, divided into overlapping, fragmented cultures, hybrid selves, continuously dissolving and emerging social states?

Asad (2003: 15); emphasis in the original.

Contents

Illustrations

MAP

FIGURES

Acknowledgements

Research is a relationship, to echo the words of Jean-Paul Sartre. Indeed, this book is the result of the relationships that I have established over the years with many people. When I first mentioned that I wanted to switch research fields from Africa's smallest country, the Gambia, to the 'giant of Africa', Nigeria, several people reacted with shock. To echo the words of the Nigerian novelist Chibundu Onuzo (2017) in her immersive novel *Welcome to Lagos*, Lagos still evokes images – not completely unjustified but also not accounting for the megacity's versatility – of 'armed robbers, ritual killers, drug dealers' (68). The late Yoruba scholar J. D. Y. Peel reacted less alarmed: 'As a robust woman, you will be fine in Lagos'. Indeed, my research went well, which had less to do with my alleged 'robustness' and more with the enormous network of people who welcomed me, answered my many questions, took me along on their spiritual journeys, and gave me an insight into their lives. Unfortunately, I cannot mention them all by name here.

My former PhD supervisor, Peter Geschiere, put me in touch with the late political scientist Abubakar Momoh. Abu generously opened his house to me. He, his wife Tawa, and their son Muchin turned out to be the perfect hosts. Because their family home was far from my fieldwork sites, they helped me move to central Lagos, where I spent part of my field research with Tawa's mother, Mama Alhaja, in whom I found a loving host. Their driver, Mr K., traversed me safely through the hectic Lagos traffic. Abu's sudden death came as a great shock; may his soul rest in peace.

Abu introduced me to my research collaborators, Mustapha Bello and Tobi Oshodi. The description 'research collaborators' does not do justice to their input: my research benefitted tremendously from their insightful comments, their deep knowledge of Lagos, and their comradeship. On several occasions their students acted as research assistants. Other colleagues and friends to whom I owe much are the late Lateef Adetona (may his soul rest in peace), Amidu Sanni, Danoye Laguda, Selome Kuponu, Taiwo Olunlade, Olumuyiwa Falaiye, Imam Busairi,

Funke Adeboye, Ronke Christiana, Funke Oduwole, Ridwan Balogun, Oludare Ogungbe, and Folajimi Oyawoye. My special appreciation goes to the award-winning photographer Akintunde Akinleye, with whom I had the privilege to collaborate.

I wish to thank Tela Tella, the Lady Apostles, and the rest of the Tella family for welcoming me so warmly in *Ifeoluwa*, and Samsindeen Saka, Shadiat Popola, and Pastor Tunde for offering me hospitality in *Oke Tude*. Mustapha Bello introduced me to NASFAT's leadership and membership, which was the beginning of an extensive collaboration. Chief Ifabunmi introduced me to Ifa and to his group, *Ijo Orunmila*. Thanks to Bob, Mr Akindele, the Lawson family, Edith, and Dr Ademola for acquainting me with their deep spiritual insights. I am also grateful to Dr Daniel Olukoya and his team of 'prayer warriors' for allowing me access to the prayer camp of Mountain of Fire and Miracles Ministries (MFM) along the Lagos–Ibadan Expressway. Without them, and the hundreds of religious practitioners whom I met during my fieldwork, my research would not have been possible.

Other colleagues and friends to whom I am greatly indebted for their intellectual input and encouragement over the years are Adeline Masquelier, Ebenezer Obadare, Asonzeh Ukah, Benjamin Soares, Karin Barber, Insa Nolte, Stephan Lanz, Jochen Becker, Mamadou Diouf, Kai Kresse, Abdoulaye Sounaye, Louis Brenner, Egodi Uchendu, Murtala Ibrahim, Adeyemi Balogun, Murray Last, Adam Higazi, Hansjörg Dilger, Abdulkader Tayob, Dorothea Schulz, David Garbin, Simon Coleman, John Hollingworth, Joy Onyejiako, Angelica Baschiera, Jörg Haustein, Edward Simpson, David Mosse, Trevor Marchand, John Campbell, and Andrea Cornwall. Sedat Sag and Nikki Ditrolio of the North London Boxing Club, Özlem Biner, Wendy Willems, Carolien Janson, Mee Beran, Maryse van den Muysenberg, and Denise van Kesteren provided a welcome distraction from writing.

I have greatly benefitted from readings of an earlier version of this manuscript by Peter Geschiere, Birgit Meyer, and Richard Fardon. In all I have found sharp mentors and dear friends. Many of the ideas in this book have developed in conversation with Birgit, who kindly invited me to the workshops and seminars she organized as part of her research project Habitats and Habitus: Politics and Aesthetics of Religious World Making (2012–17). Although J. D. Y. Peel did not live long enough to read my manuscript, his magisterial work on the interactions between Christianity, Islam, and 'Yoruba religion' in south-western Nigeria provides the context and foil for this study of religious pluralism in Lagos. His scholarship and generosity have been a great source of inspiration. I am especially indebted to Adeline Masquelier and the two anonymous reviewers for their careful reading of my manuscript and their incisive comments. They have taught me some invaluable lessons about how to write in a more readable way. Stephanie Kitchen of the International African Institute and Maria Marsh, Thomas Haynes, and Dhivya Elavazhagan of Cambridge University Press provided excellent editorial assistance.

I wish to thank the Departments of Anthropology, African Studies, Religious Studies, and Theology at SOAS University of London, Leiden University, Utrecht University, the University of Göttingen, the University of Bergen, the University of Oxford, the University of Cambridge, the University of Edinburgh, the University of Leeds, the University of Kent, Leibniz-Zentrum Moderner Orient (ZMO), Freie Universität Berlin, Humboldt University Berlin, the participants in the Satthertwaite Colloquium organized by Richard Werbner in 2016, and the participants in the conference of The European Society for Intercultural Theology and Interreligious Studies in Sarajevo in 2019 for comments on earlier versions of the chapters in this book. I acknowledge the input of the students who took my New Religious Movements and Religions on the Move modules at SOAS and thank them for being my 'guinea pigs': many of the ideas presented in this monograph have been tested on them. I also found the discussions with my former PhD student Alina Apostu enlightening.

My research was made possible by generous research grants. The research that took place between 2010 and 2011 was funded by the Federal Ministry of Education and Research (BMBF) in Bonn, Germany, under the auspices of ZMO in Berlin. The research in 2013 was conducted as part of the project 'Global Prayers: Redemption and Liberation in the City', funded by Forum Transregionale Studien in Berlin, under the auspices of SOAS. The research in 2017 was conducted as part of the project 'Religious Reform, Faith-Based Development and the Public Sphere in Sub-Saharan Africa (Lagos, Dar es Salaam and Cape Town)', funded by the German Research Foundation (DFG), under the auspices of Freie Universität Berlin. Special thanks go to Gabriele Hänsel for navigating me through German bureaucracy. I thank SOAS for granting me a term of research leave during the writing of this book.

Some material and passages presented in Chapter 3 appeared in the articles 'Unity through Diversity: A Case Study of Chrislam in Lagos' (*Africa*, 2016b, 86 (4): 646–72) and 'Introduction: Towards a Framework for the Study of Christian–Muslim Encounters in Africa' (part of a special issue co-edited with Birgit Meyer in *Africa*, 2016, 86 (4): 615–19). Some material and passages presented in Chapter 4 appeared in the article 'Crossing Borders: The Case of NASFAT or "Pentecostal Islam" in Southwest Nigeria' (*Social Anthropology*, 2020, 28 (2): 418–33) and 'Modern Love in Lagos: Dating the Halal Way' (in *Femmes d'Afrique et emancipation. Entre normes sociales contraignantes et nouveaux possibles*, edited by Muriel Gomez-Perez and published by Karthala, 2018). Some of the photographs appeared in 'The Spiritual Highway: Religious World Making in Megacity Lagos (Nigeria)' (produced with Akintunde Akinleye for *Material Religion: The Journal of Objects, Art and Belief*, 2015, 11 (4): 550–62). I would like to thank representative of the Fela Kuti estate Catie Ginsburg for allowing me to reprint the cover of Fela Kuti's album *Shuffering and Shmiling* as the book's cover image.

This is a book about belief, or rather the absence of belief. I wish to thank my mother, Martie Janson, for always believing in me, although at times I gave up the belief that my research would result in a monograph, and for her unwavering support; she is my everything. My late father, Kees Janson, who is missed greatly, always accompanies me in spirit. Wil Pieëte showed me another dimension of 'being related'. I dedicate this book to my parents and to Willy with all my love, gratitude, and respect.

Glossary

Aborisa	'the one who propitiates *orisa*', referring to practitioners of 'Yoruba religion'
adura	prayer
Aladura	a cluster of churches founded by African religious innovators who triggered a series of revivals in Nigeria between the 1920s and 1930s
alafia	an all-round state of well-being, including health and prosperity
Alasofunfun	'White Garment Churches', i.e. African independent churches
alfa	Muslim cleric
asalatu	Muslim prayer group
ase	a concept that is believed to invoke divine forces
awo	secret
babalawo	diviner, priest of Ifa
bid'a	unlawful innovation, deviation from the Prophet Muhammad's path
danfo	minibus
da'wa	invitation or call to Islam
dhikr	remembrance of God by recalling His names
du'a	supererogatory prayer
ebo	sacrifice
egun	spirit possession
ese	a verse of Ifa sacred literature
esin	religion
hadith	account of what the Prophet Muhammad said or did
hajj	pilgrimage to Mecca
halal	lawful in Islam
haram	unlawful in Islam
hijab	veil
HU	the 'holy name of God' in Eckankar
ide	beads

Ifa	the name of an *orisa* and a Yoruba divination system
ile Ifa	'house of Ifa' or shrine
ilu	town, community
Imale	Yoruba term for Muslims
Iwe Odu Mimo	Holy Book of Divination Verses
jalbu	the preparation of amulets by Muslim clerics, 'spiritual consultancy'
jihad	holy war
jinn	evil spirit
Ka'aba	the most sacred site in Islam
karma	the spiritual principle of cause and effect
Mahanta	the Living ECK Master, i.e. the leader of Eckankar
Mahdi	the prophesied redeemer of Islam
malam	Islamic scholar
oba	king, ruler
obi pipa	Yoruba ritual of 'casting the lots'
odu	a chapter of Ifa literature. Each *odu* has a corresponding sign that appears in divination
olaju	enlightenment, development, progress
Olodumare	the Yoruba High God
Olorun	God Almighty
Oluwo	High Priest
Onibuko	Yoruba term for Christians
opele	divination chain used by Ifa priests
oriki	praise poetry
orisa	deity
Orunmila	the deity in charge of divination
sadaqat	alms
Sallah	the end of Ramadan celebration
Shari'a	Islamic law
sin	worship
Sunna	Prophetic traditions as recorded in the *hadith*
tafsir	Qur'anic exegesis
tahajjud	Muslim night vigil, all-night prayer meeting
tankara	term used in NASFAT for Qur'anic recitation
tariqa	Sufi order
tawhid	oneness of God; core principle in Islam
tude	ritual of 'running deliverance' as practised by Chrislamists

umma	global Muslim community
wahala	'trouble' in Pidgin English
wuridi	Muslim prayer session
zakat	religious tax in Islam that is mandatory for affluent Muslims

Lyrics: *Shuffering and Shmiling* by Fela Kuti

Suffer suffer suffer suffer
    Suffer for World
    Na your fault be that
    Me I say na your fault be that
    Suffer suffer for World
Enjoy for Heaven
    CHORUS: Amen
    Christians go dey *yab* [talk]
    CHORUS: Amen
    'In Spiritum Heavinus'
    CHORUS: Amen
    Moslems go dey call
    CHORUS: Amen
    'Allah wa Akbar'
    CHORUS: Amen
Open your eye everywhere
    Archbishop *na miliki* [have a good time]
    Pope na enjoyment
    Imam *na gbaladun* [enjoy]
Archbishop dey enjoy
    Pope self dey enjoy
    Imam self dey enjoy
    My brother *wetin* [what] you say? (2x)
    My sister wetin you go hear? (2x)
    Archbishop dey for London
    Pope dey for Rome
    My people – them go dey follow Bishop
    CHORUS: Amen
    Them go follow Pope
    CHORUS: Amen
    Them go follow Imam
    CHORUS: Amen

Them go go for London
CHORUS: Amen
Them go go for Rome
CHORUS: Amen
Them go go for Mecca
CHORUS: Amen
Them go carry all the money
CHORUS: Amen
Them go *juba* [worship] Bishop
CHORUS: Amen
Juba Pope
CHORUS: Amen
Juba Imam
CHORUS: Amen
Them go start to *yab* [talk to] themselves
Every day – for house
Every day – for road
Every day – for bus
Every day – for work
My people my people my people
Every day my people inside bus
CHORUS: Suffering and smiling
Forty-nine sitting ninety-nine standing
CHORUS: Suffering and smiling
Them go pack themselves in like sardine
CHORUS: Suffering and smiling
Them dey faint, them dey wake like cock
CHORUS: Suffering and smiling
Them go reach house water no dey
CHORUS: Suffering and smiling
Them go reach bed power no dey
CHORUS: Suffering and smiling
Them go reach road go-slow go come
CHORUS: Suffering and smiling
Them go reach road police go slap
CHORUS: Suffering and smiling
Them go reach road army go whip
CHORUS: Suffering and smiling
Them go look pocket money no dey
CHORUS: Suffering and smiling
Every day na the same thing
CHORUS: Suffering and smiling

Suffer suffer for World
    CHORUS: Amen
    Enjoy for Heaven
    CHORUS: Amen
    Christians go dey *yab*
    CHORUS: Amen
    'In Spiritum Heavinus'
    CHORUS: Amen
    Moslems go dey call
    CHORUS: Amen
    'Allah wa Akbar'
    CHORUS: Amen
How many many you go make
    CHORUS: Many many
    Suffer suffer for world
    CHORUS: Amen

Source: The Shrine – the unofficial website for Fela Kuti and
Afrobeat music

1   Introduction
Reforming the Study of Religious Reform

> Religions are lived, and it is in their living, in the full and tragic necessity of people's circumstances, that we encounter them, study and write about them, and compare them, in the full and tragic necessity of our circumstances   Orsi (2012: 13).

'Welcome to Lagos; here everything is possible' were the words with which my research collaborator Dr Mustapha Bello greeted me when I first arrived in Nigeria's former capital in 2010. That 'everything is possible' in this megacity I soon discovered when we drove by a three-storey building that, as Mustapha pointed out to me, hosted a mainline church, a Pentecostal church, and a mosque. Although he described himself as a 'die-hard Muslim', Mustapha did not seem to have any problem with a mosque sharing the same space with a church. Underlining the pragmatism that characterizes Lagosians, he argued that this was an 'economic use of space'. While in this particular building different religious institutions occupied different floors, I also came across movements mixing Islam and Christianity, sometimes in interaction with 'Yoruba religion',[1] during the course of my nine-month ethnographic field research in Lagos.

Although 'Yoruba religion' – which is premised on the belief that the material world is continuously affected by unseen powers such as the *orisas* or personalized deities – still plays an important role, Islam and Christianity have dominated the religious landscape in south-west Nigeria, a region called Yorubaland, since at least the 1950s. Islam arrived in what today is called Nigeria as early as the eighth century. Despite its expansion, Islam remained marginal until the time of Usman dan Fodio's jihad in Hausaland (modern northern Nigeria), which resulted in the creation of the Sokoto Caliphate; the largest state in

---

[1] As I will discuss in Chapter 5, there is no such separate entity as 'Yoruba religion'; what is called 'Yoruba religion' in the literature is a tradition that is very much part of Yoruba Islam and Christianity. For lack of a better alternative, I use 'Yoruba religion' in inverted commas (see also Brenner 1989).

West Africa until it was conquered by the British in the early twentieth century. The Sufi orders triggered a movement of mass conversion to Islam in Nigeria in the late nineteenth and early twentieth centuries. While Islam was already firmly rooted in Nigeria, Christianity started expanding only in the nineteenth century. Whereas the Muslim penetration of Nigeria has traditionally been associated with African traders and missionaries, Christian evangelists from Europe and the United States found it much harder to find acceptance in local communities. After a slow start, however, the nineteenth century witnessed an evangelical revival. The 'social gospel' (Shankar 2014) of Western education and medical mission proved to be the ultimate proselytizing instrument, as a result of which Christianity emerged as the dominant religion in Nigeria by the end of the colonial period.

The years just after the Nigerian Civil War (1967–70), when the growth in oil revenues raised hopes for Nigeria's national development, were a time of religious revival, when Islamic reformist and Pentecostal Christian movements mushroomed (Vaughan 2016). Whereas Islam and Christianity had initially developed largely independently, they now became competitors for converts and access to state facilities and distribution of resources. Within the context of the Muslim–Christian competition for supremacy in Nigeria, Christianity – and Pentecostal Christianity in particular – moved centre stage with the inception of democratic rule in 1999, and has been more or less hegemonic ever since (Obadare 2018). According to Marshall (2009), Nigeria is the cradle of the 'Pentecostal revolution' in Africa, that is, the source from which many of the doctrines and rituals associated with Pentecostalism on the continent have originated. These doctrines and rituals aim at individual and collective renewal through a process of conversion based on the idiom of new birth: becoming born-again means becoming a new person, set free from one's personal sinful past and corrupt cultural traditions. In this spirit, Pentecostalism carries the promise of hope: the hope of a better life, if not in this world then at least in the hereafter. Indeed, the Nigerian Pentecostal theologian Nimi Wariboko (2014) explains the upsurge of Pentecostalism in Nigeria by arguing that it presented itself as a moral alternative to the failed promises of the postcolonial state and as capable of moving the country into economic development.

Since the 1970s, Pentecostalism has profoundly changed the religious landscape in Nigeria, resulting not only in political cleavage along religious lines but also fuelling religious borrowing. In an effort to win converts and occupy urban space, mainline Christian and even Muslim movements in the south-west have copied styles and strategies from the religious superpower, Pentecostalism. Hence, it could be argued that the

Figure 1.1 Christian–Muslim interactions in Lagos.
Photographer: Akintunde Akinleye

Pentecostal revolution has provided the impetus for Muslim reform. Religious competition may thus induce mutual appropriation without religion automatically becoming weaponized. In this spirit, my monograph aims to develop a new comparative framework for the study of religion that is not organized around demarcation and separation, but is devoted to drawing out similarities and differences, overlaps and tensions, between religious traditions.

Despite the mutual appropriation between Islam and Christianity, Nigeria is often portrayed in the media, as well as in the academic literature, as a country torn by violence between Muslims and Christians – an image that has gained more currency since the upsurge of the militant Islamist group Boko Haram in north-eastern Nigeria in 2002. This rivalry, I argue, is just one aspect of Muslim–Christian manifold relations. This is not to say that I smooth over the detrimental effect of religious clashes. There is plenty of religious difference, also in the peaceful Yorubaland, but the case studies I present illustrate that difference does not automatically lead to violence or polarization; religious divergence could as well be the ground for a range of modes of copying, competition, and reciprocal exchange (Larkin 2016: 635) (Figure 1.1).

Highlighting that in practice the boundaries between religious traditions are not as sharply demarcated as depicted in the media and academic literature, many of the Lagosians with whom I worked during my field research described themselves as 'religious shoppers' who, contrary to Mustapha Bello who self-identified as a committed Muslim, had changed their religious allegiances or shifted between them. Whereas Rohregger (2009) uses 'religious shopping' as an etic term to refer to multiple religious affiliations within Christianity, my interlocutors used it as an emic term for multiple religious affiliations not only within but also across religious denominations. Because religious shopping is for Lagosians part of a local stock of images that they draw on in everyday living, it is well suited as a tool to study religion through the lens of pluralism: an analytical concept referring to the coexistence of different religious traditions in one site where religious practitioners engage simultaneously with different religious traditions (Eck 2007; Bochinger 2013; Berger 2014; Soares 2016).

A 39-year-old Yoruba man nicknamed 'Prince Charles', because he descends from a royal family, narrated his life story characterized by religious shopping,

I used to have a booming business in electronics imported from China. I made big money, lived in a huge mansion, and owned three cars, but I lost everything. At the time of my birth, my family had made a pact with *Mami Wata*.[2] In return for wealth, I was ordained to make a sacrifice before the age of 40. I'm turning 40 this year and I still didn't sacrifice. That's why things started going wrong. Since I don't want to return to my ancestors' traditional beliefs, I tried to turn the tide by shopping from one church to the other. I even worshipped in the Hare Krishna temple. One day I went to visit an old friend from university, who is a drug lord. Although I know that drug trafficking is Satanic, I was so desperate that I wanted to work for him. My friend taught me how to swallow kola nuts, as a way to prepare me for swallowing cocaine as a drugs courier to Europe. Close to my friend's place, I noticed a whitewashed compound with strange symbols on the fence. This made me curious and I decided to go inside. It must have been God calling me. That's how I discovered Chrislam [a Yoruba religious movement that mixes Christian and Muslim beliefs and practices; see Chapter 3]. Because Chrislam combines the best of both [Christianity and Islam], I'm expecting my breakthrough any moment.

As this narrative illustrates, religious shopping not only refers to moving in and out of religious movements but also to the mixing of elements from divergent religious traditions: in Prince Charles's case 'Yoruba

---

[2] Mami Wata is a mermaid-like spirit that is worshipped throughout West Africa known for her spiritual power and sumptuous seductions, luring her devotees with luxuries into her water kingdom (Bastian 1998).

Figure 1.2 Lagos as an urban apocalypse.
Photographer: Akintunde Akinleye

religion', Christianity, Islam, and even Hinduism. According to the self-identified religious shoppers with whom I worked, if one is in need of deliverance – understood by the Yoruba notion of *alafia*, a condition of well-being with health and prosperity as its main components – one cannot afford to be picky. Instead, one picks and chooses in the hope that by combining elements from different religious traditions one increases one's chances of having a good life. This conception of religious shopping aligns with the popular description of Yorubaland as a 'religious marketplace' (see Chapter 2), where religious practitioners act as consumers, choosing between the various religious options available to them, and where local criteria of religious value tend to prevail, inducing the religious entrepreneurs competing for a niche in the market to borrow each other's commodities.

Religious shopping needs to be studied against the backdrop of entrenched depictions of Lagos as an 'apocalyptic megacity' (Koolhaas 2001), that is, an urban landscape that evokes eschatological images of uncontrollable growth, poverty, disease, violence, and corruption (Figure 1.2). Indeed, in a context of uncertainty and instability, where one out of two Nigerians lives beneath the poverty line (Human Development Report 2006), it makes sense to strategically mobilize potency from multiple religious traditions in one's search for health and wealth by engaging in religious shopping. Thus, while Lagosians such as Prince Charles recognize religious boundaries between Islam, Christianity, and 'Yoruba religion', they cross them creatively while shopping around Lagos's religious marketplace in the hope that the mixing and matching of divergent religious elements allows them to live life more profitably, thereby converting doomsday scenarios of living in Lagos into opportunities for improvement and bliss.

Religious shopping challenges normative conceptions of religion as an integrated, internally consistent belief system.[3] These conventional notions are highly problematic because they ignore that in a pluriform religious setting such as Yorubaland, Muslims and Christians have long lived side by side, often in harmony with practitioners of 'Yoruba religion'; the boundaries between the three are not always sharply demarcated (Peel 2000, 2016a). My point here is that if we want to gain a better understanding of the dynamics of multifaith settings where Muslims, Christians, and practitioners of 'Yoruba religion' interact, align with, and copy from each other, we must bridge the common divide in the study of religion along theological boundaries and go beyond ready-made binary oppositions such as Islam versus Christianity, monotheism versus polytheism, and 'traditional' local versions of religion versus the 'world religions'.[4] It will then emerge that religious practice is not so much a matter of 'either/or' – a binary logic that permeates the study of religion – but rather of 'both/and' (Lambek 2008).

By analysing how religious shoppers mix and match divergent religious elements and cross religious boundaries, this book sheds light on practices of religious pluralism that transcend the either/or binary logic. By critically engaging with religious pluralism, I am answering Sanneh's (1975) call for a better grasp of interreligious encounters: 'It is important for us to begin to build on the rich legacy of personal meeting and

[3] Although the scholarly emphasis on religion as a consistent belief system has long been criticized (e.g. MacGaffey 1983; Ottenberg 1984; Fabian 1985; Hackett 1989; Kirsch 2004; Lambek 2008; McIntosh 2009, 2019; Spies 2013, 2019; Peel 2016a; Soares 2016; Nolte and Ogen 2017; Werbner 2018), there is still a tendency to study religious traditions as distinct.

[4] Both 'traditional' and 'world religion' are controversial concepts for various reasons. Although 'Yoruba religion' is often referred to in terms of an African Traditional Religion (ATR), the label 'traditional' misrepresents the religious reality on the ground. A significant proportion of the Yoruba population still participates in indigenous as well as Muslim and/or Christian rituals, which questions the conventional 'traditional' religion versus 'world religion' dichotomy (Peel 2016a; see Chapter 5). Unlike what the label of 'world religion' suggests, Masuzawa (2005) criticizes it as an apparatus of nineteenth-century European intellectual thought that constructs other religious traditions outside the West as reflections of itself.

communal encounter that is a hallmark of Christian–Muslim relations in numerous parts of Africa' (108). Sanneh's prediction that interreligious encounter, which he illustrated with a vignette of a Christian man reciting a Muslim prayer, heralded the arrival of an 'age of religious convergence' (107) has not come true. Three decades later, Soares (2006: 1) wrote in his landmark volume on Muslim–Christian encounters in Africa that the dynamics of their interactions are still not properly understood.[5] Around the same time, Larkin and Meyer (2006) proposed to look at reformist Islam and evangelical Christianity in West Africa as doppelgangers: 'enemies whose actions mirror each other and whose fates are largely intertwined' (287).[6] In their opinion, rather than taking for granted the opposition between Islam and Christianity, we should explore their convergence.

While these authors have moved away from ingrained conceptions of religion as bounded and distinct, there is still a persistent tendency in African studies to approach Muslim–Christian relations on the continent in terms of either religious conflict (a tendency that has gained more currency since 9/11 and the upsurge of Boko Haram) or what scholars attempting to advance ecumenical ideas have called 'interfaith dialogue'. Although these two approaches represent opposites, they suffer from the same limitation: they take religious boundaries for granted. Challenging the tendency to study Muslim–Christian interactions one-dimensionally in terms of either conflict or cooperation, this monograph maps the actual intersections between Muslims and Christians and how they relate to practitioners of 'Yoruba religion'. In a nutshell, my main argument can be summarized as follows: in order to fully understand how religion is practised in a multifaith setting, we must tackle the compartmentalization of the study of religion by taking religious pluralism – as manifested in the practice of religious shopping – as our starting point. This entails that we approach religion first and foremost as lived practice and experimental mixing.

---

[5] In his follow-up article, Soares (2016) concludes that even if it is now acknowledged by some scholars that it is no longer sufficient to study different religions as separate units, the study of Muslim–Christian encounters is only beginning to receive the attention that it deserves.

[6] For the study of Islam and Christianity as mirror images in Sub-Saharan Africa, see also Loimeier (2005); Cooper (2006); Marshall (2009); Janson and Akinleye (2015); Obadare (2016); Janson (2016b); Ibrahim (2017a, b). However, according to Peel (2016b) in a critical response to Larkin and Meyer's (2006) study, there are irreconcilable differences between Islam and Christianity, notably in the call for shari'a law and an Islamic state. Yet, although not taking jihad as their model to bring about religious reform, many current Pentecostal churches dream, more or less openly, about a Christian nation (Marshall 2009); hence the title of Obadare's (2018) *Pentecostal Republic*.

Living Religion

While doing research in the Gambia, I learned that many Muslim youths portray themselves as 'Born-Again Muslims' (Janson 2014, 2016a). Issued from the Christian lexicon, the 'born-again' concept they use to refer to themselves signals, as they explained to me, the influence of Chrislam preachers from Nigeria on local constructions of religious identity. I was intrigued by these itinerant preachers who practise a mixture of Christianity and Islam and wanted to know more about them. Having quickly exhausted my leads in the Gambia, I decided to go to the source. In 2010 I switched research fields from Lilliput nation the Gambia to the 'giant of Africa', that is, Nigeria.[7] The move was quite a culture shock, not only because of the scale of my new field site but also because – being raised in a scholarly tradition that perceives religions as mutually exclusive – I initially found myself somewhat uneasy with Chrislam and analogous movements that mix religious traditions.

I was not the only one who felt uneasy: every time I presented my research data on religious pluralism at conferences and seminars in the United Kingdom and Europe, my listeners' primary reaction was laughter.[8] They seemed to feel unsettled, not knowing how to make sense of pluriform religious movements such as Chrislam, thereby reducing them to something trivial against the backdrop of the more 'serious' religions, that is, Christianity and Islam. This reaction of downplaying pluriform religious movements that cannot be easily pigeonholed was very different from the response of many Lagosians when they heard that I was conducting research on movements that mix elements from various religious traditions. Although they did not necessarily agree with these movements, they echoed Mustapha Bello's words in the opening vignette and dryly remarked: 'Welcome to Lagos', thereby suggesting that religious pluralism is immanent in the ways Lagosians practise their faith.

My Western colleagues' and my own initial uneasiness with religious pluralism could be explained by the conventional Abrahamic understanding of religion as a bounded regime. Movements such as Chrislam propose a comparative model to escape mono-religious approaches, and provide an emic perspective on religious pluralism that forces us to rethink our assumptions of internal consistency and boundedness. To overcome essentialist notions of religion that are

---

[7] With its approximately two hundred million inhabitants, Nigeria is Africa's most populous country.
[8] Once the reaction to my presentation about Chrislam was less lighthearted. Afterwards, I received hate mail accusing me of heresy.

grounded in Western ideologies, the first step is to substitute the concept of 'religion' for the more fluid notion of 'religious tradition'. Rather than using reifying terms such as 'Islam' and 'Christianity', comparative religion scholar Wilfred Cantwell Smith (1962) understood the religious lives of individuals and groups to be derived from what he called 'cumulative religious traditions', which evolved under the diverse influences of historical and cultural contingency.[9] Instead of autonomous entities defined along the boundaries of a distinct content, a focus on religious traditions invites us to study religions in relation to each other. Religious encounters are then no longer viewed as encounters between discrete entities along a conflict-cooperation continuum but as relational processes, accounting for the incoherence, inconsistency, and unpredictability of lived religious practice, thereby allowing a more accurate picture of the dynamics of religious pluralism in Lagos.

However, substituting 'religion' for 'religious tradition' does not lead us much further if we stick to the common bifurcation between Islam and Christianity in the scholarship on religion. As Meyer and I have demonstrated in a special issue of *Africa* (Janson and Meyer 2016), the division of labour in studying religion along these lines is highly problematic because it ignores the fact that, despite the differences in the historical development of Islam and Christianity, in multifaith settings religious groups and individuals have long coexisted. This prompts us to develop a more inclusive anthropology of religious pluralism (Lambertz 2018: 33n.17),[10] that is, an anthropology that shifts the attention from a narrow analysis of Islam and Christianity as separate units structured around

---

[9] Along similar lines, Jonathan Smith (1998) – another early critic who engaged in the deconstruction of the category of religion – argued that religion has been invented by scholars of religion, '"Religion" is not a native term; it is a term created by scholars for their intellectual purposes and therefore is theirs to define. It is a second-order, generic concept that plays the same role in establishing a disciplinary horizon that a concept such as "language" plays in linguistics or "culture" plays in anthropology. There can be no disciplined study of religion without such a horizon' (281–2).

[10] According to Bochinger (2013), given its normative connotation we should refrain from using the term 'pluralism' and use 'plurality' (*Vielfalt*) instead. Whereas pluralism seeks to promote the peaceful living together of various religious traditions, plurality describes actual religious encounters, whether peaceful or not. In other words, whereas pluralism refers to an ideology, plurality serves as a descriptive term (Berger 2014: 1). My approach to religious pluralism is more in line with that of political philosopher Connolly (2005), for whom 'deep pluralism' embraces both the descriptive *and* normative. As I will show in Chapter 2, for the Yoruba people religious pluralism denotes lived practice as well as an ideology for peaceful coexistence, referred to as *olaju*.

distinctive theologies towards a perspective that focuses on the ways in which religious practitioners live religion.[11]

A focus on lived religion entails that we rethink the ingrained conceptualization of religion as doctrine, belief, and dogma, which is dictated by what Asad (1993) calls a 'Protestant legacy' that needs to be located historically but should not be taken as being universally valid, and concentrate instead on practice and being-in-the-world. This move away from orthodoxy (correct belief and doctrinal conformity) may help us in better understanding Lagosians' religious shopping. For religious shoppers such as Prince Charles, religion is less a matter of belief and doctrinal conformity and more of orthopraxy (correct religious practice), which allows them to navigate between religious traditions and mix elements from different traditions. On my question why Lagosians felt attracted by the new religious movements that are central in this book, an often-heard response was, 'They give me the tools to solve my problems'. Rather than belief, many Lagosians tend to privilege the performative power of religious practice that helps them cope with the contingencies of urban life – a life in which, according to several interlocutors, 'one doesn't know in the morning if and what one's going to eat in the evening'. Since religion is in this context of precarity not primarily about doctrine but about practical concerns, the pragmatic mixing of diverse – and sometimes contradictory – religious elements is permitted as long as it helps to overcome the challenges faced in everyday urban living.

Here it should be noted that the 'everyday' in Lagos is not akin to the taken-for-granted version of 'life as usual'. Rather, it stands for disorder and precariousness (see also Vigh 2009; Adebanwi 2017). To my common 'How are you?', the typical answer was not, as one would expect in small talk, 'I'm fine' but 'I'm managing' or, in Pidgin English, *Body dey inside cloth* (literally meaning 'I'm still wearing clothes'). Although this response made me tongue-tied, it is an obvious answer in a context of uncertainty caused by the dire economic situation. The Nigerian economy went into a downturn following the slump of the oil market in the 1980s, but, according to the International Monetary Fund (IMF) and the Central Bank of Nigeria (CBN), has plunged into recession since 2016 (Noko 2016). The current economic recession is a popular topic of discussion in the press and in *danfo*s, the minibuses that are an essential mode of public transportation in the lives of millions of Lagosians. Without any prompting, my fellow passengers often shared their views regarding the causes of the Nigerian recession. President Buhari's poor

---

[11] Scholars who have focused on lived religion include Marsden (2005); McGuire (2008a); and Schielke and Debevec (2012).

economic planning was held responsible for the current crisis, 'Although we're one of the world's largest oil producers, our mineral riches haven't resulted in an improvement in the quality of life for the majority' was an often-heard complaint. The inflation rate reached its nadir of nearly 19 per cent in 2016, resulting in the skyrocketing of consumer goods prices to the extent that, for instance, a bag of rice has become unaffordable, and not only for the poor. Lagosians were startled when in March 2017 a doctor parked his SUV in front of the Third Mainland Bridge, which connects Lagos Island with the mainland, and committed suicide by jumping into the Lagos Lagoon. This was the first of a series of (attempted) suicides that were allegedly induced by the economic recession, which also affected the upper middle class, as this example illustrates.[12] As economic hardship has become part of daily life in Lagos, societal turbulence and its social manifestations – as reflected in high rates of un- and underemployment, corruption, and staggering levels of criminality – have become endemic. In such a context of economic uncertainty and unpredictability it is not surprising that many Lagosians turn to religion, which offers them the hope of a good life and the tools to cope with precarity.

In order to shed light on lived religion in a pluriform setting such as Lagos, the central research question that guides this monograph is: how can we use religion as a concept that makes boundary crossing possible without falling into the pitfall of essentializing it? And a related question: how can we engage in religious comparison, which implies some kind of unity, across and through diversity? I propose that the answer to these questions lies in studying religion as lived in everyday encounters. A focus on lived religion may eventually shift the attention from a narrow analysis of religions as mutually exclusive to the complex multi-level dynamics of actual entanglements, employed here as a term that 'works with difference and sameness but also with their limits, their predicaments, their moments of complication' (Nuttall 2009: 1).

In taking lived religion in an entangled lifeworld as my point of departure, the theoretical argument that I aim to establish is that the persistent conceptualization of religions as mutually exclusive entities constituted by a belief in God is untenable for, as Fabian (1985) claims, 'expectations regarding the logical consistency and coherence of belief systems often lead to elegant but potentially misleading descriptions' (139). In this spirit, my book is to be read as an attempt to abandon our disciplinary obsessions with 'coherence' and 'consistency' (Ewing

---

[12] See www.vanguardngr.com/2017/04/lagos-raises-alarm-increasing-rate-suicide/.

1990; Robbins 2007) in order to get to grips with the idiosyncratic ways in which religion is practised in everyday living, which are often marked by ambivalence, contradiction, and double standards rather than by neat divisions along religious boundaries. To sum up, to unlock analytical space in the nearly hermetically sealed scholarships of Islam and Christianity I aim to develop a programmatic vision for the reform of the study of religious reform – a reform that shifts the attention from a narrow analysis of Islam and Christianity as separate entities structured around distinctive theologies and orthodoxies towards a perspective that focuses on the ways in which Lagosians live religion and its ambiguities, inconsistencies, and aspirations as the constitutive moments in their lived religion.

Coping with Religious Pluralism

By studying religion through the vector of religious practice and lived experience, the entanglements between Islam and Christianity (see Chapters 3 and 4), as well as between monotheistic and polytheistic religions (see Chapters 5 and 6), come into the picture. The challenge in this monograph is to explore religious pluralism from a standpoint beyond the rather well-trodden paths that take 'syncretism' – originally a Greek word that became the preferred term for the combination of elements from two or more different religious traditions in the study of religion (Stewart 1999: 58) – as a conceptual frame. The problem here is that, as many scholars have remarked,[13] the notion of syncretism presupposes the distinctness of religious traditions and takes mixing as a deviation. But rather than religious boundedness as norm and religious fluidity as anomaly, the practice of religious shopping suggests that the mixing of religious elements is part of lived religion in Lagos. In this section I explore the shortcomings of syncretism and related analytical tools to study the complexities of religious mixing and propose assemblage as an alternative heuristic device. My broader mission is to explore the conceptual and methodological possibilities that may open if we take our lead from assemblage, and this book makes its potential evident by applying assemblage theory to a number of ethnographic case studies that shed light on religious pluralism in Lagos.

One of the reasons why scholars of religion have long found it difficult to come to terms with Islam and Christianity in Africa was their tacit partition between an orthodox version of 'world religion' and a syncretic

---

[13] See e.g. Droogers (1989); Shaw and Stewart (1994); Gellner (1997); Stewart (1999); Leopold and Jensen (2004); McIntosh (2009, 2019); Gez et al. (2017).

'African' version – a dilution of the 'pure' religion with 'traditional' African beliefs and practices (Chidester 1996; Meyer 2004). In such a view, the adjective 'African' came to stand for an adulterated form of the 'world religions' imported from the Arab Muslim world and the Western world. Underscoring the pejorative connotation of syncretism, Shaw and Stewart (1994) write, '"Syncretism" is a contentious term, often taken to imply "inauthenticity" or "contamination", the infiltration of a supposedly "pure" tradition by symbols and meanings seen as belonging to other, incompatible traditions' (1). At stake here is the power to identify 'true' religion and to authorize some practices as 'truthful' and others as 'false' or 'syncretic'.

Despite its pejorative connotation, syncretism remains in wide circulation today. According to McIntosh (2009: 185), its persistence can be explained by its relevance to popular explorations of 'bricolage' (Lévi-Strauss 1966; Mary 2005), 'creolization' (Hannerz 1987; Palmié 2006), and 'hybridity' (Clifford 1988; Bhabha 1994). These conceptions of cultural and religious mixing dismantled older anthropological assumptions of cultural boundedness, fixity, and homogeneity. Still, they share with syncretism a derogatory connotation: while bricolage emphasizes the mixing of dissonant elements, thereby having the connotation of chaos and disorder, creolization and hybridity carry a colonial baggage of racism and debasement (Abou-El-Haj 1991: 143; Stewart 1999: 41). Although each of these concepts is accompanied by a longstanding debate, my main concern is that they cannot analyse religious traditions that coexist without turning them into a coherent belief system. Because their underlying principle is commensurability (Spies 2013), the outcome of syncretization, bricolage, creolization, and hybridization is viewed as a new entity, thereby highlighting coherence and consistency. Rethinking our ingrained classificatory schemes will help us deal with instances where Lagosians refer to Islam, Christianity, and 'Yoruba religion' without feeling the need to choose between those traditions, and where religious elements are juxtaposed without necessarily being synthesized.

In an effort to overcome notions of religious pluralism that tend to be reductionist and static because they conceptualize diversity as the many sub-forms of a single instance or the parts of a 'pure' whole, Spies (2019) argues for a theory of religious diversity that sees religions not as discrete units brought into interaction – sometimes clashing, sometimes mixing – but rather as ongoing processes constituted by their interrelations. Her example of the mission work of a Nigerian Pentecostal church in Madagascar – an island with multiple religious traditions and cultural influences – demonstrates how religious actors and communities can be understood as products of continuous relational processes. Because a relational approach to religion does not differentiate types of religion, it is better suited for grasping what Spies calls 'the fuzziness, dynamics, and complexities of everyday life' (66–7).

In a similar vein, McIntosh (2019) developed a theory of relational religion grounded in the complex character of religious practice and the fluid nature of everyday life in East Africa. The ritual practice of the Giriama people on the Kenyan coast is one of two separate systems of supernatural power – 'traditional' religion and Islam – that do not overlap or bleed into each other; each has its own spiritual forces and its own terms of address. This complex type of ritual practice is, according to McIntosh, not well described by the term 'syncretism'. Rather than the reconciliation of diverse practices into a syncretic whole, what we see here is that religious pluralism preserves discontinuity between loci of religious power – a model she calls 'polyontologism'.[14] Polyontology is a form of pluralism that recognizes the ontological reality of distinct sources of religious power. Hence, in polyontologist practices plural ontologies are not modelled as ultimately one, nor are their associated deities or forces semiotically aligned or equated (117). In other words, while differences between the two systems are recognized by the Giriama, they do not remark on the apparent contradiction in their religious practice because they are not preoccupied with an imperative notion of singular truth in religion (119n.5).

Taking my cues from the pioneering work by Spies and McIntosh, I propose assemblage as an alternative conceptual frame to shed light on the practices of religious pluralism that I encountered during my field research in Lagos. In their *A Thousand Plateaus*, the philosophers Deleuze and Guattari (1987) define assemblage as the causally productive result of the intersection of two open systems – what they call a 'machinic process' – resulting in 'multiplicity'. In French *assemblage* – connoting mixing, collating, or joining – is not a static term; an assemblage is not a set of predetermined parts that are then put together into an already conceived structure (Wise 2005: 77). To paraphrase Deleuze and Guattari (1987), we do not know what an assemblage *is* until we find out what it can *do*, 'we will call an assemblage every constellation of singularities and traits deducted from the flow – selected, organized, stratified –

---

[14] For a version of polyontologism in Mozambique, where the Makhuwa people toggle between 'traditional' religion and Pentecostalism, see Premawardhana (2018). Premawardhana attributes the Makhuwas' religious fluidity to an underlying existential mobility. In many parts of East Africa and the wider Indian Ocean region, mobility has long been a way of life, which explains the reluctance of peoples such as the Makhuwa to root themselves in a single religious tradition.

in such a way as to converge (consistency) artificially and naturally; an assemblage, in this sense, is a veritable invention' (406). Put differently, assemblage refers to a collection of heterogeneous elements that is not fixed, but is constantly being made, remade, and unmade.

Deleuze and Guattari's understanding of states of temporal instability, combined with the rhizomatic as a productive property of the interaction of open systems, has influenced the use of assemblage by social scientists as an anti-structural concept that connotes emergence, heterogeneity, the decentred, the evanescent, and the ephemeral (Marcus and Saka 2006: 104–5). For example, anthropologists Collier and Ong (2005) define assemblage as,

[T]he product of multiple determinations that are not reducible to a single logic. The temporality of an assemblage is emergent. It does not always involve new forms, but forms that are shifting, in formation, or at stake ... assemblage implies heterogeneous, contingent, unstable, partial, and situated (12).

In a similar vein, for sociologist Sassen (2006) the power of assemblage lies in understanding how something as heterogeneous as nation-states hold together without ceasing to be heterogeneous. These authors' stress on non-coherence is in line with Derrida's (1982: 3–27) use of assemblage, which points to the normalcy of incongruity in life in the postmodern era. Similar to the social sciences and humanities, in the arts assemblage – a term that, according to Blier (2018: 96–7), was invented by Picasso for an art form made from recycled materials – is used as a composite concept denoting fragmentation and improvisation. Over the past two decades, assemblage has acquired a range of different meanings in different disciplines but, according to cultural theorist Venn (2006), the different usages all emphasize 'adaptivity rather than fixity or essence ... co-articulation and compossibility rather than linear and discrete determination, multilinear time and the temporality of processes' (107). Of particular relevance to my study is the primacy that assemblage accords to emergence, heterogeneity, and open-endedness. Taking this course, it offers a theoretical tool that begins from the diversity of parts and sheds light on the specific ways in which religious formations emerge across and through differences.

Inspired by Deleuze and Guattari, I employ assemblage theory as a lens through which to study the fluid nature of the religious configurations that have cropped up in Lagos since the religious revival of the 1970s. In these configurations Islam, Christianity, and 'Yoruba religion' are not assimilated but exist side by side, representing distinct loci for achieving a life of success, wealth, and good health. For example, the practitioners of Chrislam, who self-identify as Chrislamists, do not consider Christianity and Islam contradictory but rather complementary and this explains why they, to some extent, retain rather than reconcile the distinctions between the two religious traditions. As will be shown in Chapter 3, Chrislamists believe that by combining Christian and Muslim beliefs and practices they can be blessed in multiple ways. Also, the Muslim mass organization *Nasrul-Lahi-il Fathi* Society of Nigeria (NASFAT) mixes Islam with Pentecostal styles and strategies. Chapter 4 illustrates that, in the case of NASFAT, the assemblage of Muslim and Christian beliefs and practices has, somewhat paradoxically, preserved its Muslim distinctiveness. Rather than mixing two mono-theistic traditions, Chapter 5 illustrates that the adherents of The Indigenous Faith of Africa (IFA), *Ijo Orunmila Ato*, deliberately man-oeuvre between 'Yoruba religion' and Christianity, appropriating the perceived powers of both. The adherents of the Grail Movement and Eckankar, two new religio-spiritual movements in Lagos that I discuss in Chapter 6, even go a step further in that they mix not only Islam, Christianity, and 'Yoruba religion' but also elements from the 'Eastern' religions and non-religious sources in their search for spiritual self-development. The extended case studies illustrate that in Lagos's pluri-form setting, far from being reasoned away as in syncretism, the incon-sistencies between Islam and Christianity on the one hand, and between religious monism and polytheism on the other, are embraced in order to simultaneously access various types of redemption and enhance one's chances of achieving a good life. The underlying idea is that different religious traditions solve different problems and may therefore coexist, without causing conflict and without the need to synthesize into a single belief system.

To sum up, the merit of taking assemblage as a conceptual frame is that it allows studying religion as lived, which necessitates the mixing of elements that may be inconsistent, ambiguous, or contradictory, rather than as a bounded, coherent belief system. Because assemblage connotes emergence rather than resultant formation as in syncretism, it highlights the agency and creativity involved in the process of mixing. As such, assemblage supports an actor-centric, pragmatic analysis of religion. Assemblage operates through religious shoppers, who are the experts at assemblage because they are not constrained by notions of religious boundary. Although they may acknowledge the existence of religious differences, to them, other than in syncretism, these differences do not necessarily stand for discrepancies. Furthermore, assemblage emphasizes improvisation. The uncertainty and unpredictability of urban living may then no longer evoke eschatological registers of apocalypse (Koolhaas 2001), but can be seen as conditions for stimulating ingenuity and

resourcefulness. In brief, by studying different modes of religious pluralism in terms of assemblage rather than syncretism, I intend to move
beyond essentializing notions of religion, and focus instead on processes
of emergence and becoming, or, as I would like to put it, processes of
living religion. Taking this course, a focus on assemblage may overcome
not only the compartmentalized research on religion in pluriform settings
where one scholar studies 'Islam', another 'Christianity', and a third
'African Traditional Religion' (ATR) but also goes a step further by
dissolving 'religion' as a unified category (see also Spies 2019: 76).

Urban-Religious Assemblages

Contrary to the religiously homogeneous northern and south-eastern
parts of Nigeria, called Hausaland and Igboland respectively, religious
pluralism is considered in Yorubaland in the south-west not a sign of
heresy but a source of pride. Indeed, Laguda (2015: 51) notes that the
more groups a Yoruba belongs to, the more respect he earns in the
community. While practices of religious pluralism characterize lived
religion throughout Yorubaland, the assemblage of multiple religious
traditions occurs first and foremost in urban contexts (Albera 2012:
227). Hence, Yorubaland's teeming centre Lagos[15] – dubbed 'the centre
of one of the largest urban areas in the world' (Ukah 2013: 179) – is a
good place to think about assemblage as a form of lived religion.

The religious movements that form the core of this monograph have
wider relevance beyond Lagos; several have branches elsewhere in
Yorubaland and beyond. Still, this monograph needs to be read as an
urban ethnography. Lagos is not only the economic centre of
Yorubaland; it is also the hub for religious interaction and experimentation among urbanites who inhabit an environment that produces a
dizzying array of challenges and opportunities. By examining how
Lagosians mobilize religion as everyday technology of survival this book
sets out to analyse the place and function of religion in the production
and maintenance of urban life. I propose that Lagos's status as a 'hypercity'[16] needs to be studied in tandem with the hyper-religiosity and ever-

---

[15] According to the Yoruba historical tradition, Ile-Ife is the centre of the Yoruba cosmos: it
is considered the first city in the world, the birthplace of the gods and the place where the
orisa first came to the world (Olupona 2011). Still, Lagos is seen as the economic and
financial centre of Yorubaland because it produces some 40 per cent of Nigeria's GDP
(Ukah 2016: 526). Although Lagos has a multi-ethnic population, it is regarded as
culturally more Yoruba (see Chapter 2).

[16] The United Nations Center for Human Settlements uses the term 'megacity' for urban
agglomerations with more than 10 million inhabitants (UNCHS 1996). Since, according

shifting dynamics of religious pluralism that one encounters there. To put it differently, Lagos is not just the *mise en scene* for practices of religious pluralism but also produces impromptu forms of religion that are not self-contained but are shifting and in flux, making the hypercity an 'urban-religious assemblage' (Lanz 2013) in and of itself. My focus on urban-religious assemblages entails that we study how Lagos has produced new forms of religiosity and how these have inscribed themselves in urban space.

Although its particular religious constellation makes Lagos an ideal laboratory for a cultural anthropologist whose aim it is to develop an anthropology of religious pluralism, I am still not sure whether I like or hate my fieldwork setting. In this, I resemble Lagosians who have a popular saying about their city, 'Love to hate her, or hate to love her.' Underscoring Lagosians' ambivalent attitude to their habitat, Mustapha Bello said, 'Whereas visitors to other Nigerian cities are greeted with a banner with the words "Welcome to city so and so", visitors to Lagos are welcomed with "This is Lagos".' This scanty welcome needs to be interpreted as 'nobody will care for you, and you have to struggle to survive' (Packer 2006). Indeed, everyday living in Lagos is characterized by a constant battle against traffic, pollution, poverty, crime, and corruption. Elucidating what life is like in Lagos, my friend, a professional working for a multinational, told me that she wakes up every morning at 4am to reach her workplace at Lagos Island (due to the costs of living, she cannot afford to rent there) before rush hour, and she stays till late at night when traffic has slowed down. Her journey takes so long not only because of the traffic but also because of the many road blocks. She sighed, 'Yesterday, I was stopped by the traffic police because of an imaginary problem with my headlight; today, I might be stopped on my way home because of another minor issue. You have to play the game; only after paying a bribe you can continue your journey. That's Lagos for you!' My friend's journey is not only stressful because of the corrupt traffic police but also because of the danger of armed robbers, who operate late at night. Still, she considered herself lucky because, unlike many of her peers who are either un- or underemployed, she has a good job. It is not merely suffering and doom, however, that is the order of the day in Lagos. In her essay *At Home in Lagos*, the iconic Nigerian novelist Chimamanda Ngozi Adichie (2019) describes Lagos's upbeat side: its striving and trying, a city that is forward-looking and pulsing, which intimidates with its high-end estates and stylish people. Resolving the

to recent estimates, Lagos has a population of over 20 million, it counts as what urbanists call a 'hypercity' (Nas and Samuels 2006).

tension between the two popular images of the city, its impossibility and extraordinarity, Adichie concludes, 'Lagos is Lagos'.

It is not easy to describe life in Lagos to those who have never been there. I think Smith's (2007) description that in Lagos 'the volume is turned up – sometimes too high' (xii) is appropriate. Despite several attempts by former Lagos State Governor Babatunde Fashola (2007–15) to implement a law that prohibits religious organizations from using loudspeakers at night, Lagos's soundscape is marked by 'religious noise' (Larkin 2008a).[17] Lagos's huge population and process of rapid urbanization contribute to a sense of life that is not only loud but also turbulent and hectic, where survival depends on improvisation, risk-taking, and wit. Such an extreme urban environment necessitates urban-ites to act as what is called a 'hustler' in English or a *cascadeur* in French,

a daredevil, someone with courage, ready to take risks and deal with life's risks. … The disabling factors that constantly impact urban dwellers' lives force them to be flexible and master the tricky skills of improvisation and excel in the mental gymnastics necessary to transcend or outlive the moment and survive on a daily basis (De Boeck and Baloji 2016: 76).

In an economy marked by hustling, many of my interlocutors considered multiple religious belonging and the mixing of divergent religious trad-itions an example of the resourcefulness of Lagosians who, by appropri-ating Muslim, Christian, as well as Yoruba practices, increase their chances of having a good life. In other words, religious shopping is a necessary condition for 'living the city' (Macamo 2018: 7).

As several studies have illustrated (e.g. Coleman 2009; Ukah 2013, 2016; Marshall 2014), Pentecostalism in Nigeria is about urban space. Pentecostalism not only needs the city – the site of illicit temptation – against which to position itself ideologically but also requires urban infrastructure, such as large warehouse-style halls and massive prayer camps, to engage in dramatic prayer rituals and evangelical practices that form the basis of its appeal. In this spirit, Lagos's cityscape and the Pentecostal upsurge have jointly produced urban renewal and religious transformation. Although the transformation of Lagos's cityscape seems to be driven by Pentecostalism, it is certainly not the only mode of urban identification. Lagos has to a large extent been shaped by Islam, such as

---

[17] Despite a new law that bans the use of externally placed speakers by religious organizations, which was implemented by Lagos State Environmental Protection Agency (LASEPA) in May 2016, 'religious noise pollution' is an often-heard complaint in Lagos. Mustapha Bello and his wife have written several angry letters to the Lagos State Government, complaining that the night vigils organized by the Pentecostal church in their street prevent them from sleeping.

in its architecture and soundscape, where Qur'anic recitation and tape-recorded sermons endeavour to drown out Pentecostal preaching and hymns. My Pentecostal neighbour's reaction that he felt 'intimidated' by the height of the minarets of the mosques in our neighbourhood and the call for prayer (*adhan*) 'vomited out' of loudspeakers five times a day shows that architecture and media technologies have created a contested socio-religious space in Lagos. Indeed, to paraphrase Larkin (2016), these are part of 'the common ecology of urban life' (635) through which Islam and Christianity compete but also copy from one another. Apart from the sacrifices at crossroads, that is, locations betwixt and between the worlds of the living and the deities, 'Yoruba religion' plays a much less visible and audible role in Lagos than Christianity and Islam.

Other than the Pentecostal megachurches and the Muslim mass organization NASFAT, most of the urban-religious assemblages I present in this book are much smaller, composed of a few hundred or even a few dozen adherents. For instance, the oldest Chrislam movement has only some fifty followers. Its leader prefers having a small membership so that he can lead his movement as a 'spiritual family'. In a similar vein, a female leader prided Eckankar's exclusivism by saying that 'it's not for everyone'. Their small size raises the question of representativity. Although the religious-urban assemblages that are central here may not all be representative of the large-scale religious upsurge taking place in Lagos today, I argue that they can be seen as symptoms of wider religious shifts and transformations that are difficult to map because of the persistent tendency among scholars of religion to emphasize religious boundaries. What appear as marginal phenomena may then be central for my aim to develop new analytical perspectives that enable a better understanding of the ways in which urban Muslims, Christians, and practitioners of 'Yoruba religion' live religion and engage with each other in various configurations and modalities beyond the conflict-cooperation continuum. By taking such a course, the case studies have the potential to illuminate not just a unique Yoruba experience, but to raise wider questions about Muslim–Christian encounters and pluralism as a social situation and a political disposition in an entangled world in which people with different ethnicities and worldviews live together.

Religiosity and urbanity have in common that they are both about the 'engineering of certainty' (Mbembe and Nuttall 2004: 361). The reasons why people turn to religion often overlap with their motivations to migrate to the city: they strive for a better life. By paying attention to Lagosians' aspirations and imaginings of a good life, I seek to answer Robbins' (2013) call for an 'anthropology of the good' that overcomes the discipline's reliance on a metanarrative of 'suffering'. This metanarrative has deeply encroached on urban ethnographies, in which African cities are described as dangerous, dirty, and dysfunctional.[18] My ethnographic account of religious assemblages in Lagos seeks to complicate such facile generalizations by considering the astonishing creativity and the tactics of improvisation that religious shoppers tap in navigating the city.[19]

Navigating Lagos

I employ assemblage not only as a frame for conceptualizing modes of religious pluralism and the interlocking of religiosity and urban space but also as a methodological tool. As a methodology, assemblage may offer a fresh perspective on Lagos's vibrant cityscape as emergent from multiple overlapping and intersecting religious practices, infrastructural fragments, and social processes. Because the practices, fragments, and processes that constitute the megacity are always in flux, my field research, which took place between 2010 and 2017 (approximately nine months altogether), necessitated a mobile and flexible method. By navigating Lagos, I explored the co-production of the cityscape and religious lifeworlds. Below I map how I navigated my field site and the obstacles I met along the way.

When I switched research fields from the Gambia to Lagos, the scale of my new field site necessitated that I broaden my fieldwork method. Whereas I was used to conducting participant observation in demarcated villages and small towns, and interviewing interlocutors whom I selected via snowball sampling,[20] I now had to find a way to conduct ethnographic research in a megacity where livelihoods are provisional, where forms of social interaction are shifting, and where residents are constantly on the move, often changing their religious affiliations along the way. Making research methods responsive to the dynamic realities of religion in motion, Capps (1979) proposed that the methodology in the study of religion must be mobile enough to come to terms with the 'change factor', 'the moving, inconstant, spontaneous, irregular, discontinuous, non-forensic, once-only, explosive, surprise element'

---

[18] For a warning against such stereotyping, see Masquelier (2019).
[19] Here I use 'navigation' in the sense of Vigh (2009) as referring to how people act in uncertain circumstances, using a combination of wit and flexibility that allows them to adapt to a landscape of fluctuating opportunities.
[20] Snowball sampling is a technique used in the social sciences where research participants with whom contact has already been made use their social networks to refer the researcher to other interlocutors. In large fieldwork settings, snowball sampling is less useful.

(185; cited in Chidester 2018: 152). Although Capps called for a methodological turn in the study of religion as early as the 1970s, anthropologists and other scholars of religion still seem to have difficulties in coping with flux, focusing instead on 'enduring essences, stable structures, or recurring patterns' (Chidester 2018: 157).

To get a better sense of both the ephemerality and sacrality of the city, De Boeck (2013) proposes that urbanists 'circumambulate' urban space. This reminds of de Certeau's influential essay *Walking in the City* (1984), in which he understands walking as a way to read the city from the street-level, as a lived complexity that requires alternative maps based on wandering (Mbembe and Nuttall 2004: 361). Whereas walking is a mundane activity, circumambulating has the connotation of walking around something sacred, as part of a ritual such as in *tawaf* when pilgrims circle the Ka'aba (the most sacred site in Islam) seven times. Lagos, where car wrecks on the tarmac are common sights, does not lend itself particularly well to walking. Marshall writes, 'People don't *flâne* or stroll, or even walk, in Lagos. They trek, they rush from place to place, dash across expressways and fight for seats in taxis and buses' (2014: 112n.8). Inspired by De Boeck's circumambulation method, I hired a *kabu kabu* – an unlicensed taxi – to navigate Lagos's cityscape and chart its religious topology. My research budget did not allow me to hire a licensed taxi.[21] Moreover, unlike a licensed taxi that is painted yellow, a *kabu kabu* looks like an ordinary passenger car and therefore allowed me to observe Lagos's citylife relatively anonymously, as a 'voyeur' (de Certeau 1984).[22]

I spent a great part of my field research on the road stuck in 'go-slows' and 'no-go's', Nigerian slang for traffic congestion. While annoying, these traffic jams provided me a window into the various ways Lagosians shape their religiosity: in their use of space (Muslims blocking the streets during Friday prayers and Christians blocking the streets during Pentecostal crusades), architecture, billboards (since most road users have resorted to religion to avert the dangers of the road, religious billboards seem to have replaced traffic signs), sounds, the sacrifices placed at crossroads (a common practice among practitioners of

---

[21] Ironically, in a city where as part of everyday survival strategies residents constantly stretch the boundaries between the legal and illegal, I engaged in an illegal activity myself by hiring an unlicensed taxi. Once the driver and I were arrested, but after paying a bribe to the traffic police we were on the road again.

[22] Koolhaas (2002) rented a presidential helicopter to 'decode' Lagos from an aerial vantage point. The difficulty of decoding Lagos from the ground is summed up in the words of a local official overseeing Lagos Island: '[In Lagos], the problem is everything is happening everywhere' (Packer 2006).

'Yoruba religion'), apparel, and the paraphernalia that are used to mark religious identity (like the prayer beads on my driver's rear-view mirror). My circumambulation of Lagos helped me to get a better overview of the jumble of neighbourhoods and religious sites, and eventually to develop a spiritual map with which to read the city, pointing out relations between mosques, churches, and other religious organizations that at first sight seemed to be separate locations.

Although I began by observing Lagos's religious citylife from behind a car window – somewhat similar to de Certeau's (1984) operation of 'window shopping' – my focus on lived religion meant that I soon had to exchange the comfort of the *kabu kabu*'s backseat for participant observation in Lagos's pluriform religious landscape. During my ethnographic research, I adopted an actor-centred and practice-oriented approach, focusing less on religious worldviews and more on how religious practitioners live and do religion. To explore religion through the vector of religious practice, I found Droogers' (2014: 69–77) 'methodological ludism' useful. Methodological ludism is premised on the anthropological method of participant observation, which involves a double perspective, combining involvement and distance, an insider's and outsider's perspective. 'Ludism', which is derived from the Latin word for play, offers a way out of these two seemingly opposing perspectives. Indeed, Droogers proposes ludism as a method of dealing with alternatives. In play, actors are capable of dealing simultaneously with different identities and realities. By assuming the role of *homo ludens*, the anthropologist can put him- or herself into the religious actors' view of reality, if only for a moment.

Just as my method enabled me to shift easily from one perspective to another, for my research participants religion was fundamentally about testing possibilities. Given that for them religious truth does not reside permanently in one religious tradition, occasionally changing their religious affiliation and participating in different religious traditions simultaneously was considered profitable. In short, methodological ludism opened up a playful approach to research that allowed for a better understanding of different points of view without seeing them as conflicting. By means of methodological ludism, semi-structured and biographical interviews with both religious shoppers and religious entrepreneurs, discourse analysis of sermons, religious pamphlets, mission statements, and visuals, I have recorded ethnographic case studies that shed light on the inherent pluralism of religious life in Lagos.

While for my interlocutors truth did not necessarily reside in one religious tradition, for my research collaborator, Mustapha Bello, Islam represented the only truth. Although Mustapha realized that engaging in an ethnographic research project implied that he needed to work with people whom held radically different religious beliefs than him, in practice he found it sometimes difficult to conduct participant observation in movements whose religious practices he condemned.[23] Although at times our different positions – Mustapha portraying himself as someone who 'eats, drinks, and sleeps Islam' and me having anthropology as my only 'faith' – stood in the way of our collaboration, they also posed an interesting methodological dilemma: in order to understand a particular religious tradition, how far can and must one identify with it and participate in it? (Droogers 2014: 63). Rather than letting our different positions compromise our collaboration, we tried to use our different worldviews productively, which resulted in a table talk at the Global Prayers Congress in Berlin in 2014, during which we spoke openly with each other and with the audience about the possibilities and impossibilities of a collaboration between a religious scholar and a scholar of religion.[24] Our joint conclusion was that differences should not preclude mutual understanding.

Many Lagosians would no doubt portray Yorubaland as a model of religious tolerance and ecumenism. However, a growing number of Lagosians tend toward a more reformist-oriented form of religion, which is less tolerant of other faiths. What we thus see in Yorubaland is that religious pluralization goes hand in hand with religious fundamentalization (see Chapter 6). As such, we should be careful not to idealize Yorubas' religious tolerance. Moreover, Mustapha's reformist stance shows that Yorubaland's particular religious constellation does not mean that religious differences do not matter. Rather than focusing on only religious similarities and overlaps in our comparative framework, we should also consider religious differences (Peel 2016b; see Chapter 4). Still, the fact that Mustapha's mother was a Christian before she married his father and converted to Islam, that his sister converted to Christianity upon her marriage, and that some of his close friends are Christians makes him, in his own words, 'open minded' and distinguishes him from 'hardcore' Hausa Muslims from the north.

Since my mission during my field research was to transcend rigid boundaries between allegedly mutually exclusive categories (Islam versus

---

[23] When Mustapha left on pilgrimage to Mecca, I collaborated with his colleague, Dr Tobi Oshodi. Where my research necessitated that I collaborated with Christians, I found helpful research assistants in their students. Other than Mustapha Bello, Tobi Oshodi, and the public figures who appear in the media, all other names in this monograph are pseudonyms in order to protect the privacy of my interlocutors.

[24] See www.youtube.com/watch?v=6mWcjrMcTsg.

Christianity and 'traditional' religion versus 'world religion'), in my fieldwork method I have also tried to cross boundaries. In circumambulating Lagos, I have traversed not just geographical boundaries but also religious ones. Furthermore, I have transgressed disciplinary boundaries by bringing insights from anthropology, African studies, religious studies, philosophy, and urban studies into conversation with one another. Finally, I have attempted to expand the scientific research method by crossing boundaries between ethnographic and artistic modes of representation, as exemplified by my collaboration with the Nigerian award-winning photographer Akintunde Akinleye.[25] According to De Boeck (2013), a performative turn has taken place in the social sciences. Vice versa, the arts have appropriated social scientific methods of observation and documentation (Enwezor et al. 2002; Lanz 2013: 31–2).[26] Along similar lines, Akinleye's and my collaboration resulted in the study of religion as a set of aesthetical and spatial practices of world making that explores how religion 'takes place' in daily practice and how urban dwellers are engaged in making religion 'happen' (Knott 2005).

Expanding the field of academic output, Akintunde and I have presented our research data not only at academic conferences and seminars and in written publications but also in a travelling photo exhibition and catalogue (Akinleye and Janson 2014) and a visual essay (Janson and Akinleye 2015). Here it should be noted that the Research Excellence Framework (REF), the system for assessing the quality of research in UK higher education institutions, still measures academic output largely by conventional means, i.e. written publications. Although the crisis that occurred in anthropology in the 1970s and 1980s made anthropologists more aware of the political implications of our modes of representing the Other, and opened up the discipline to the possibilities of more varied forms of representation (Marcus and Cushman 1982), these have yet to be recognized by those judging the quality and impact of our work (see also De Boeck 2013: 560–1). By developing creative research methodologies that go beyond the predominance of textual methods, we can build intellectual space for a study of religion through the lens of lived experience.

---

[25] Akintunde Akinleye is the first Nigerian photographer to have been awarded a prize in the World Press Photo, the Netherlands, in 2007 (https://widerimage.reuters.com/photographer/akintunde-akinleye).

[26] An example is *Documenta 11*, the contemporary art exhibition curated by the late Nigerian curator Okwui Enwezor, which constituted a formative moment in the rapprochement between the arts and the (social) sciences (Enwezor et al. 2002).

Structure of the Book

To provide a historical, political, and socio-economic context for the emergence of the religious assemblages described in this book, I begin with outlining the pluriform religious setting in south-western Nigeria, an area known as Yorubaland, with Lagos as its economic, financial, and cultural hub. Taking this course, Chapter 2 serves as scene setting for the rest of the book. Challenging the tendency to study Muslim–Christian encounters one-dimensionally in terms of either conflict or cooperation, Chapter 3 presents three Chrislam movements whose religious leaders all come from a Muslim background and copy heavily from Christianity, particularly Pentecostalism. The Pentecostal movement, with its appealing emphasis on this-worldly blessings and healing, has become so vibrant in Nigeria today that even Muslim organizations appear to be increasingly Pentecostalised. A case in point is NASFAT. In Chapter 4 I argue that contrary to Chrislam that assembles Christian and Muslim beliefs and practices, NASFAT is more about copying Pentecostal prayer forms while emphasising Muslim doctrine. The case of NASFAT thus illustrates that religious assemblage does not imply that religious differences do not matter.

Although Christianity and Islam dominate the religious landscape in Lagos, 'Yoruba religion' still plays a vital role. In Chapter 5 I show how the adherents of The Indigenous Faith of Africa (IFA), *Ijo Orunmila Ato* – a movement that was founded in 1920 by an Anglican Yoruba after he had a vision in which the *orisa* Orunmila appeared to him – have revived 'Yoruba religion' by appropriating Christian elements. Challenging the evolutionary perspective that typifies the study of religion in Africa, Chapter 5 studies 'Yoruba religion' and Christianity as contemporaries. Chapter 6 calls for a critical investigation of the very notion of 'religion' itself. Exogenous religio-spiritual movements such as the Grail Movement and Eckankar, who assemble elements from Islam, Christianity, 'Yoruba religion', and the 'Eastern' religions, as well as non-religious sources, show that religion is increasingly becoming more diffuse and elusive in its meanings in Lagos's competitive religious marketplace. Finally, Chapter 7 draws together the book's larger argument about religious pluralism and raises questions for a comparative study of urban religion that takes assemblage as its lens.

Here it should be noted that although the case studies in this book focus on single denominations, they illustrate that Lagosians move in and out of these denominations, and where they affiliate with a specific denomination they borrow religious elements from others, thereby making a plea for a pluralistic approach to religion that stresses boundary crossing. By and large the case studies ask: How can we capture the encounters between Muslims and Christians beyond the conventional conflict-cooperation continuum? How can we compare religious movements of various sizes without reducing comparison to a shallow exercise of finding similarities? How can we study modes of religious mixing without sticking to syncretism as a conceptual frame? Why and how do Lagosians mix different religious elements, and which reactions do such mixtures generate? How do processes of religious pluralization and fundamentalization relate? How do religious assemblages transform Lagos's cityscape, and how, conversely, does Lagos generate novel forms of religion and invite processes of religious assemblage? These questions are matters of practical, daily concern for Lagosians, and it is in considering the complex processes of living religion in Lagos that we will see how these questions are answered.

In her ethnography of Bedouin lifeworlds, Abu-Lughod (1993) lucidly notes that,

> [T]he dailiness, by breaking coherence and introducing time, trains our gaze on flux and contradiction; and the particulars suggest that others live as we perceive ourselves living – not as automatons programmed according to 'cultural' rules or acting our social roles, but as people going through life wondering what they should do, making mistakes, being opinionated, vacillating, trying to make themselves look good, enduring tragic personal losses, enjoying others, and finding moments of laughter (27).

Drawing on Abu-Lughod, my monograph searches for the moments of laughter in Lagosians' lived religion. In his song *Shuffering and Shmiling* (1978), the legendary Nigerian Afrobeat musician Fela Kuti honours the struggle of Nigerians to maintain human dignity in the face of overwhelming difficulties in their day-to-day lives by stressing the importance of humour and laughter. The movements that are central in this book suggest that humour plays a critical role in religious experience and that seeing religion as pertaining to the 'serious' is a Western ethnocentric perspective. Perhaps the assemblage of divergent religious traditions is, to some extent, meant to be humorous?[27] It is in this playful way that Lagosians navigate the uncertainties, insecurities, and aspirations that mark everyday reality in the megalopolis.

---

[27] This does not in any way mean that I am not taking my interlocutors' religious practice seriously, or that I downplay the hardship of urban living. My point is that by paying attention to the humour involved in Lagosians' reflection on, and practice of, religion, we may gain a better understanding of lived religion and counterbalance the images of misery and doom in many ethnographies of African cities.

2 The Religious Setting
Muslim–Christian Encounters in Nigeria

> As big as Nigeria is, it sometimes seems too small to contain its astonishing fury of human activity (Smith 2007: xi).

'What's Wrong with Nigeria?'; 'Nigeria in Crisis'; 'Nigeria's Religious Riots Continue'; 'Boko Haram: World's Deadliest Terror Organization': this is just a random selection of national and international newspaper headlines on Nigeria. As Smith (2007: xii) points out, conflict and violence are so closely associated with the image that people (not only outsiders but also Nigerians themselves) have of Nigeria that a common phrase in Pidgin English to characterize the nation is 'Nigeria is a war'. And yet, Muslim–Christian relations in Nigeria are not just marked by clashes. For centuries, there were high levels of social interaction between Muslims, Christians, and practitioners of 'Yoruba religion', and interfaith marriages and conversions were common (Peel 2000, 2016a; Soares 2006; Nolte and Akinjobi 2017).[1] The point I want to emphasize in this chapter is that if we aim to understand Muslim–Christian encounters in Nigeria beyond the ingrained conflict-cooperation continuum, we must pay attention to how Muslims and Christians actually live their religion and how their ways of living religion relate to each other.

Whereas initially Islam and Christianity developed largely independently, the second half of the 1970s marked a reversal in Muslim–Christian relations. This is not to say that Nigeria was free from religious tension before the 1970s. In the early nineteenth century Usman dan Fodio led a jihad that resulted in the creation of the Sokoto Caliphate. This was just one among several jihadist movements that disseminated Islam through violence. In recent decades, however, incidents of religious violence have increased in number, spread geographically, and

---

[1] According to Nolte and Akinjobi (2017), interfaith marriages are more common in south-western Nigeria than in any other part of Africa. Since a woman is expected to submit to her husband's religious authority, interfaith marriages often involve interfaith conversion.

affected larger portions of the Nigerian population (Falola 1998: 5). The Muslim–Christian conflict, in particular, has come to play a decisive role in Nigerian politics since the country's return to civil rule and the beginning of political liberalization in 1999.

Summarizing in a nutshell the state of politics since colonial rule, Nigeria became a formally independent federation in 1960. From 1967 to 1970 it was ravaged by a civil war, known as the Biafran War. The Igbo leadership of the secessionist state of Biafra wanted to separate from the Northern-dominated federal government. Thereafter Nigeria alternated between democratically elected civilian governments and military dictatorships, until it achieved a democracy in 1999. As Obadare (2018) points out, the democratic process since 1999 coincided with the upsurge of Pentecostalism as a political force in Nigeria, as manifested in the rising political influence of Pentecostal leaders. Muslims felt marginalized and competed in increasingly violent ways with Christians for access to the state and its resources. In the current conflict, the religiously plural south-western part of Nigeria, that is, Yorubaland, is something of an exception (Map 2.1). Muslims, Christians, and practitioners of 'Yoruba religion' have lived together here relatively harmoniously since the nineteenth century, making the region an 'icon of ecumenism' (Peel 2000). This chapter charts Muslim–Christian interactions historically as well as geographically.

Whereas Nigeria is divided almost equally between Muslims and Christians,[2] along a predominantly north–south axis, Muslim–Christian relations in the south-west are dynamic and they occur in a context where Muslims and Christians mutually enhance and transform each other. As emerged in Chapter 1, many Yoruba describe their religious practice in terms of 'religious shopping'; an emic term referring to multiple religious affiliations across religious denominations and the mixing of elements from divergent religious traditions. This self-identification is in line, as I will elaborate in this chapter, with the popular description of Yorubaland as a 'religious marketplace' where religious shoppers pick and choose from the religious traditions that are available to them (Peel 2011).

Yorubaland is not the only multi-religious setting in either Nigeria or (West) Africa at large.[3] There are small Muslim communities within

---

[2] Because of the political sensitivity of religion in Nigeria, the 1963 Census was the last to include information on religious affiliation. At that time, the census reported that Muslims accounted for 47.2 per cent of the population, Christians for 34.5 per cent, and other religions 18.3 per cent (Population Census of Nigeria 1963: 37).

[3] For notable studies of African settings where religious encounters are not just marked by antagonism and where religious practitioners participate in each other's social and

Map 2.1 Map of Yorubaland

Igboland and elsewhere in the south-eastern (mostly Christian) part of Nigeria. Even in a Muslim-majority setting such as Hausaland in northern Nigeria, where religious hierarchies are explicit and politically legitimated, Muslims and Christians have long cooperated (Shankar 2014). Hence, Yorubaland is not an exceptional setting. But whereas elsewhere multi-religious communities are often small-scale and geographically demarcated, in Yorubaland – a vast region with a population of over 35 million people (Peel 2016a: 3)[4] – practices of religious mixing occur on a large scale. Indeed, religious pluralism is part of the lived experience of every Yoruba. Moreover, there is the unusual situation in Yorubaland

ceremonial life, see for example Atiemo (2003); Cooper (2006); Mwakimako (2007); Frederiks (2009); Langewiesche (2011).
[4] The Yoruba are the second largest ethnic group in Nigeria, and among the largest ethnic groups in Africa.

that we can compare not just two but three religious traditions within a single framework.

Yorubaland's economic and financial hub is Lagos. Urban settings are well suited to illustrate how people from different socio-religious backgrounds share public space and borrow each other's traditions. Indeed, Nigerian best-selling novelist Chimamanda Ngozi Adichie (2019) portrays Lagos in her essay *At Home in Lagos* as a city of 'blurred boundaries',

Lagos has a Muslim population but, like all of southern Nigeria, it is a predominantly Christian city. Drive past a gleaming modern building and it might be a bank or a church. ... Pentecostal Christianity is fashionable, prayers are held before corporate board meetings, and 'We thank God' is an appropriate response to a compliment, or even merely to the question, 'How are you?'.

Lagos's estimated population of over 20 million represents an assemblage not only of Muslims and Christians but also of immigrants from around the continent and the world. Although multi-ethnic and highly diverse, Lagos is seen as culturally more Yoruba. The cultural 'ownership' of Lagos, while contested, is exemplified by the celebration of the popular *Eyo* festival, referring to the white-clad masquerades that represent the spirits of the dead, which is a week-long celebration of Yoruba culture in Lagos. In an effort to promote Yoruba culture, the previous Lagos State Governor Akinwunmi Ambode (2015–19) ratified the Yoruba Language Preservation Law, which sees the Yoruba language as the cultural vehicle for communication. As a result, the teaching of Yoruba is now compulsory in both public and private schools in Lagos State.[5] In such a setting of 'unity through diversity' (Janson 2016b; see also Chapter 3), the weaponization of religion is unlikely and religious pluralism is the norm rather than the exception.

In this chapter I begin with a historical overview of the spread of Islam and Christianity in Nigeria. I then trace the reconfiguration of Muslim–Christian relations in the late 1970s, and argue that while Muslim–Christian relations have grown tenser in Yorubaland since the 1980s, the region remains a beacon of religious amity in the current era of religious conflict. By analysing Yorubaland as a religious marketplace and the Yoruba as religious shoppers, I show the limits of existing approaches that understand religious difference as a ground for religious violence and open an avenue for a more nuanced analysis of interreligious encounters. The consumerist approach to religion, whereby religious shoppers mix and match different religious traditions, is most

---

[5] See www.vanguardngr.com/2018/02/lagos-preservation-yoruba-language/.

visible in Yorubaland's economic hub Lagos. My analysis of religious pluralism in Lagos aims to give a new impulse to urban studies of Lagos. Redressing the one-dimensional generalization of the pathological city on the brink of collapse, I discuss how religious entrepreneurs are actively involved in urban restructuring plans to convert Lagos from a 'Sin City' into a 'Prayer City' (Ukah 2013, 2016). The case studies in the following chapters need to be read against the backdrop of Lagos as a Prayer City, which is predisposed to produce religious assemblages and avert Muslim–Christian conflict.

The Expansion of Islam and Christianity in Nigeria

Although officially the Federal Republic of Nigeria – the world's second most religious country, according to the 2017 Gallup International poll[6] – is a secular state, religion has come to dominate Nigerian politics since the return to civil rule in 1999. According to a popular adage, there are two profitable professions in Nigeria: pastor and politician, often practised by one and the same person. This section explores the unfolding of Nigeria as a federal republic through the lens of its religious history and the interplay between religion and politics.

As early as the eighth century, Islam arrived in what is today called Nigeria through the trans-Saharan trade routes. Under the influence of the dispersion of Islam by North African traders, there emerged small pockets of Islam. Islam remained confined to the elite composed of traders and local rulers till the late eighteenth century, when the religion was popularized through the Sufi orders. Under the influence of Sufi clerics, Islam became less scriptural and Arabized; more responsive to local demands for magico-spiritual services as in the production of amulets and the delivery of special prayers; and reconciled to local culture (Peel 2000: 189, 197–202).

The *Qadiriyya*, which derives its name from 'Abd al-Qadir al-Jilani – a Sufi scholar of twelfth-century Baghdad – is the oldest Sufi order in Nigeria. It was established in the north of what is now Nigeria in the early seventeenth century. Among its most influential adherents was Usman dan Fodio. Religious competition started in 1831 when the Senegalese scholar Alhaji Umar Tall came to Sokoto in northern Nigeria and was able to win followers for the *Tijaniyya* – a Sufi order that was founded in the Maghrib by Ahmad al-Tijani (d. 1815) and that claimed spiritual supremacy (Loimeier 2007: 44–6). Since then, the

---

[6] See www.gallup-international.bg/en/Publications/2017/373-Religion-prevails-in-the-world.

Qadiriyya and Tijaniyya have witnessed fierce dissension over doctrinal matters. Rivalry decreased, however, with the emergence of a reformist-oriented Islam in Nigeria in the late twentieth century, when the Sufi leaders shelved their disputes and formed a 'coalition of convenience' (Loimeier 1997: 308) in order to be able to better resist the danger posed by the new enemy from within the Nigerian Muslim community.

The nineteenth century was to mark the height of Muslim influence due to the jihad of Usman dan Fodio, which started in 1804 and triggered the establishment of the Sokoto Caliphate. This caliphate, which covered a large area of Hausaland in northern Nigeria and extended to Ilorin on the northern Yoruba border, created *dar al-Islam* (the abode of Islam): the region where Islam was practised and shari'a law ruled (Last 1967). A century later, the Sokoto Caliphate was conquered and mostly incorporated into northern Nigeria by the British colonial rulers. It could be argued, however, that the legacy of Dan Fodio's jihad endures to this very day, in that the Sokoto Caliphate has deeply shaped the political-religious order of northern Nigeria ever since (Vaughan 2016).

Islam made advances not only into northern Nigeria but also into the south-west in the nineteenth and twentieth centuries. Unlike in the former region, Islam in Yorubaland was disseminated through peaceful, decentralized means, including traders and itinerant Muslim preachers (Danmole 2008: 203–4). These Muslim preachers were less critical of 'Yoruba religion', structured around the belief in *orisas* or deities and the practice of *Ifa* divination, than their Christian counterparts. Ifa was – and to some extent still is (see Chapter 5) – an essential element of 'Yoruba religion', which was based on a divination system that was found widely throughout Sub-Saharan Africa and that ultimately derived from Islamic sources (Bascom 1969; Brenner 2000). This explains why Ifa priests could easily adapt their Ifa corpus to suit the newly adopted Islam by, for example, reconfiguring the *orisas* as Muslim angels (*malekas*) (Peel 2000: 195–6). This flexibility gave Yoruba Islam a more tolerant orientation, which minimized religious tension and violence in the region. Unlike their northern Muslim fellows, Yoruba Muslims did not call for shari'a law to displace local law or to subvert local authorities. Consequently, Yoruba Islam was considered less 'orthodox' than that practised in northern Nigeria. In this context, Danmole (2008: 205–6) speaks of a push toward the 'Yorubacization' of Islam, contributing to both the expansion and the legitimacy of Islam in south-western Nigeria.

If non-conflictual traditions shaped Yoruba Islam, the late twentieth century marked a diversification of the Muslim field in Nigeria with reformist, sometimes militant, Muslim organizations striving to change the ways in which Islam had long been practised locally. The *Ahmadiyya*

Movement in Islam, which was brought to Lagos by missionaries from the Punjab in 1916, was the first to 'modernize' Islam by enhancing the development of secular education. The growing international pressure on the Ahmadiyya, which was suppressed as heretical based on the claim of its founder Mirza Ghulam Ahmad to be the *Mahdi* (the prophesied redeemer of Islam) – a claim that contradicted the Prophet Muhammad's unique position as the last prophet – led into a crisis among Ahmadis in Nigeria (Fisher 1963). In 1923, a group broke away and formed the *Ansar-Ud-Deen* Society of Nigeria, which soon grew into one of the most successful organizations that attempted to reform Islam through education. After modest beginnings, in the late 1960s almost half of the educational institutions in Nigeria were run by Ansar-Ud-Deen (Reichmuth 1996: 383).

In 1978 the *Jama'at Izalat al-Bid'a wa-Iqamat as-Sunna* – Hausa for the Society for the Removal of Innovation and Reinstatement of the Sunna, or Izala for short – rose to prominence in northern Nigeria with a series of attacks against Sufism that up to that point had effectively dominated Islam (Loimeier 1997; Kane 2003). In its efforts to reform Nigerian Muslim society, Izala fought against a broad range of Sufi practices that it labelled un-Islamic, such as amulets, saint veneration, supererogatory prayers, and conspicuous life-cycle rituals. It rejected these practices as unlawful innovation (*bid'a*) and pleaded instead for the preservation of the *Sunna*, the Prophetic traditions. In order to maintain a 'true' version of Islam, the main concern of Izala's spiritual leader, Abubakar Gummi, was to unite Muslims politically. During the Shagari civil administration of Nigeria's Second Republic (1979–83), Izala became a political force to contend with because its leadership could deliver the block votes of its followers. However, since the mid-1980s factionalism and the prolonged hold on power of the Nigerian military combined to diminish Izala's initial political momentum (Umar 2001: 136).

Whereas Izala was populist, reformist movements that succeeded Izala took a more radical political stance. Since the Iranian revolution in 1978–9, a number of activist Muslim groups have originated from the Muslim Students Society of Nigeria (MSSN), which advocated radical political solutions for Nigeria. MSSN was founded in Lagos in 1954. It soon grew into a national organization that rejected the Nigerian constitution and anything secular (Kenny 1996: 344). Some of the groups that originated from MSSN, particularly the followers of Sheikh Ibrahim El-Zakzaky – the MSSN leader at Ahmadu Bello University in Zaira, Kaduna State, in the late 1970s – were stigmatized as Shi'i on account of their sympathies toward Iran, which supported them. However, El-

Zakzaky insisted that he and his followers were not Shi'i Muslims but belonged to the Nigerian Muslim Brothers (*Ikhwan*) (Loimeier 2007: 55–8). The latter represented an Islamic trend different from Izala's modernist interpretation of Islam. They rejected the Nigerian constitution, flag, and legal institutions, accepting only shari'a law (Kenny 1996: 344).

The most militant Islamist group in contemporary Nigeria is the *Ahl al-Sunna li-l-Da'wa wa-l-Jihad*, that is, the Association of the People of the Sunna for Proselytization and Armed Struggle, popularly known as Boko Haram, which means something like 'Western education is *haram* (unlawful in Islam)' in Hausa. Most studies trace its origins to Maiduguri, the capital of Borno State in north-eastern Nigeria, from where, since its foundation in 2002, it has carried out numerous attacks on police stations, security forces, and other state targets (see Anonymous 2012; Higazi 2013; Mustapha 2014). Boko Haram changed its policy after the execution of its spiritual leader and founder Muhammad Yusuf in police custody in 2009. Under Abubakar Shekau's leadership, it became more organized and sophisticated in its armed campaign, using guerrilla tactics and terrorism that pose a real challenge to the Nigerian state. A raid on Bauchi prison in September 2010, in which Boko Haram freed over 700 prisoners (including many of its members), was a key moment in the movement's increased radicalization. Since then, more than 36,000 people have lost their lives in Boko Haram's insurgencies in Nigeria and its surrounding countries of Niger, Chad, and Cameroon.[7]

Explanations for Boko Haram's emergence and violence vary, but the social inequality argument seems most popular among scholars and (inter)national commentators. They claim that the disparity in wealth between northern and southern Nigeria explains why deprived young northerners joined Boko Haram. However, Thurston (2016: 7) argues that economic deprivation alone cannot explain Boko Haram's growth. Its emergence needs to be interpreted as another example of reformist Islamic movements insisting on the radical transformation of Nigerian society, going back several centuries (Vaughan 2016: 223). Indeed, Last (2014) studies Islamic reformist groups in northern Nigeria as part of a tradition of dissidence. At its root, dissidence in these groups depends on what is considered *bid'a* or unlawful innovation. By re-enacting the *Sunna*, the Prophetic traditions, they try to establish *dar al-Islam* that is

---

[7] The Council on Foreign Relations' Nigeria Security Tracker keeps a tally of violent deaths in Nigeria by state, month, and perpetrator: www.cfr.org/nigeria/nigeria-security-tracker/p29483.

kept free of *bid'a*. Irrespective of their common origin, many Nigerian reformists have denounced Boko Haram's worldview and violence.

That Islamic reformist organizations with political aspirations are not necessarily militant is illustrated by the *Jama'atu Nasril Islam* (JNI), which was founded in 1962 by Ahmadu Bello – the late *Sardauna* (the Premier of northern Nigeria) of Sokoto – with the aim of coordinating Islamic efforts in Nigeria and becoming the mouthpiece of all Muslims in the country. Because of an internal division, JNI could no longer speak for the entire Nigerian Muslim community. The Nigerian Supreme Council for Islamic Affairs (NSCIA), which has been vocal on questions of shari'a and the violence between Muslims and Christians, was founded in 1973 (Kenny 1996: 345). The multiplicity of Muslim identities and positions regarding political Islam shows the inadequacy of our analytical categories, including the ingrained dichotomy between Sufism and reformist Islam, to capture the complexity of the different ways of being Muslim in present-day Nigerian society (see also Masquelier 2009).

While Islam had already firmly taken root in Nigeria at the start of the nineteenth century, Christianity was just beginning to lay its foundations. Until the eighteenth century, attempts to spread Christianity met with only limited success. Compared with their Muslim counterparts, the Christian missionaries laboured under great disabilities. Whereas Muslim missionaries were usually fellow Africans, who settled down in local communities and travelled with relative ease, the Christian missionaries were 'a few ailing Europeans, struggling to keep alive in the swampy creeks and depending on sailing vessels for communication with their bases in Europe' (Ajayi 1965: 4). However, the Christian missionaries' appropriation of Western education soon gave them a lead on their Muslim counterparts.

After a slow start, the first half of the nineteenth century witnessed a missionary revival (Falola 1998: 32). Protestant missionaries began the first major implementation of Christianity in the aftermath of the British ban on the exportation of slaves from Nigeria in 1807. Still, a lively slave trade to the Americas continued until the 1860s. Colonial officers and missionaries worked hand in hand to replace the institution of slavery with something more 'civilized' by British and Christian standards of the time (Ryan 2006: 196). For the missionaries, slavery was not just an inhuman practice that had to be replaced, but a sin that had to be abolished. In this way the evangelical revival supported the anti-slavery movement (Ajayi 1965: 9). For the enslaved, Christianity served as a 'social leveler' (Ayandele 1966: 84), and liberated slaves became an essential part of the missionary movement. The most notable among them was Samuel Ajayi Crowther, who played a key role in the Anglican Church Missionary Society (CMS) – the largest mission at that time. In 1864, Crowther was acclaimed as the first indigenous African bishop of the Anglican Church, thereby becoming the figurehead of African nationalism (182, 205–6).

Internal problems within the CMS, including the split between European and African missionaries, offered an opportunity for the first Roman Catholic missionaries to gain ground among the Igbo population of Onitsha and its environment in eastern Nigeria (Ryan 2006: 197–9). Bishop Shanahan's understanding of the Igbo religion contributed to the outstripping of the Protestant missions by the Catholics in Igboland, although the former preceded the latter by four decades. Shanahan was an Irish priest of the Society of the Holy Ghost Fathers, who arrived in Onitsha in 1902 and went from village to village on foot. Based on the knowledge he acquired during his tours, he concluded that the Igbo religion did not need to be destructed but rather transformed. Hence, Shanahan made the Igbo understand Mass in terms of spirit worship and God in terms of Chukwu, the supreme being of the Igbo religion (Ayandele 1966: 265). Ayandele concludes that in statistical terms, the Igbo responded most enthusiastically to Christianity. By 1910, the number of Christians in eastern Nigeria had outnumbered those in the south-west. Whereas in the latter region Christianity competed with 'Yoruba religion' and Islam, Islam did not have much impact in Igboland (343–5).

Bishop Crowther was determined in his effort to missionize northern Nigeria, but out of fear of anti-missionary risings among the Muslim population, Lord Lugard's colonial administration did not allow Christian missionaries to operate in predominantly Muslim areas, except on expressed voluntary invitation to missionaries by the rulers of such areas. As a result of this policy, Christian missionaries gave up the hope of converting northern Nigeria and focused instead on preventing the Islamic frontier from extending further. With this goal in mind, Christian missions were sent to the Middle Belt, stretching across central Nigeria, in the early 1900s. Middle Belt Nigerians were considered 'pagans', who had to be prevented from falling to Islam. Schools and health clinics were magnets that attracted new converts in the Middle Belt, but traditional religious beliefs turned out to be difficult to eradicate (Falola 1998: 35–6).

By the end of the colonial period, Christianity had emerged as the dominant religion in eastern Nigeria, and as a major religion in west, central, and southern Nigeria (33). Only the north remained relatively closed off from Christian influence. As a result, Western education – the ultimate proselytizing instrument – developed slowly in northern

Nigeria, which explains the huge regional divergences in wealth up to this very day. However, the foundation of leprosariums and health dispensaries by Christian missionaries in northern Nigeria meant that former slaves, poor migrants, and workers started seeing opportunities and upward social mobility in the new religion, resulting in Christianity slowly making inroads in northern Nigeria in the 1930s (Shankar 2014).

Although the Christian missions were making progress in Nigeria under the aegis of colonial rule, the missionaries complained that while they had grown in numbers, they had not 'grown in grace' (Peel 2016a: 84). Compared to the mission churches, the African Independent or *Aladura* Churches were more successful in winning converts' hearts because their mode of worship was considered to be more 'African' (Peel 1968). The *Aladura* are a cluster of churches[8] founded by African religious innovators who triggered a series of revivals – involving healing through sanctified water, witchcraft confession, mass destruction of idols, and prophecy – between the 1920s and 1930s. Their basic aim was to make the power of prayer (*adura*; which explains their name) more available than it was in the mission churches for this-worldly objectives such as health, fertility, protection against witchcraft and danger, prosperity, and success (Peel 2016a: 79).

Gradually, the Pentecostal churches took over from the *Aladura* churches, resulting in the 'Pentecostalization' of Nigerian society (Marshall 2009). The Pentecostal movement first made an appearance in Nigeria in the 1930s, when the leaders of the *Aladura* churches came into contact with the Apostolic Church, a British denomination that originated from the Pentecostal movement. Thus emerged a grouping of churches distinguished by the practices of drawing in the Holy Spirit and speaking in tongues, as well as by a concern for effective prayer and visionary guidance, and for an 'African' style of worship. Over the 1950s and 1960s, the influence of American Pentecostalism grew, with leading evangelists conducting revivals in Nigeria and Nigerian pastors visiting their various headquarters in the United States. But the Pentecostal movement did not achieve a firm foothold in Nigerian society until the 1970s. Oil revenues permitted the expansion of higher education, which facilitated Pentecostalism's earliest constituency of students. Due to worsening economic and political conditions as a result of collapsing oil prices in the 1980s, Pentecostalism expanded faster. By the mid-1990s, the Redeemed Christian Church of God's (RCCG) monthly

---

[8] Examples include the Cherubim and Seraphim (1925); the Church of the Lord, Aladura (1930); and the Christ Apostolic Church (1930). These churches still have considerable constituencies today (Adogame 2010: 485).

'Holy Ghost Nights' had become the largest gathering of any kind ever held in Nigeria, attracting tens of thousands of worshippers (Ojo 1988: 179–84; Peel 2000: 314). Over the past three decades, Nigeria has become the site of Pentecostalism's greatest explosion on the African continent, which made the Nigerian Pentecostal theologian Nimi Wariboko (2014) conclude that we cannot understand Nigeria without understanding Pentecostalism and vice versa.

Just as Islam does not form a homogeneous movement in Nigeria, Christianity is made up of different denominations that are involved in a struggle to convert souls. With the end of the Nigerian civil war in 1970, the climate was conducive to ecumenical interactions among churches, resulting in the formation of the Christian Association of Nigeria (CAN) in 1976 (Enwerem 1995: 76–88). Over the years, CAN has grown into a political organization, which repeatedly called attention to the alleged dominant Muslim influence in national politics. For instance, in 1989 CAN went to court to seek the state government's withdrawal from organizing and subsidizing the pilgrimage to Mecca, which it interpreted as a deliberate instance of Muslim favouritism (Falola 1998: 174).[9] Thus, whereas Islam and Christianity initially expanded separately from each other, since the 1970s – a time of great political and economic turmoil – Muslim–Christian interactions have become increasingly disruptive in Nigeria, as we will see in the next section.

Muslim–Christian Conflict

Before giving a succinct historical overview of religious conflict in Nigeria, it should be noted that since the 1970s there has been competition, as well as higher levels of radicalization, not only between but also within the different religious traditions. As indicated earlier, in their efforts to reform the way Islam has long been practised locally, reformist movements, beginning with Izala, fought against a broad range of Sufi practices that were labelled un-Islamic, thereby facilitating increasing religious polarization among Muslims (Loimeier 2007). Furthermore, over recent decades Pentecostalism has drawn many Nigerian Christians from the *Aladura* churches, the Protestant churches, and the Roman Catholic Church, promising them spiritual rebirth. The Pentecostal upsurge has thus played a central role in the increasing political cleavage along interdenominational lines (Marshall 2009). As such, Muslim–

---

[9] Due to the budget deficit, President Buhari announced the end of governmental sponsorship of both the pilgrimage to Mecca and Jerusalem in July 2015 (www.pmnewsnigeria.com/2015/07/13/buhari-to-end-fg-sponsorship-of-pilgrimage/).

Christian confrontations are not the only source of religious conflict in Nigeria.

A second caveat is that historical analyses show that Muslim–Christian interactions in northern Nigeria – the current hotbed of Muslim–Christian conflict – have been more complex than the dominant conflict paradigm suggests. For example, Shankar (2014) claims that colonial northern Nigeria was 'a place of religious collaboration, experimentation, puzzlement, and sympathy' (144). She points to the cooperation between Christian missionaries and their Muslim northern hosts before the 1930s, as exemplified by Ethel Miller, the first white woman to work for the CMS, and Abdullahi Bayero, the Emir of Kano, who collaborated in their opposition to the consumption of alcohol by the residents of Kano (67). Complicating the politically motivated narrative of Muslim–Christian conflict, Shankar writes, 'The history of Northern Nigerian Christianity, and especially the notion that Christians can genuinely be Hausa, Fulani, or Kanuri (predominantly Muslim ethnic groups), does not readily fit the usual political narratives, whether British colonial, Islamist, secular, or even those that dwell on Christian victimization' (xv). Although there is an increasing 'economy of panic' (Last 2007) surrounding Muslim–Christian relations in contemporary Nigeria, northern Muslims and Christians still engage in religious dialogues, as exemplified by the Interfaith Mediation Centre (IMC) that was founded by Imam Muhammad Ashafa Nuruddin and Pastor James Wuye in Kaduna in 1995. Their Centre's mission is to mediate between northern Muslims and Christians in order to create a peaceful society.[10]

Most analysts date the beginning of Muslim–Christian confrontations in Nigeria to 1978, when a new constitution was adopted after power temporarily shifted from the military regime to civil politicians (e.g. Kenny 1996; Falola 1998; Ryan 2006). Conflicts arose over the question of whether Nigeria would become a secular state or subscribe to the shari'a legal system. Christian anxiety over Nigeria becoming an Islamic state increased in 1986 when the military government of General Ibrahim Babangida tried to promote Nigeria from observer status to full membership in the Organization of the Islamic Conference (OIC) – an intergovernmental organization that was established in 1965 with the aim of encouraging international Islamic solidarity. Eventually, Babangida's government announced that the question of

---

[10] Nuruddin and Wuye have taken their experience in communal mediation in Nigeria to Kenya, and they regularly speak abroad. Their story is featured in the documentary *The Imam and the Pastor*, produced by FLT Films (www.fltfilms.org.uk/; www.imcnigeria .org).

Nigeria's full membership in the OIC had been deferred. Nevertheless, this incident raised a storm among Christians that lasted for decades (Hunwick 1992: 150).

The battle over shari'a law paved the way for the violence of the 1980s. The most notable crisis occurred in 1987 in the College of Education in Kafanchan, Kaduna State, when Christians belonging to the Federation of Christian Students organized what they called 'Mission'87 in Jesus Campus', a title they proclaimed with a banner at the entrance to the college. The college's Muslim students removed the banner and protested against the talk given by a Muslim convert to Christianity, who in their opinion misinterpreted Qur'anic verses and falsified the prophecy of Muhammad. The struggle between the Muslim and Christian students led to violence in other urban centres in northern Nigeria and the Middle Belt, leaving many dead and churches and mosques destroyed. There have been numerous incidents of Muslim–Christian tension on college campuses over the years (Kenny 1996: 358–60; Falola 1998: 179–87).

Though the Yoruba continued as a beacon of religious cordiality, also in Yorubaland relations between Muslims and Christians grew tenser than they used to be before the 1980s. For instance, in 1985 the highest-profile public Muslim–Christian confrontation that the Yoruba had known erupted over the so-called Ibadan-cross controversy. The dispute was triggered by a speech delivered by Chief Moshood Abiola at the opening of a new mosque, funded with Saudi money, on the campus of the University of Ibadan. Not far away from the mosque stood, since 1954, a large white cross, close to the Catholic chapel. Abiola asked for the cross to be demolished. Other issues of Muslim grievance arising from marginalization in a university whose staff and students were largely Christian came into the dispute, which continued for many months. However, unlike in northern Nigeria, the situation did not culminate in violence. The Minister of Education intervened and a compromise was reached: the cross stayed, but a concrete screen was erected to block the mosque's view of the cross, and a Muslim emblem (the crescent) was erected near the mosque. The peaceful resolution of the conflict demonstrates the strength of Yoruba consensus (Falola 1998: 175–8; Peel 2016a: 147).

In the 1990s, a major incident of religious violence occurred in Nigeria every four months on average (Falola 1998: 194). In March 1991, a huge riot broke out in Kano. CAN had organized a revival led by the German evangelist Reinhard Bonnke. Pamphlets purporting to 'claim Kano for Christ' were distributed even in the Muslim quarters. This took place not long after the government had refused the South African Muslim preacher Ahmed Deedat – who was known for using Christian styles of communication to strengthen Muslim defenses against Christian evangelism – a visa to visit Kano because it was feared he would stir up trouble (Larkin 2008b). Muslim resentment against Bonnke's rally was overwhelming, especially because it was planned to take place in the public Race Course. On receiving Muslim complaints, the government, concerned not to foment unrest, decided to relocate the event. Bonnke never actually made it on the stage as angry mobs of Muslim youths went into the Christian quarters of Kano, killing, looting, and burning churches.[11] The next day Christians organized their retaliation, burning many Muslim businesses and mosques (Kenny 1996: 358–9; Falola 1998: 194–211).

Between 1992 (the run-up to the presidential election to vote for the civilian successor to General Ibrahim Babangida) and 1999 (the commencement of the Fourth Republic under the leadership of President Olusegun Obasanjo), Muslim–Christian relations increasingly became dominated by the political situation in Nigeria (Obadare 2018). Since 2000, a new field of conflict has been added to the long list of Muslim–Christian clashes: the introduction of shariʿa law to twelve of the northern states (Loimeier 2007: 65–9).[12] But although the issue of shariʿa contributed to the existing anxieties among Christians about being dominated by Muslims, Loimeier warns not to consider shariʿa law as the sole instigator of Muslim–Christian clashes. For example, Muslim–Christian tensions have occurred in Plateau State in central Nigeria where shariʿa has not been implemented. The conflicts in Plateau State are mostly linked to disputes over land and access to resources between settlers and immigrant groups (Higazi 2008). This demonstrates that conflict in Nigeria is instrumentalized for a variety of reasons. Where Muslim–Christian conflicts prevail, it would be more prudent to indicate the cause of these conflicts as a mixture of different factors, with religion being only one; many of them are rooted in colonial and postcolonial development. In addition to the uneven access to state facilities and distribution of resources, other factors contributing to interreligious conflict included the effects of the civil war, the foreclosure of democratic debate by the military regimes that succeeded one another until 1998, the manipulation of religion to accentuate ethnic differences as a tool to retain political power, and the difficulties of managing plural identities

---

[11] When Bonnke visited southern Nigeria in 2000 to lead the Great Millennium Crusade – purportedly attended by six million people – he was told publicly by the Council of *Ulamas* to stay away from the north of the country (Hackett 2001: 194–5).

[12] These states are Zamfara, Niger, Sokoto, Gombe, Kano, Kebbi, Jigawa, Katsina, Yobe, Bauchi, Bornu, and Kaduna.

in a federal state system (Falola 1998; Last 2007; Loimeier 2007; Nolte et al. 2010; Vaughan 2016).

Muslim–Christian relations have deteriorated further because of the violent attacks against Christians in which Boko Haram is involved. While initially it attacked mainly security forces – the alleged symbol of the immorality and corruptness of the secular Nigerian state – after the killing of its leader Yusuf in 2009 it started attacking Christians. Here it should be noted, however, that although the media frequently report on Boko Haram's attacks of Christians, it would be wrong to describe the insurgencies solely in terms of Muslim–Christian conflict.[13] As Mustapha (2014) points out, Boko Haram and other militant Islamist groups in north-eastern Nigeria have targeted fellow Muslims more frequently than Christians. Still, convinced that the state and Christians collaborate to target Nigerian Muslims, Boko Haram have killed Christians and sought to enflame Muslim–Christian tensions since 2009 (Thurston 2016: 18). On Christmas Eve 2010, Boko Haram insurgents bombed a church in Jos – the ethnic and religious fault line that divides the mainly Muslim north from the largely Christian south. In January 2012, Boko Haram gave a three-day ultimatum to all Christians to leave northern Nigeria and summoned all Muslims to leave southern Nigeria. In this way, the militant group aimed to bring about a sharper division of Nigeria into a northern Muslim bloc and a southern Christian enclave (Higazi 2013). In April 2014, Boko Haram invaded Chibok, a mainly Christian village in the northeastern state of Bornu, and abducted nearly all the girls at the Government Girls Secondary School Chibok.

President Goodluck Jonathan – who long viewed Boko Haram as more of a northern than a national problem – was accused of being slow and inadequate in undertaking action to release the kidnapped Chibok schoolgirls.[14] In the lead-up to the presidential election, the scale of insecurity in northern Nigeria became an electoral problem for Jonathan's ruling party (Obadare 2018: 115–21). With the election of the Muslim ex-General Muhammadu Buhari as president in March 2015, a new chapter in Muslim–Christian relations commenced. Concerns about Islamization and northernization re-emerged, and Buhari felt pressured to select Yemi Osinbajo, a senior pastor of the RCCG, as his vice-presidential candidate (129–30). However, the

---

[13] Remarkably, at least one notable pastor has been involved in Boko Haram, and Christians from the north-east and Delta region have been found within its ranks (personal communication with Murray Last, September 2015).

[14] In an attempt to bring international attention to the Chibok girls' abduction, Michelle Obama posted an image of herself on social media, posing with a sheet of paper that said '#BringBackOurGirls'. More than five years later, many of the girls are still missing.

political marriage of convenience between Muslims and Christians exemplified by the Buhari–Osinbajo alliance has done little to mitigate the problem of religious conflict in Nigeria.

The aforementioned shows that religious difference may erupt in religious conflict, but the opposite may also be the case. The intricate pattern of Muslim–Christian relations in Nigeria is far more diverse than the conventional conflict-cooperation continuum assumes. As Apostolov (2004) points out, this continuum identifies Muslims and Christians as distinct groups with neat boundaries. As the next section illustrates, scholars should be careful, though, not to treat Muslims and Christians as monolithic communities that interact as hostile, demarcated blocs.

Yorubaland as Religious Marketplace

According to Peel (2000: 278), the term 'Yoruba' was a missionary invention adopted by the CMS as an ethnic designation to apply to the people of south-western Nigeria (and some from Benin, Togo, and Sierra Leone) who shared the same language, cultural traditions of common origin (from the Yoruba cradle of Ile-Ife), and symbols and customs surrounding religious and political authority. In addition to similarities in language and culture, religious coexistence is considered the ultimate signifier of Yorubaness (Laitin 1986; Peel 2016a; Nolte and Ogen 2017). Since the nineteenth century, Islam, Christianity, and 'Yoruba religion' have existed side by side within a setting of shared community values, in contrast to the situation in the rest of Nigeria that is religiously much more homogeneous. Laitin (1986) elucidates this particular situation as follows: 'Muslim and Christian Yorubas see themselves culturally as Yorubas rather than as Muslims or Christians' (97). That Yoruba attach more value to common ethnicity than to religious affiliation explains the 'nonpoliticization of religious differentiation' (Laitin 1986) in Yorubaland.

Yoruba's nonpoliticization of religious differentiation has been subsumed under the denominator of tolerance. For instance, Peel (2016a) describes Yorubaland in terms of a 'culture of tolerance' (133). However, this label somewhat obscures the multiple ways in which the Yoruba engage with the three different religious traditions, 'they reject, borrow and appropriate each other's practices, and sometimes they convert to each other's religions' (Nolte and Ogen 2017: 4). Everyday social interaction in Yorubaland extends beyond tolerance towards what my interlocutors described in terms of religious shopping and what has been portrayed in the literature as religious pluralism. Underlining the mode of religious pluralism that typifies Yorubaland, a Christian reverend told me, 'If a Yoruba man has a problem, his father will go to the mosque to pray for him, his mother will seek support in the church, and his aunty might visit a shrine to request the *orisas* to help.' This narrative illustrates that Muslims, Christians, and practitioners of 'Yoruba religion' do not merely tolerate each other, but that religious boundaries are readily transgressed in everyday living.

The complex Yoruba value of *olaju* may help us further in understanding lived religious practice in Yorubaland than the culturalist notion of tolerance. Generally speaking, *olaju* – derived from the Yoruba verb *laju*, meaning 'to open the eyes' – refers to a social state of increased knowledge (acquired through education) and awareness, which is a condition for progress and development (Peel 1978: 144). Because religion is understood as an important form of knowledge, it is a significant part of *olaju*. According to Peel, *olaju* is associated with missionaries and other people coming from outside such as traders, who 'brought light to darkness' (146–7). In this spirit, *olaju* provides us with an understanding of otherness not as a threat but as a potential resource to learn from (Nolte and Ogen 2017: 11). Certainly, the openness towards (religious) others associated with *olaju* helped the establishment of first Islam and later Christianity in Yorubaland.

The Yoruba spirit of *olaju* is reflected in the celebration of religious festivals and holidays. Mutual participation in each other's ritual festivities is a standard feature of Yoruba social life, as well as a source of cultural pride. For instance, an elderly Christian told me that during Christmas he asks a Muslim butcher to slaughter a ram for him in the *halal* way (lawful in Islam), so that his Muslim relatives and neighbours can also partake of the meal. Similarly, Christians take part in the festivities at the end of Ramadan. Tellingly, the Christian children in the neighbourhood where I lived referred to *Sallah* (the end of Ramadan celebration) as the 'Muslim Christmas'. When I was invited to celebrate *Sallah* in a Yoruba Muslim household, it struck me that the majority of the guests were Christian. Noticing my surprise, my host explained, 'Of course you find more Christians than Muslims here; Muslims stay at home to entertain their guests.' These narratives illustrate the degree to which religious boundaries are put to social use in Yorubaland.

The family situation of my research collaborator Dr Tobi Oshodi is another telling example of Yorubaland's particular religious constellation. Tobi's Muslim father married a Christian wife (Tobi's late mother), and after her death he remarried another Christian woman. Tobi's elder brother is a Muslim scholar who spends his leisure time listening to tape-recorded sermons, while his younger half-brothers, who are DJs and live in the same family house in Lagos, play popular music, and his half-sister, who is a member of a Pentecostal choir, practises her Christian hymns. Tobi married a woman from an *Aladura* church who converted to Islam on their marriage. Because of their mixed family situation, the wedding took place in a wedding hall instead of a mosque or church. Tobi and his wife raise their two daughters as Muslims. Although he self-identifies as a 'liberal Muslim', Tobi goes by his Yoruba rather than his Muslim name so that even those who are close to him cannot immediately tell his religion. Tobi's family situation asserts Laitin's (1986: 141) argument that cross-cutting cleavages have made the politicization of religion in Yorubaland difficult.

Social life is not the only domain in Yorubaland where religious boundaries are transgressed. Health and wellbeing is another arena in which religious practitioners are engaged in pluralism. For example, when a Muslim or Christian Yoruba has a health problem (physical and/or mental), it is likely that s/he will consult – sometimes in private – a divination priest or *babalawo*. A member of NASFAT – Yorubaland's largest Muslim organization – explained to me that although he knows that consulting *babalawos* is 'un-Islamic', still he believes it is effective. Another Muslim interlocutor told me that he considered consulting *babalawos* for healing purposes to be part of his 'culture': 'Like a doctor diagnoses the cause of an illness in your culture, in our culture the *babalawo* diagnoses the root of a problem.' The secularization of 'Yoruba religion' by taking it out of the category of religion and presenting it in terms of culture has, as Peel (2016a: 221–2) pointed out, been a common reaction among practising Muslims and Christians in recent years to honour what makes the Yoruba distinctive as a people.

As became apparent in the previous section, politics is a sphere that as a rule is dominated by religious conflict. However, also in the Yoruba political arena the spirit of accommodation prevails. Take, for example, the traditional institution of kingship. The role of the *oba* (king) has been at the apex of administration before the imposition of colonial rule. The *oba* was regarded as a divine ruler, who stood above the many spiritual practices within his kingdom. As such, *obas* were – and still are – recognized as the heads of all religions, which implies that they are expected to participate in multiple religious practices (Oyeweso 2017). As Nolte and Ogen (2017: 10) point out, the title of 'head of all religions' represents both an ideology of power that projects the king's authority over all sections of society, and a reminder of the need to accommodate those who make up society. In this sense, religious transgression is a strategy of both power and democracy.

Here it should be noted that the fact that religious boundaries are blurred in social interaction and medical and political life in

Yorubaland does not mean that religious differences are downplayed. According to Nolte and Ogen (2017: 6), among the Yoruba religious difference is valued in itself, as *difference*. The Yoruba engage with religious difference in multiple ways. For example, several interlocutors explained to me that they had become 'better Muslims' or 'true Christians' after closely observing the religious other: they had grown up in extended families composed of Muslims, Christians, and sometimes practitioners of 'Yoruba religion', and because they had been confronted with religious pluralism on a daily basis they knew much better how they wanted to shape their own religious identity. The opposite also occurred: a middle-aged Christian convert, Adam, told me that, when he was still a Muslim, he found it hard to observe the Islamic principles. He could not keep fast during Ramadan, and praying five times a day was simply 'too much' for him. Through growing up in a family with Christians, he had experienced the 'joyful side of being a Christian'. But, as Adam emphasized, he still respects Muslims a lot, 'Because I know how hard it is to be a Muslim, I respect them. Had I grown up in the north, my attitude would have been completely different.'

Although religious boundaries are easily transcended in socio-political interaction, the aforementioned narratives illustrate that religious diversity is acknowledged: many Yoruba Muslims and Christians do not shy away from asserting their moral superiority to their fellow countrymen. The fact that *babalawos* are often visited at night for others not to notice suggests that 'Yoruba religion' evokes tropes such as 'paganism' and 'occultism' – a tradition that a 'pure' Muslim or Christian does not want to be associated with. With the upsurge of reformist Islam and Pentecostal Christianity in the 1970s, 'Yoruba religion' was attacked as 'demonic' (Danmole 2008). Practitioners of 'Yoruba religion' counteracted these attacks by 'modernizing' themselves, that is, by appropriating elements from Islam and Christianity (see Chapter 5), thereby crossing boundaries again.

To shed light on Yorubaland's pluriform religious landscape in which religious traditions are readily broached, Peel (2011) used the metaphor of the religious marketplace on which religious practice is determined by the forces of supply and demand (Figure 2.1). This metaphor is well chosen because it captures both of the aforementioned aspects of Yoruba religious dynamics: the cross-cutting of religious boundaries as in religious shopping and the valuing of religious distinctness. As on the marketplace, there is a variety of religious commodities on offer in Yorubaland, adapted to a range of tastes and contexts. Religious entrepreneurs compete for customers, who act as consumers, choosing

Figure 2.1 Lagos's religious marketplace.
Photographer: Akintunde Akinleye

between the various religious options available to them. Local criteria of religious value give the competing religious entrepreneurs an incentive to copy effective elements from each other. Somewhat paradoxically, competition on the religious marketplace thus simultaneously creates homologies and market segmentation (Peel 2016a: 173–4, 182). Put differently, in a situation of religious pluralism, competing religious entrepreneurs try to cultivate their own religious market niche by copying each other's religious commodities.

In addition, the metaphor of the religious marketplace keys well into the pragmatics of 'Yoruba religion'. As I will further discuss in Chapter 5, the predominant feature of 'Yoruba religion' is that it assigns primacy to preventing misfortune and maximizing good fortune, thus ensuring the well-being of both the individual and the community. In this view, the trying out of different religious commodities is encouraged as it helps religious shoppers confront the contingencies of everyday living. But although it is a useful concept to get to grips with Yorubaland's inbuilt multiplicity, some scholars of religion have contested the utility of the religious marketplace metaphor. While several sociologists argue, following Weber, that an economic analysis can improve our understanding of aspects of religious practice (e.g. Ekelund et al. 2006), others have problems with the notion of religion as a commodity (e.g. Riesebrodt

2010). And whereas several scholars of religion assume that religion is rational behaviour based on a weighting of costs and benefits (e.g. Horton 1975a,b; Gooren 2006), according to others it is irrational (e.g. Malinowski 1948; Stark 1999). Nevertheless, over the past three decades market theories of religion have become so widespread that observers have begun talking about a paradigm shift in the study of religion (e.g. Iannaccone 1992; Beyer 1997). To sum up, whereas religious difference is often linked with conflict, the openness on Yorubaland's marketplace towards difference as a potential resource to gain from has enabled the assemblage of divergent religious traditions, as cultivated by the practice of religious shopping. Yorubaland's commercial hub Lagos is a good place to study this transactional religious practice.

Lagos's Conversion from Sin City into Prayer City

Although many government institutions were relocated to the federal capital of Abuja – a newly created city designed for government bureaucracy – in 1991, Lagos remains Nigeria's economic centre. Despite its infrastructural deficiencies, the megacity has grown at such rate that, according to a United Nations' projection, it is the third largest city in the world in the twenty-first century. Lagos is therefore often taken as an archetype for the urbanization process at work in the Global South: it is seen as the 'icon of West African urbanity' and the 'paradigm and pathological extreme of the West African city' (Koolhaas 2001: 652). A fundamental paradox is that Lagos's demographic expansion has taken place in a context of far-reaching economic decline – a situation that has been described as acute 'over-urbanization' (UN-Habitat 2010: 278). The acuteness of the lack of housing for Lagos's fast-grown population is illustrated by the fact that Lagosians have created homes literally everywhere: on and under bridges, on the beach, in the water (Makoko is an enormous floating slum in Lagos Lagoon), on swampland (Lekki, the highbrow part of Lagos, is composed of former swampland), and even in the ocean (Eko Atlantic City, a planned upscale city, is currently being constructed on land reclaimed from the Atlantic Ocean).

Originally called Eko, Lagos was developed into a centre of the slave trade and gateway to Brazil by Portuguese traders starting in the sixteenth century, and was renamed after its lagoon (Ukah 2013: 180).[15] If Lagos's proximity to the Atlantic Ocean has shaped its economic character, its political character has been built since British gunboats seized the

---

[15] Lagos is a city of 3,577 square kilometres, of which 787 are lagoons, lakes, and creeks (Ukah 2013: 180). It was therefore once known as the 'Venice of West Africa' (Gandy 2005: 36).

island in 1861 to protect Britain's commercial interests. In 1884 the Berlin Conference conferred the protectorate of the region on Britain. In 1914, the Northern and Southern Protectorates were forcibly amalgamated to create the unified colony of 'Nigeria', a name allegedly selected by Flora Lugard – the wife of colonial administrator Frederick Lugard – with Lagos as colonial capital (Gandy 2005: 42–3). At the time of Nigeria's independence in 1960, Lagos was a bustling centre for trade and commerce of just under a million. Besides being Nigeria's premier city, in 1967 Lagos also became a state capital that played host to the bureaucratic establishment of Lagos State – at that time one of 12 states, and today one of 36 states in Nigeria's federal system.

In the wake of the Nigerian Civil War (1967–70), Lagos's population expanded vastly due to huge waves of migration from eastern (Igbo) parts of the country (Gandy 2006: 380). During the oil-rich 1970s, Nigeria's economy became stronger and Lagos became a target and a magnet. The onset of the global recession in the 1980s and the collapse in the oil price led to the doubling of Lagos's population. Migrants from the countryside flocked to the city, which made the informal economy expand (Gandy 2005: 46). As Adichie (2019) points out, 'If Lagos has a theme it is the hustle – the striving and trying.' Poor Lagosians often combine three to four jobs in the informal economy to earn a living. The middle class too usually has a side hustle. For example, I met schoolteachers organizing not only private home lessons but also using the school as a market to sell goods, ranging from food items to imported clothes. Many of my colleagues at the University of Lagos and Lagos State University worked as pastors and imams at the weekends. One colleague had started a side hustle as a 'marriage counsellor'. Although he offered his services free of charge, the 'gifts' he received from satisfied clients (including his students) formed a welcome addition to his salary as a lecturer. As such, it is difficult to draw sharp boundaries between the informal and formal economy in Lagos: in fact, the informal economy has become formalized.

Due to overcrowding, living conditions in Lagos deteriorated during the late 1980s and 1990s and the number of slum settlements grew.[16] Lagos's slums, which are constantly under threat of being bulldozed by Lagos State Government's Task Force,[17] stand in sharp contrast with the upscale districts of the Lekki peninsula, Ikoyi, and Victoria Island.

---

[16] Lagos now extends far beyond its original lagoon setting to encompass as many as 200 slums, ranging in size from clusters of shacks underneath highways to entire districts (Gandy 2006: 372).

[17] The Lagos State Environmental Sanitation Enforcement Agency, or 'Task Force', was established in 1991 to address the problems of poor sanitary conditions and slum settlements.

Nowhere is the contrast between the poor and the rich more striking than when driving on the Third Mainland Bridge, connecting Lagos Island and the mainland, where the tall buildings on the 'Manhattan' of Lagos Island and the soaring luxury apartments form a stark contrast with the waterside slum of Makoko and the old Yoruba neighbourhood Ebute-Metta further west, where 77 per cent subsist on less than a dollar per day (Omezi 2014: 277–8).

Indeed, the average Lagosian lives in what Barnes (1986) calls an 'environment of scarcity' (4). Access to water provides one of the most poignant indicators of social inequality. Fewer than one in twenty Lagosian households are directly connected to the municipal water supply, leaving the majority reliant on a combination of boreholes, standpipes, illegal connections controlled by local gangs of 'Area Boys', and exorbitantly priced water from private vendors (Gandy 2005: 50). A friend, who worked as a sales manager, introduced me to the complex 'water economy' in her household in the business district of Lagos: blue barrels contained expensive drinking water bought from a private local vendor called 'water lord'; white barrels contained less expensive water used for cooking bought from another water lord; the water in black barrels was drained from a local borehole and was used for washing; buckets with collected rainwater were used for flushing the toilet. Besides the water supply, Lagos's electricity supply is notoriously erratic. The National Electric Power Authority (NEPA) is therefore popularly known as 'Never Expect Power Always'. There were several periods during my fieldwork that I had electricity only twice a week and when an electricity pole broke in the neighbourhood where I was staying, we did not have electricity for weeks. Those who can afford it buy a generator. Many of the hustlers whom I met during my fieldwork complained that it is difficult to run a small business if most of one's earnings go on buying fuel. After the government removed the fuel subsidy in 2012, the price of fuel more than doubled. Since most Nigerians regard cheap fuel as the only benefit they get from the nation's oil wealth, this led into a protest movement in Lagos known as 'Occupy Nigeria'.

As Smith (2007: xii) observes, debating and analysing Nigeria's many woes, including the poor water and electricity supply, is a popular obses-sion. During my field research, many Lagosians gave me – mostly unsoli-cited – their opinion about national issues, complaining that since the economic collapse of the 1980s, the country has been deteriorating to an anomy ruled by incompetent leaders pursuing wealth and power for self-interest. My interlocutors' pessimism fits in with the trend in African Studies that stresses the dramatic erosion of the state since the economic crisis and the Structural Adjustment Policies (SAPs) of the 1980s and

1990s.[18] In these studies, Nigeria is often considered to be the exemplar 'crippled state' (Osaghae 1998), with Lagos as 'rebel city' (Harvey 2012) situated at the front line of struggles over access to resources.

Despite lacking basic amenities and public services, Lagos continues to function owing to the self-regulating system of civil society actors who operate in the twilight zone between state and society, public and private, formal and informal, and legal and illegal (Fourchard 2011: 43). That the boundaries between the formal and informal, as well as between the legal and illegal, are easily blurred is illustrated by the local gangs of Area Boys – an infamous Lagosian youth culture that emerged at a time when the labour market dwindled in the mid-1980s. Although Area Boys are often portrayed in the literature as a bunch of reckless drug addicts and petty criminals, this description is, according to Momoh (2000), one-sided. Because Area Boys exploit local markets and motor parks – two of the main sources of revenue of Lagos State – they actually play an important role in the shaping of the city (Fourchard 2011: 49–52). They act as watchdogs who are simultaneously antagonistic to the government and co-opted by it, thereby mirroring the dualism that characterizes Nigerian politics.

In the words of Fourchard (2011), Lagos is 'a celebration of informality which cannot be reduced to disorder as it generates economic dynamism and reveals the capacity of Lagosians to develop their own infrastructures' (41). The celebration of informality has become a popular theme in urban studies in recent years as reflected in the work of, for example, Simone (2004), Meagher (2010), and De Boeck and Baloji (2016). Rather than studying the informal economy as a pool of un- or underemployed workers, these authors consider it a promising site of economic activity and dynamism that creates jobs and opportunities. Their appraisal of informality challenges mainstream urban studies, which have long concentrated on urban planning, public regulations, and services. The reform of urban studies has brought about a flurry of interest in Lagos, focused around major international art exhibitions that portray the megacity as a laboratory of urban ingenuity (Gandy 2005: 37).[19]

The increasing interest in Lagos can be divided into two divergent modes of analysis and interpretation. The first approach is what Gandy calls an 'eschatological evocation of urban apocalypse', marked by

[18] See e.g. Bayart (1993); Young (2004); Bach (2006); Ferguson (2006); Piot (2010).
[19] Lagos has become the subject of artistic shows such as *Century City* (2001) in London; *Africa's: The Artist and the City* (2001) in Barcelona; and it featured prominently in the 2002 *Documenta 11* in Kassel (Enwezor et al. 2002).

uncontrollable growth, chaos, pollution, noise, poverty, corruption, unsanitary conditions, and disease, portraying Lagos as the stereotype of urban dysfunction (38). The second approach, by contrast, is far more upbeat, focusing on the novelties and ingenuity of the megacity. Exemplified by the Dutch architect Rem Koolhaas and his Harvard School of Design's Project on the City (2001), this approach also emphasizes the chaotic aspects of Lagos's development, but does so in order to highlight the homeostatic complexity of newly evolving socio-economic structures outside state regulation (Gandy 2005: 39). In this context, Simone (2004) speaks of a city not on the brink of collapse, but rather a 'city yet to come'. From such a view, Lagos is considered not a threatening anomaly but a precursor to a new kind of urbanism hitherto ignored within the teleological discourses of Western modernity and development (Pieterse 2011). Instead of Lagos catching up with the Western world, the West may be catching up with Lagos, 'To write about the African city is to write about the terminal condition of Chicago, London or Los Angeles' (Koolhaas 2001: 653).

Whereas the first approach maps Lagos as a 'Leviathan' (Liotta and Miskel 2012: 3–4), ignoring Lagosians' potential for resilience and resourcefulness, the second treats it as a living art installation and neglects that for most Lagosians the endless 'go-slows' (Nigerian slang for traffic congestion) and frequent blackouts are a source of nuisance rather than of aesthetics. In this monograph I attempt to reconcile the two approaches, which both reflect lived reality in Lagos. Despite its dysfunctions and disruptions, Lagos instils hope in the lives of its inhabitants: it is a place of opportunities where, to quote my research collaborator Mustapha Bello, 'everything is possible'. As sites where hope is being materialized, religious entrepreneurs have invested in urban renewal and religiously owned real estate over the past three decades, thereby configuring Lagos in a 'city of God' (Ukah 2016), where religion and the infrastructure of prayer hold a pre-eminent place.

The New Republic (1993) magazine described Lagos as '[i]mpoverished, filthy, steamy, overcrowded and corrupt', and 'the ultimate incarnation of the modern megalopolis gone to hell' (July 12: 11; cited in Hackett 2011: 129n.14). That Lagos is widely associated with immorality was also apparent in the stories about child kidnappings, abductions from taxis and buses, ritual killings, and trade in body parts that I read in the local press, and that I overheard in *danfo*s or minibuses.[20] In an effort to

---

[20] Smith (2007: 215), who recorded similar stories in south-eastern Nigeria, interprets them as expressions of discontent about corruption and inequality, which reconfigure political issues as morality tales.

Figure 2.2 Mountain of Fire and Miracles Ministries' (MFM)
Prayer City.
Photographer: Akintunde Akinleye

rehabilitate Lagos, former Lagos State Governor Babatunde Fashola
(2007–15) started his Beautify Lagos campaign, planting trees, creating
gardens and parks, and commissioning local artists in 'beautification
projects'. Contributing to Lagos's urban renewal, many religious entrepreneurs have invested in prayer camps – spectacular sites where hundreds of thousands of worshippers flock to attend prayer services – that
have cropped up along the Lagos–Ibadan Expressway, which connects
Nigeria's first and third largest cities (Akinleye and Janson 2014; Janson
and Akinleye 2015) (Figure 2.2).

The 120-kilometre long Lagos–Ibadan Expressway was opened in
1978 at the peak of the oil boom, a period known as 'paradise on wheels'.
It now carries around 250,000 vehicles per day. Due to increased traffic,
in combination with poor maintenance, from the 1990s decline set in
(Olusina 2012). While it has failed as the artery linking the north and
south of Nigeria, the Expressway has succeeded as a stage for the performance of public religiosity, earning it the moniker the 'Spiritual
Highway'. The real estate market is tight and land is scarce in Lagos.
Land is more affordable along the Expressway, which has become part of
the sprawling metropolis. Having morphed into permanent prayer,

living, working, and production sites, the prayer camps along the Expressway are being projected as model cities for Christians and Muslims.[21] A Pentecostal pastor who invested in a plot of land near the Lagos border explained to me,

Lagos's hustling and bustling prevents urban residents from living a spiritual life. That's why churches searched for a refuge where they can serve God without the burden of city life. In prayer camps we have found a place where we can concentrate on God and interact with Him.

Muslims reacted to the construction of the Christian prayer camps by building their own camps. A NASFAT official elucidated the establishment of NASFAT's prayer camp as follows, 'Since we didn't want to remain behind the Pentecostal churches, we followed their example and bought land along the Expressway. ... We are investing heavily in developing our camp.' Providing all kinds of services that are lacking in Lagos, ranging from electricity and water, a clean and secure living environment, and employment opportunities to redemption, the Christian and Muslim prayer camps along the Lagos–Ibadan Expressway serve as urban alternatives to Lagos (Ukah 2013: 194–6).

That the prayer camps not only compete with one another for precious land and visitors but that their proximity to one another also induces religious shopping became clear during a conversation with an unemployed university graduate in Mountain of Fire and Miracles Ministries' (MFM) Prayer City. The young man told me that to increase his chances of being 'delivered' and finding a job, he attends the Holy Ghost Service in RCCG's Redemption City on the first Friday of the month, followed by the Power Must Change Hands programme in MFM's Prayer City on the first Saturday of the month. Although being a Pentecostal, he confided to me that he sometimes even attends prayer assemblies in NASFAT's prayer camp on the first Sunday of the month. This transactional approach to religion forms the rationale behind my analytical focus on religious assemblage. Within a context marked by precarity, the picking and choosing of religious traditions is as much part

---

[21] Prayer cities are not the first cities set up by religious organizations. In Yoruba cosmology, many cities and towns (*ilu*) had a divine purpose in their establishment; the most famous of which is Ile-Ife, the 'City of 201 Gods' (Olupona 2011). Moreover, prayer cities are not the first model cities in and around Lagos. In 1977, the Nigerian petro-state poured money into FESTAC Village, accommodating the international participants in the Second World Black and African Festival of Arts and Culture. Offering all sorts of municipal services, FESTAC became a model township and masterplan of national development (Apter 2005: 49–50).

of everyday living in Lagos as the hustling for opportunities to make a living. It may be concluded then that by visiting multiple prayer camps along the Lagos–Ibadan Expressway, Lagosians make the Spiritual Highway a true crossroad. At this crossroad prayer camps act as road builders in rendering meaningful the unstable flux of life in Lagos.

Conclusion

This chapter made a plea for a conceptual reconfiguration of Muslim–Christian encounters in Nigeria. Rather than studying them in terms of conflict and war, the south-western part of Nigeria, called Yorubaland, resembles a religious marketplace where Muslims, Christians, and practitioners of 'Yoruba religion' not only compete with but also borrow from one another. Although the rest of Nigeria is religiously more uniform, it emerged that Yorubaland is not an exception. Also in northern Nigeria, which is portrayed in the media as the hotbed of Muslim–Christian clashes, there has been evidence of cooperation and mutual borrowing. Hence, there is need for comparison with other regions where religious traditions coexist. This will provide a more accurate picture of the complexity of the interactions between Muslims and Christians in Africa at large, and Nigeria in particular, beyond either peaceful cooperation or conflict, which is violent or latent.

Resonating with Guyer's (1996) claim that Yoruba society fosters its members' potential for inventiveness, this chapter has explored how the Yoruba put religious difference to work in everyday living. It emerged that rather than tearing Nigeria apart in a Muslim north and a Christian south, religion provides the Yoruba with a tool to mould their cultural identity and to deliberately manoeuvre between Islam, Christianity, and 'Yoruba religion' in order to tackle the challenges of urban living. Yoruba's ability to (re)negotiate religious differences is in line with the complex Yoruba value of *olaju*. *Olaju* has the connotation of 'enlightenment': a virtue with a strong liberal connotation as in 'interfaith dialogue'. However, the pluriform religious movements that form the core of this book do much more than bringing Islam, Christianity, and 'Yoruba religion' into dialogue: they appropriate each other's religious beliefs and practices, reject them, and combine elements from different religious traditions in new assemblages.

While the current upsurge of reformist Islam and Pentecostal Christianity in Nigeria endorses distinctive forms of piety and identification that may easily come into conflict with each other, practices of religious pluralism persist particularly in Lagos. The challenge is thus to develop a new conceptual framework that is devoted to drawing out similarities, differences, and entanglements between Islam, Christianity, and 'Yoruba religion' in Lagos's pluriform religious landscape. The case studies of the different modalities of religious assemblage that have emerged in Lagos over the past few decades facilitate this mission. It is to these case studies that I now turn.

3   Moses Is Jesus and Jesus Is Muhammad
The Chrislam Movement

> Under conditions of globalization, moreover, all the world religions
> draw not only upon their own traditions but also increasingly upon
> one another. Intercivilizational encounters, cultural imitations and
> borrowings, diasporic diffusions, hybridity, creolization, and
> transcultural hyphenations are as much part and parcel of the global
> present as Western hegemony, cosmopolitan homogenization, religious
> fundamentalism, or the clash of civilizations   (Casanova 2008: 119).

Globalization makes it difficult to understand religions as separate and
distinct entities. At the same time, global dynamics involve new forms of
state management of religion (Berger 2014). As we have seen in
Chapter 2, under conditions of globalization Islam and Christianity
spread in Nigeria. However, they did not exist as bounded religions.
The most prominent example of religious cross-fertilization in contem-
porary Nigeria is Chrislam: a series of religious movements that combine
Christianity and Islam, which emerged in Lagos in the 1970s. A paradox
of Nigerian politics is that pluriform religious movements such as
Chrislam warrant the country's secular status (Ilesanmi 1997).
Chrislam could emerge because Section 10 of the 1999 Constitution of
the Federal Republic of Nigeria states that 'the Government of the
Federation or of a State shall not adopt any religion as State Religion'.[1]
Nevertheless, the secular state recently banned one of the Chrislam
movements as 'unlawful', thereby reinforcing normative conceptions of
religion. Opposing conventional understandings of secularism, religion
and politics mutually shape each other in Nigeria (Vaughan 2016;
Obadare 2018). In this chapter, I address the question of how to

---

[1] In addition, Section 38 states that 'Every person shall be entitled to freedom of thought,
conscience and religion, including freedom to change his religion or belief, and
freedom ... to manifest and propagate his religion or belief in worship, teaching,
practice and observance.' Somewhat paradoxically, the Constitution's preamble
describes Nigeria as a 'sovereign nation under God'. Although constitutionally secular,
many Nigerians claim that the state is actually 'multireligious' (Ilesanmi 1997).

approach religious pluralism conceptually in Nigeria's secular political field, and I take Chrislam as my ethnographic case study to answer this question.[2]

During a sermon, Tela Tella – the founder of Nigeria's oldest Chrislam movement *Ifeoluwa* – proclaimed, 'Moses is Jesus and Jesus is Muhammad. Peace be upon all of them; we love them all.' One of his followers, who called himself a 'Chrislamist', told me after the sermon, 'You can't be a Christian without being a Muslim, and you can't be a Muslim without being a Christian.' These powerful statements reflect well the basis of Chrislam, namely the mixing of Christian and Muslim beliefs and practices. Here I focus on the two most prominent Chrislam movements in Lagos: *Ifeoluwa* was the first, and *Oke Tude* is the most popular. In addition to their Yoruba names, the founders and their followers use 'Chrislam' as a concept for self-designation. Despite their inclusive conception of religion, premised on the belief that 'Christianity and Islam are one', there is surprisingly little interaction between *Ifeoluwa* and *Oke Tude*. Although Tella preaches unity, he rejects other forms of Chrislam, such as *Oke Tude*, as 'inauthentic'. *Oke Tude*'s founder, Samsindeen Saka, claims not to know Tella and to be the sole inventor of Chrislam. Somewhat paradoxically, inclusion and exclusion work here side by side.

Although the religious mixing in which Chrislamists engage entails the crossing of religious boundaries, there is the ingrained need or wish to fix religions and to emphasize their unique features (Spies 2019). The tension between the relationality of fluid religious traditions and their definition as separate, fixed traditions is illustrated by a third Chrislam movement: The Chosen Kingdom of God, which was founded by Jamiu Yusuf in 2010.[3] While Tella and Saka's mixing of Christianity and Islam has not caused much upheaval, the Lagos State Government determined The Chosen Kingdom of God an 'unlawful society', resulting in the imprisonment of Yusuf and his disciples. The case study of Yusuf's banned Chrislam movement thus demonstrates that an inclusive

---

[2] This chapter is a revised and longer version of my article in *Africa* (Janson 2016b). Whereas my article focused on only *Ifeoluwa* and *Oke Tude*, here I also pay attention to a third Chrislam movement, which I study within a context of secularization.

[3] There are other movements in Lagos that mix Christian and Muslim beliefs and practices. An example is Malaika's Saint Peter's Church (New Jerusalem). During her Sunday services, Malaika (meaning angel in Arabic) sits on a throne, praising Allah and speaking an 'angelic language' (i.e. glossolalia), while sipping from a bottle of beer. Malaika's style of worship seems closer to the *Aladura* church than to mainline Christianity or Islam. Here I limit myself to those movements that refer to themselves as 'Chrislam'.

religious practice may result in exclusion by the established religious and political authorities.

Because the Yoruba attach more value to common ethnicity than to religious affiliation (Laitin 1986: 97; see Chapter 2), Chrislam can be considered a typical Yoruba phenomenon: it is the shared ethnicity that makes the mixing between Christianity and Islam possible as well as acceptable. A member of *Oke Tude* claimed that if Chrislam were to have emerged in Hausaland in northern Nigeria, 'the founders and their followers would have been dead by now, because unlike the Yoruba, northerners are extremists.' As noted in the previous chapter, in an attempt to prevent the outbreaks of violence in northern Nigeria Imam Muhammad Ashafa Nuruddin and Pastor James Wuye founded the Interfaith Mediation Centre (IMC) in Kaduna in 1995. Unlike the IMC's pioneers, the Chrislam leaders do not situate their movements against the backdrop of religious violence plaguing Nigeria, but rather against the unstable flux of life in Lagos. Although they see it as their task to bring unity between Christians and Muslims, their movements are not examples of what scholars attempting to advance ecumenical ideas have called 'interfaith dialogue' (Hock 2004). Rather than establishing an ecumenical faith, the Chrislam leaders see it as their mission to mix Christian and Muslim beliefs and practices in an effort to bring about 'deliverance' in Lagosians' lives, as expressed through success, wealth, and good health. Here, it should be noted that Chrislam is not represented by the Nigeria Inter-Religious Council (NIREC), which was established with the aim of promoting greater understanding among Nigerian Christians and Muslims in 2000. In an interview, the Muslim co-chairman of NIREC depicted Chrislam as a 'heretic sect' that was unrelated to NIREC's higher aim of 'laying the foundations for religious harmony'. His Christian fellows saw in Chrislam the apocalyptic sign that 'the drama of the end-time is unfolding'.

Pluriform religious movements such as Chrislam are not a new phenomenon in Africa.[4] Indeed, Turner (1979) considered the encounter or interaction of two different types of religion a necessary cause for the emergence of all religious movements in Sub-Saharan Africa. Succeeding generations of Africanists had more problems with this interaction model, describing what in Turner's terms are new religious movements as syncretic forms of 'African Christianity' or 'African Islam'.

---

[4] Most of the cases described in the literature concern the mixing of African Traditional Religion (ATR) with either Islam or Christianity, and not so much the fusion of two monotheistic religions (but see Atiemo 2003) or the three in one conceptual frame (but see Peel 2016a).

I suggest that Chrislam provides a rationale for scrutinizing the very concept of syncretism and propose assemblage as a heuristic device for shedding a fresh light on Chrislam's religious mixing. My main point in this chapter is that assemblage thinking allows us to foreground the ongoing and open-ended processes through which new religious formations such as Chrislam, in which divergent religious elements are mixed without becoming unified in a new synthesis, emerge and transform.

I begin with a history of the two most influential Chrislam movements, *Ifeoluwa* and *Oke Tude*, which I study within the larger socio-cultural context and political economy of Lagos. The underlying idea in Chrislam's assemblage of Christianity and Islam is that to be a Christian or Muslim alone is not enough to guarantee success in this world and the hereafter; therefore, Chrislamists participate in Christian as well as Muslim rituals, appropriating the perceived powers of both. Appropriation is always a process of translation, whereby elements from one religious context are interpreted into another one. This raises questions such as: What is acceptable religious mixing? And when does religious mixing turn into heresy? The case studies of *Ifeoluwa* and *Oke Tude* help us to answer the first question. To answer the second question, I conclude with the case study of Yusuf's banned Chrislam movement. What we see here is that Nigeria's secular state polices religious pluralism. By analysing religious pluralism at the individual, institutional, as well as national level, the case studies in this chapter challenge both the common bifurcation between Christianity and Islam and the conventional religious–secular divide in the scholarship on religion, thereby opening a new avenue for conceptualizing lived religion and religious mixing as assemblage.

Ifeoluwa: The Will of God Mission

The oldest Chrislam movement, *Ifeoluwa*, was founded in Lagos in 1976 by a Yoruba named Tela Tella. The name *Ifeoluwa*, Yoruba for 'The Will of God' or 'The Love of God', was revealed to him by divine revelation. After receiving the revelation, he meditated for 21 days at the spot where he later built his mission. In addition to *Ifeoluwa*, Tella refers to his mission as 'Chrislam' – a term that he coined to create awareness of unity among Christians and Muslims. Similar to Islam, *Ifeoluwa* is based on five pillars, with love being the first one. The others are: mercy, joy, good deeds, and truth. Tella sees himself as God's will incarnated in a human being, who has been ordained to enlighten the world, 'I'm the will of God personified. The word of God is Jesus. The motor of my mission is love, peace, and abide. My followers abide by the laws, rules, and regulations of *Ifeoluwa*. I'm an instrument in the hands of God.'

According to Tella, God communicates with him via divine revelations, which he conveys through glossolalia. Until the world is ready to receive these revelations, Tella lives a secluded life with his two wives (the Lady Apostles), their children (the Prayer Warriors), a parrot, and a couple of white doves[5] on the 'Mountain of Power':[6] a whitewashed compound in Agege, a densely populated suburb in Lagos. The whitewashed walls contrast with the grubby neighbouring compounds, and the smell of incense within the compound forms a stark contrast with the smell of the street's open sewage system. On the compound's fenced wall, *Ifeoluwa*'s symbols are painted: a slate shaped like that used in Qur'anic schools on which students learn to write Arabic with a Christian cross in the middle, and a heart signifying love.

Tella has a small congregation, composed of about fifty lower middle-class followers, who meet every Saturday. Similar to many other Nigerian religious movements, youths outnumber elders and women outnumber men in the congregation. A long-term *Ifeoluwa* member (whose husband is a Muslim who does not attend *Ifeoluwa* services) explained, 'Men don't care. We women are more concerned about our children, families, and businesses. That's why you find more women in Chrislam – but not only here: in all religious movements in this country women are over-represented.' Since Tella believes in the principle of '50–50', or gender equity, both men and women hold leading positions in *Ifeoluwa*. Nevertheless, directives of the Holy Spirit forbid women to attend services during their menstruation.

Because Tella avoids the spotlight, it was initially not that easy to meet him. During our first interview, it started raining, in which Tella saw the sign that God disapproved of my research. But when the sky cleared up quite suddenly, he concluded that God loved me and that was the beginning of an intensive collaboration. During one of many interviews, Tella explained why his congregation meets on Saturday, and not in a mosque or church but in a temple,

I don't want to lean on Friday since Friday is for the Muslims, and I don't want to lean on Sunday since Sunday is for the Christians. Therefore we congregate on Saturday, which is the Sabbath.[7] In previous years, services took place on both

---

[5] The white dove symbolizes peace; an idea that originated with Christianity, where it symbolizes the Holy Spirit.

[6] 'Mountain' has a strong reference to Mount Sinai in Egypt, where, according to Christian and Jewish traditions, Moses received the Ten Commandments.

[7] Besides the Sabbath, I did not come across other references to Judaism in *Ifeoluwa*.

Fridays and Sundays but because people accused me of practising my faith half-way, I decided to switch to Saturdays ... *Ifeoluwa* is unique. I don't love Jesus more than the Prophet. I love them all and they love me.

To prevent accusations of favouring Christians above Muslims or vice versa, Tella refused to talk about his religious background. Nevertheless, it is generally known that he was a Muslim before founding Chrislam. All he was willing to tell me about his past was that he travelled widely, and during his many journeys he met with people of all walks of life and all religions. These encounters inspired him in his mission to bring about love and peace among worshippers, regardless of their faith, ethnicity, and race.

Tella's temple is composed of a garage-like white building with, in the middle, a colourful altar that is separated by a curtain from the prayer ground, where, as in a mosque, the congregation sits on the floor. On the wall above the altar the Arabic word *nur*, meaning 'light', is written. Unlike in a mosque, there is no *muezzin* who calls for prayer: a bell is rung, while Tella's parrot voices '*Ase*': a Yoruba word that is believed to invoke divine forces. The Saturday service starts with singing songs from the three *Ifeoluwa* hymn books. According to Tella, these songs came to him by divine revelation, 'Bach nor Beethoven could have composed the songs of *Ifeoluwa* – it's God who composed them.' The singing is accompanied by African drums, a Western drum kit, and a keyboard.

After the singing of the *Ifeoluwa* songs, the creed is recited in Yoruba,

> *I believe in God Almighty*
> *I believe in Jesus Christ*
> *I believe in all the Messengers of God*
> *I believe in the Holy Spirit*
> *I believe in the Day of Resurrection*
> *I believe in* Ifeoluwa *and his precepts*
> *May God help me to do His will*
> *Amen*

Tella then enters the temple accompanied by his disciples, who hold burning candles and ring bells with which to summon the angels. It is believed that God has elevated God's messenger, *Ifeoluwa*, above all mankind, and the angels of God prostrate to him. Resembling the Muslim practice of *tawaf*, when pilgrims to Mecca circumambulate the Ka'aba (the most sacred site in Islam) seven times,[8] Tella circumambulates the Holy Spirit Square – an open space decorated with a cross –

---

[8] *Tawaf* is believed to demonstrate the unity of Muslims in the worship of God, as they move in harmony around the Ka'aba, while supplicating to Allah.

Figure 3.1 Tella sitting on his throne with the Bible in one hand and the
Qur'an in the other hand.
Photographer: Marloes Janson

seven times while holding both a Bible and a Qur'an (Figure 3.1).
According to Tella, the holy scriptures are incomplete, 'What many
people don't know is that the true story of Jesus' birth is
missing from the Bible.' To complement the Bible and Qur'an, Tella is
working on his own Holy Book, the *Ifeoluwa* Book, which is kept in a
velvet-lined box on the altar. Since he does not consider himself a
religious scholar, the book contains none of his own theologies but only
divine revelations.

After circumnavigating the Holy Spirit Square, Tella delivers a sermon
in Yoruba and English recounting passages from the Bible, Qur'an, and
Ifeoluwa Book. I heard Tella elucidating his message of love in a way that
recalls the Pentecostal theology of the Prosperity Gospel,[9]

God doesn't love one religion more than another. Among all religions,
Christianity and Islam are closest to each other. Christians and Muslims should

---

[9] According to the Prosperity Gospel, God bestows spiritual and material blessings on
those He loves, whereas the Devil is responsible for poverty.

love each other, but instead they hate each other. Because they don't open their hearts for love, they have problems. God means love. The way to reach God is through love. Once you receive my message of love and disseminate it to others, you will prosper in life. If you want prosperity in your business, radiate love. If you want success in your life, you must spread the gospel of love.

The service ends with a joint prayer. Unlike Muslims, who pray five times a day, *Ifeoluwa*'s congregation prays only twice a day. Tella explained, 'My adherents are required to pray every three hours. But because life in Lagos is hectic, I have been pleading on my adherents' behalf for God's grace to accept prayers twice a day. They don't have time to pray more than twice a day, but they love God constantly in their hearts.' This pragmatic approach to religion is characteristic of Chrislam, as we will see in this chapter. The closing prayer, during which *Ifeoluwa* adherents gesticulate wildly with their arms to open the way for deliverance, is followed by testimonies and thanksgiving. Similar to Pentecostal services, the testimonies recount the 'miracles' experienced by Tella's followers when they accepted God's love in their lives, in the form of healing, finding a spouse, the birth of a baby, finding employment, or a windfall. After the service, the congregants assemble to receive *manna*, that is, blessed food.

In addition to the weekly service, which lasts for about three hours, *Ifeoluwa*'s congregation assembles every Thursday to attend a night vigil. The purpose of the vigil is to maintain a closer relationship with God and to develop spiritually. Other weekly events are the Friday Victory Hour, during which the sick get healed. *Ifeoluwa* is portrayed as 'the Jesus of our time' to whom God has attributed Jesus's healing powers. Once a year *Ifeoluwa*'s followers set out on a pilgrimage to the 'Mount of Authority' in Tella's home town in Ogun State, where they pray and fast uninterruptedly for three days. Tella's daughter told me, 'Like Muslims have their pilgrimage centre in Mecca and Christians in Jerusalem, we have our pilgrimage centre on the Mount of Authority. We are proud that God has chosen Nigeria as Chrislam's pilgrimage centre.' Another annual event is the Dancing Anniversary, when Tella – who, similar to King David, has been commanded by God to dance for Him – dances and brings out the religious paraphernalia that are normally kept inside the temple. This is an important event for the congregation, who receives special blessings on that day. In addition, the anniversary of the *Ifeoluwa* mission is celebrated annually and the last Sunday of December the Harvest Thanksgiving Day takes place.

Somewhat paradoxically, despite Chrislam's inclusive conception of religion, Tella seems to draw on the idiom of the secret society – a socio-religious institution in Nigerian society that provides collective solidarity and security for its members – as the basis for his mission.[10] Membership is modelled on an initiation rite during which members undergo a cleansing ritual that washes away their sins and requires years of spiritual training. Initiation is expected to elicit a higher spiritualty and new moral lifestyle that will promote social harmony. Just as membership in a secret society is constrained by restricted knowledge, membership of *Ifeoluwa* is restricted by the observance of eighty rules and regulations concerning codes of moral behaviour (such as 'any member who wears *Ifeoluwa*'s uniform should not rebuke or speak against any religion'), dress codes (Tella's female followers are obliged to cover their heads and all followers must dress modestly), and food taboos derived from the Old Testament and the Qur'an (members must avoid drinking alcohol, abstain from eating fish without scales, such as catfish, and pork; only *halal* meat is allowed). Like in Islam, several rules and regulations emphasize the importance of 'purity' (women must stay away from the temple during their menstruation plus one extra day, after which they must sanctify themselves; members must take a bath after sexual intercourse and stay away from the temple for at least six hours).

During their spiritual training, the initiates, who are called 'Dove Members', earn different spiritual ranks, symbolized by coloured belts worn on their white gowns,[11] and religious paraphernalia such as prayer staffs and swords. These religious items are believed to protect them against spiritual attacks by evil forces, and enable them to heal fellow worshippers. Dove Members assemble every Wednesday for a three-hour prayer session to call upon the power of the Holy Spirit. In order to reach a higher spiritual level that brings them closer to God, they fast on Fridays – the most holy day in the Muslim calendar.

Tella acknowledges that *Ifeoluwa*'s strict rules and regulations prevent his adherents from committing themselves wholeheartedly. Adherents often attend weekly services for some months, but, when the problem that brought them to *Ifeoluwa* has been resolved, they return to their former church, mosque, and/or shrine. As a result, there is a high level of fluctuation among the congregation. To pierce the cloud of secrecy surrounding his mission and to attract more adherents, the *Ifeoluwa*

---

[10] During the economic crisis in the mid-1980s, and especially during the coercive and repressive military regimes of the 1990s, secret forms of organization (re-)emerged in Nigeria (Gore and Pratten 2003). One of the most popular of these secret organizations is the Reformed Ogboni Fraternity: a Christianized version of a precolonial Yoruba political institution.

[11] The wearing of white gowns by *Ifeoluwa* worshippers is a reminder of the dress code in the so-called White Garment Churches (*alasofunfun*) – that is, *Aladura* churches – as well as in certain Muslim prayer groups, such as NASFAT.

mission has recently built a website and joined Facebook.[12] On the website a remarkable story has been recorded: during the midst of the COVID-19 pandemic, Tella received a 'divine message' from an angel that descended on the Mountain of Power to summon him to come out to the world. Upon this divine revelation, he issued a press release on 25 April 2020, to ordain his adherents and all the religious leaders worldwide to follow ten instructions, composed of special prayer formulas.[13] These prayer formulas address all believers and instruct them to point their swords or staffs of authority, Bibles, and Qur'ans upwards to the sky while prostrating and reciting six times 'Jehovah, take this evil away from us' in the language best known to them. The press release also states that 'Jehovah' can be substituted for 'Allah' by those speaking Arabic or *Olorun* (God) by Yoruba speakers. By following these instructions, the global pandemic could be put on hold and peace would rule.

Although *Ifeoluwa*'s recent publicity has led to a small increase in worshippers attending weekly services, and a modest international following intrigued by the idea that Chrislam might be the solution to the Israel–Palestine conflict, Tella intentionally wants to keep his congregation small so that he can rule it as a 'spiritual family', 'The more people, the more *wahala* ['trouble' in Pidgin English]. I don't care about numbers; I care about people being prepared to do the will of God.' Just as his mother was allegedly pregnant with him for thirteen months, Tella thinks that his mission – which aims to bring 'a new world order beyond the imagination of homo sapiens' – also needs time to flourish.

Oke Tude: Mountain of Loosing Bondage

Tella complained that a man calling himself Prophet Dr Samsindeen Saka[14] had stolen his idea and founded his own Chrislam movement in 1989. Although several of his followers advised him to take Saka to court, Tella refused, saying: 'I don't like *wahala*; God knows the truth.' In addition to Chrislam, Saka's movement is also known by its Yoruba name *Oke Tude*, 'Mountain of Loosing Bondage', a name that is redolent

---

[12] See www.facebook.com/groups/297672903678845/ and https://ifeoluwamission.org/.
[13] See https://ifeoluwamission.org/press/ifeoluwa-heals-the-world-covid-19/?fbclid=IwAR 1B4685HL3thP-gA1JnDcvo4v1sgWSxsEqngqj5_7ghzNMeua1XoQ2XrDM.
[14] Based on his power to 'see' ('seeing' is the term used in Pentecostal churches for prophecy), Saka regards himself as a prophet intermediating between God and his followers. Besides prophesying, another feature of Pentecostal churches is the growing trend towards intellectualization (Marshall 2009: 179–81). In line with this trend, Nigerian Pentecostal pastors often adopt the title of 'doctor', deliver lectures, publish books, and open universities. As reflected in his title and activities, Saka – who allegedly never finished secondary school – has been influenced by this trend.

Figure 3.2 Running *Tude*.
Photographer: Akintunde Akinleye

of Pentecostal discourse. Similar to Pentecostal churches, the basic idea behind *Oke Tude* is that worshippers' progress in life is blocked by evil powers that hold them trapped in bondage with Satan. By fasting and participating in a ritual called *Tude* or 'running deliverance',[15] during which worshippers run seven times around a replica of the Ka'aba containing a well with 'holy' *Tude* water while shouting 'Hallelujah' and '*Allah Akbar*' ('God is great'), it is believed that they can be delivered from these demonic forces. Deliverance, which is accompanied by possession by the Holy Spirit, is expressed through good health (Figure 3.2). The crutches hanging on the wall next to the well serve as proof of the healing powers of Saka, who even claims to be able to cure AIDS.[16] Physical healing is but one aspect of deliverance: there are also promises

---

[15] *Tude* resembles the *sa'i* ritual during the *hajj*, when pilgrims run or rapidly walk seven times back and forth between the hills of Safa and Marwah. This is a re-enactment of Hagar's search for water before Allah revealed the water of the Zamzam well to her.

[16] The practice of exhibiting healed members' crutches probably comes from the Catholic tradition of ex-votos. One sees a similar practice in T. B. Joshua's The Synagogue, Church of All Nations (SCOAN) in Lagos. Joshua's alleged healing powers have brought him international fame but also national condemnation. In July 2001, leading Pentecostal pastors from Nigeria and abroad gathered to condemn Joshua as an 'agent of Satan' (Marshall 2009: 18, 300n.48).

of affluence, fertility, virility, freedom from family problems, passing exams, and getting jobs when taking part in *Tude*. This deliverance ideology explains *Oke Tude*'s popularity in Lagos, especially among socially marginalized groups, including barren women and unemployed youth.

In Nigerian society, bearing children is a prerequisite for attaining complete social and moral womanhood, and childless women are often abandoned by their husbands. Women's concern with bearing and successfully rearing children may lead them to *Oke Tude*'s weekly Women Affairs Programme, which offers them the means to 'destroy the yoke of barrenness'. During the programmes that I attended, I heard dozens of women, and a few husbands, praying aloud to God to 'open my womb and let my fibroids melt down in Jesus's name'. Besides barren women, quite a few unemployed youth attend *Oke Tude*'s Prayer Warrior School, where they study the Bible and Qur'an, on Wednesdays. At a time when a school diploma is no longer considered sufficient to secure upward social and economic mobility and the promise of a more successful life, religious movements such as *Oke Tude* offer disenfranchized urban youth the spiritual means – and sometimes also the material ones, in the form of business opportunities and small loans – to bridge the gap between their aspirations and actual possibilities. For instance, a man in his early thirties told me that 'Daddy GO' (General Overseer, i.e. Saka – a title that is also used in Pentecostal churches) helped him find a job and obtain a plot of land on which to build a house for his family. Although *Oke Tude* is not an exception, because Pentecostal churches and Muslim movements such as NASFAT offer similar material support, what makes Chrislam exceptional is that, by mixing elements from both Christianity and Islam, members believe that they will be blessed multiply. Several members explained to me that Chrislam allowed them to hedge their bets by 'combining the powers in Christianity and Islam', thereby doubling their chances of achieving a 'good life': that is, a life of good health and wealth. For instance, the *Oke Tude* imam told me that he prayed eight times a day – five times in the Muslim way and three times in the *Tude* way – in order to benefit from the cumulative power of prayers.

Besides the benefits, several members mentioned the 'costs' of joining *Oke Tude*. A young veiled woman whom I met during *Oke Tude*'s Sunday service reacted hesitantly when I asked whether I could interview her. After several phone calls, she finally allowed me to visit her at her sister's place. She did not want me to visit her at home since her Muslim husband does not know that she worships in *Oke Tude* in the hope it will cure her migraine. She attends services on Sunday morning when her husband attends NASFAT prayer meetings. She feared that her husband

and in-laws would consider her an 'unbeliever' if they knew that she attended services at *Oke Tude*. Because, in Islam, apostasy is considered a sin, several interlocutors from a Muslim background did not openly present themselves as Chrislamists. But since running *Tude* made her headaches disappear, this woman took the risk of being considered an apostate.

Even Saka – who, like Tella, was born into a Muslim family, but whose father was a famous herbalist – initially found it hard to bear the costs of his Chrislam mission, which forced him to give up his booming business in herbs. However, he felt he had no other choice since he received a 'divine call' to establish his mission, 'When I was on *hajj* and rested near the Ka'aba, God showed me in a dream photographs of religious war in Nigeria.[17] He assigned me to bridge the misunderstanding between Christians and Muslims.' Although Saka made the pilgrimage to Mecca four times, for a long time he followed the example of his father – to the regret of his mother, who introduced herself to me as a dedicated NASFAT member – and worked as a herbalist. His vision encouraged him to stop his business in herbs, to divorce his five wives, and to establish a worship centre in Ojota, a lower middle-class neighbourhood on the outskirts of Lagos. On *Oke Tude*'s flyers, the location of the worship centre is indicated by means of the name of the closest bus stop. While one often sees double-parked cars in front of Pentecostal churches on Sundays, most members travel by bus to *Oke Tude*. In a country where cars are seen as a status symbol, the fact that most *Oke Tude* members do not own a car suggests that they are from a lower-class background.

From the outside, *Oke Tude*'s worship centre looks like a church, but with its pillars the inside resembles a mosque. As in a mosque, *Oke Tude* members perform ablution (*wudu*) and remove their shoes before entering the worship centre, and there are separate seating areas for women and men. A banner on the glass façade – which makes the worship centre resemble an office building – says that this is neither a church nor a mosque but 'Chrislam alias *Oke Tude*'. Initially, Saka had wanted to register his worship centre under the name of 'Chrislamherb', a portmanteau word expressing a mixture of Christianity, Islam, and 'Yoruba religion' that believes in the power of herbs for healing purposes. However, the government's Corporate Affairs Commission (CAC) that registers religious organizations did not approve of this name, which Saka then changed into *Oke Tude*. Ironically, whereas state representatives

---

[17] The fact that Saka received photographs by divine revelation is interesting in relation to the heavy mediatization of religion in Nigeria (see Chapter 4).

took offence at Saka's attempt to mix Christianity, Islam, and 'Yoruba religion', they did not see a contradiction in his bringing together Christianity and Islam.

Because many people knew him as a successful herbalist with his own television show, Saka soon attracted a congregation of a thousand or so followers who started worshipping in his centre in the hope of being delivered. In addition to his worship centre, Saka runs three smaller *Oke Tude* branches in Lagos, three in Abuja, one in Ogun State, one in Ibadan, and a house fellowship in London. According to Saka, *Oke Tude* flourishes mainly in Lagos, which he explained as a result of its pluriform setting where 'Christians and Muslims belong to the same family'. His own family situation, with his late father practising herbalism and his mother being a pious Muslim, is a case in point.

In addition to *Tude*, which takes place on an individual basis, Saka's followers engage in congregational worship. Every Sunday they assemble at 8 am to participate in a Muslim prayer session (*wuridi*) led by an imam. The imam opens the prayer session by saying 'Glory be to God the Father, the Son, and the Holy Spirit', before performing *dhikr* (remembrance of God by recalling His names) and reciting Qur'anic and Bible verses. The *wuridi* session is followed by a Christian prayer session led by a rotating group of gifted prayer leaders reciting special prayer formulas or 'prayer points' for health and wealth, and closed with a joint service led by Saka himself. Before the joint service starts, the choir sings Christian and Muslim songs in a mixture of Yoruba and English, followed by *Oke Tude*'s anthem,

> *Oh God, the Heavenly One*
> *The Creator, come and hear us*
> *May the peace of God be upon Isa (Jesus Christ),*
> *And also upon Muhammad*
> *May the peace of God be upon Samsindeen Saka and the noble prophets*
>
> *God of* Tude, *deliver us*
> *Deliver us from illness, sorrow, and the challenges in our lives*
> *God of* Tude, *deliver us*

While the singing is ongoing, Saka enters the stage dancing (Figure 3.3). Copying the style of Pentecostal pastors, he arrives at *Oke Tude*'s worship centre in a Hummer and he dresses flamboyantly in either Western suits or traditional attire. He opens his sermon – called a 'lecture' in *Oke Tude* discourse, in line with the growing trend towards intellectualization in Pentecostal churches – by quoting in both Yoruba and English verses from the Bible and Qur'an that stress the similarities between Christianity and Islam. During a service that I attended, Saka assured

Figure 3.3 Saka on stage.
Photographer: Akintunde Akinleye

his followers that, irrespective of being a Christian or a Muslim, 'God would answer our prayers because we're all children of Abraham',[18]

Who is a child of Abraham? A Muslim is a child of Abraham. 'Muslim' is an Arabic word that stands for 'believer' in general. As such, a Christian can be a Muslim too, because they are both believers. What Christians believe, Muslims believe and what Muslims believe, Christians believe. Do we have two different suns for Christians and Muslims? ... I have never visited a restaurant where only Muslims eat, nor have I ever shopped in a supermarket where only Christians shop. Because we are children of Abraham, Christians and Muslims should not fight over God; God is able to fight for Himself.

Saka concluded that 'we're all the same', which, as in a Pentecostal service, was answered by the congregation clapping and shouting 'Hallelujah', with the only difference being that '*Allah Akbar*' and '*Ameen*' were also shouted. The service ended with a joint prayer led by Saka in a mixture of Yoruba and Arabic, fusing Christian and Muslim elements such as contemplation with folded hands and prostration.

[18] Saka's conception of the Abrahamic religions seems to exclude Judaism. There are not many Jews in Nigeria, except for some Igbo communities with Judaic practices (Bruder 2008).

In addition to the worship service, night vigils take place twice a month and attract a large following. Similar to Pentecostal churches, *Oke Tude* organizes an annual 'Convention'. In order to attend these programmes, one does not have to convert. An *Oke Tude* member is only expected to buy a copy of both the Bible and Qur'an, and to run *Tude* for seven consecutive days. To this end, new members sometimes temporarily stay in *Oke Tude*'s guest house. Running this guest house is an additional source of income for Saka, who is also involved in selling second-hand cars and in the real-estate market. He has invested the money he earned as an herbalist in property, which he now sells to his adherents to whom he preaches that, 'To become successful in life, you must change your status from tenants into landlords.' In an attempt to compete with the massive Pentecostal prayer camps along the Lagos–Ibadan Expressway, Saka told me in 2017 that he had started developing '*Oke Tude* Village' along the Expressway. Another of Saka's enterprises is his bookshop, where he sells his religious pamphlets and books with imaginative titles such as 'Key to Happiness', 'Today's Success is Mine', 'Prayer Points: Your Spiritual Vitamins', and 'True Messages: Similarities in Bible & Quran', audio and visual recordings of his Sunday services, and bottles of anointing oil and 'Blood of Jesus' (a drink made out of red corn) that are ascribed healing powers. Like Pentecostal religious entrepreneurs, Saka's wish for the future is to have his own television channel, 'The whole world should know of Chrislam!'

Spirit of Hope

Although Tella and Saka claim not to have anything to do with one another, there are actually many similarities between the two Chrislam leaders and their movements. Most importantly, they both use the term Chrislam as a concept for self-designation. Tella explained, 'I coined the term Chrislam for what I'm doing: bringing unity between Christians and Muslims. Let's emphasize our similarities and leave our differences aside.' Through their mixing of Christianity and Islam, Tella and Saka aim to deliver their followers so that they will succeed in life. Therefore, Chrislam's religious mixing has to be understood not so much against the backdrop of religious violence, which is largely unheard of in Lagos, but rather against the urban contingencies such as un- and underemployment, social inequality, poverty, and disease that Lagosians face on a daily basis. The uncertainty and precarity that pervades everyday living in Lagos explains why an increasing number of the urban lower middle class, who feel frustrated by the failure of the Nigerian state to deliver welfare to its citizens, have turned to movements such as Chrislam, which provide them with the spiritual but, above all, the pragmatic means to overcome social anxiety and economic hardship.

Larkin and Meyer explain the dynamism of Pentecostal Christian and reformist Muslim movements in urban West Africa by their ability to provide 'the networks and infrastructures that allow individuals to nego-tiate the material anxieties of living in uncertain economic times' (2006: 307). In a similar vein, Chrislam's popularity can be explained by its ability to mitigate the insecurity that marks everyday living in Lagos. Chrislam is not alone in providing Lagosians with a discourse of material and spiritual security; other religious movements also promise eternal rewards for those whose lives are marked by poverty and inequality. The difference is that Chrislam is believed to offer a more powerful discourse of hope than Christianity or Islam alone. One of Saka's religious pamph-lets is entitled 'My Hope is Not Lost', encouraging readers not to lose hope in challenging times. During one of his Sunday services, he summoned his congregation to laugh. When I asked him afterwards why his congregation had spent half of the service laughing rather than praying, Saka explained,

Poverty, unemployment, illness, difficulty in finding a partner, barrenness, witchcraft attacks, and all other sorts of problems that my followers encounter on a daily basis bring them to *Oke Tude*. By making them laugh and letting them dance, they forget their problems. My lectures are like vitamins for the soul.

That this method is effective was demonstrated by a former Area Boy, who confessed that he found comfort in *Oke Tude*, 'When I joined *Oke Tude*, I stopped fighting and engaging in other sinful things; my life changed completely.' Similarly, Tella's sermons contain moral lessons that are interpreted by his followers as 'religious pep talk', instructing them in how to combat their feelings of despair and how to become successful in life.

In light of this spirit of hope, most Chrislamists rationalized their joining *Oke Tude* and *Ifeoluwa* in pragmatic terms, arguing that physical, spiritual, and/or financial problems had led them to Chrislam. An example is Peter, who narrated his moving life story in his single-room apartment where he lived with his wife and three children. My research assistant and I were offered the only two plastic chairs in the scarcely decorated room. Seated on the floor, Peter told us,

The people who, after spending time in Lagos, returned to my hometown were driving nice cars, so I thought that Lagos was the New York of Nigeria where one could earn big money. I arrived in Lagos with high hopes. But life in Lagos was not what I had expected. Instead of a paradise, it was more like hell. When I couldn't find a job, I started shopping between churches. I also briefly joined a Sufi order. ... I have been worshipping at so many different religious sites, but my prayers were never answered. When I could no longer afford my rent and my children's school fees, I tried to commit suicide but I was saved by God's voice ordering me to keep up. Shortly after my suicide attempt, somebody told me about *Ifeoluwa* and I decided to go there. When I came home after my first *Ifeoluwa* service, my wife asked me whether I was drunk. I responded to her that I was drunk with joy. My family now also attends *Ifeoluwa* services. I feel that good things are about to come to us. No condition is permanent, *kodi* [isn't it]?

Peter's narrative illustrates that Lagos is a city that offers prospects for having a good life. At the same time, it emphasizes the stereotypes of Lagos as an urban apocalypse: a place like hell. In an effort to turn hell into paradise, Peter engaged in religious shopping. Remarkably, while his religious shopping brought him to *Ifeoluwa*, it led others away from it. For example, Prince Charles, who was introduced in Chapter 1, continued his religious shopping after having worshipped in *Ifeoluwa* for nearly a year. Because Christian rituals play a prominent role in Chrislam, practising Christians such as Peter find it easy to join, while others rejoin their former religious movement when Chrislam does not bring the miracles they had hoped for. Because Chrislam is a non-doctrinal religion that does not require conversion, members' backsliding is not considered in terms of apostasy by Chrislam's leadership.

Its non-doctrinal nature explains Chrislam's popularity in Lagos. Rather than orthodoxy it emphasizes orthopraxy, offering urban dwellers such as Peter the tools to overcome their problems. For example, *Oke Tude*'s Healing School teaches its participants special prayers and other techniques to heal themselves. During one of the sessions that I attended, several participants complained about 'itching hands', a condition that was explained by the leading pastor as a metaphor for the situation they found themselves in: being poor, unemployed, and not being able to spend money. He guaranteed that as soon as they started running *Tude*, drinking *Tude* water and bathing with it, and fasting more regularly they would see changes in their lives and their hands would stop itching. This example illustrates that, as in Pentecostal discourse, 'healing' is not only significant in its literal sense but also as a potent metaphor for renewal and deliverance.

Because of its emphasis on orthopraxy, Chrislam offers more room for religious mixing than the orthodoxies of Christianity and Islam allow.[19] Opposing the conventional understanding of religion as normative

---

[19] By privileging the performative aspects of religious practice over religious belief, Tella and Saka reassert traditional religious patterns that assign primacy to preventing misfortune and maximising good fortune. The influence of the local historical religious heritage on Chrislam, which is particularly visible in *Ifeolowa*, deserves further study.

doctrine, Tella remarked, 'I don't like dogmatic teachings.' Saka went as far as defining *Oke Tude* in terms of a 'practical religion', offering members the tools to 'instant deliverance', 'People come here to fight their enemy. Their enemy is illness, barrenness, death, poverty, disillusion, frustration, failure, sorrow. We teach them how to pray to God, Abraham, Moses, Jesus, and Muhammad in order to conquer their enemy. Prayer is the key to success.' To underline that pragmatism outweighs doctrine in Chrislam, one of Saka's ministers – who introduced himself as an *alfa*-pastor (*alfa* is the Yoruba term for a Muslim cleric) – said, 'God is not interested in our faith; to Him it doesn't matter whether we are Christians or Muslims. All He is interested in is what we *do* with our religion.' Indeed, as Bayat (2007: 588) points out, marginalized urban residents cannot afford to be ideological; instead, they are more likely to side with religious movements because they effectively support them in their everyday needs.

In short, the appeal of Chrislam is to be found in the fact that it does not just promise peace and fortune in heaven; it wants to assure its members that peace and fortune can be had on earth too. This explains its expansion in Lagos, Nigeria's 'aspirational axis where dreams will live or die' (Adichie 2019). The fulfilment of Lagosians' dreams requires improvisation and experimentation, and Chrislam can be seen as part of this improvisational and experimental lifestyle. Remarkably, whereas Christian and Muslim theological doctrines put more emphasis on salvation and the afterlife, Chrislam promises a better life on earth. The general conviction among Chrislamists is that God – referred to as 'the living God' in Chrislam discourse – is immanent, and active in their lives, and concerned with solving their problems. Because God is believed not to be a remote entity but someone – a 'lover' in Tella's terms – with whom one can communicate through prayer, Chrislamists may influence Him through their ritual actions. This urges us to shift our attention from religion as a coherent belief system preoccupied with universal truth to the practicalities, complete with their incoherence and contradictions, of lived religion.

Unity across Difference

Pluriform movements such as Chrislam prompt us to question not only the categorical absolutism of our conventional conceptions of religion but also to rethink the concepts that we have long used to study religious mixing. As we have seen in Chapter 1, the mixing of elements of divergent religious traditions has been captured under the banner of syncretism. The Oxford English Dictionary defines syncretism as 'an attempted union or reconciliation of diverse or opposite tenets or practices'. The assumption in theories of syncretism is that divergence must eventually be assimilated into coherence (McIntosh 2019). This makes syncretism inadequate for understanding the ways Chrislamists practise and experience their religiosity. Whereas syncretism emphasizes coherent religious practice, Chrislamists do not strive to harmonize Christianity and Islam, and are not bothered by ontological contradictions between the two traditions. Because the available theory for understanding Chrislam's religious pluralism is limited, here I plea for assemblage as an alternative conceptual frame. Unlike syncretism, assemblage is not intended to designate an absolute category but recognizes the inconsistency, incoherence, and unpredictability that marks lived religion in Lagos.

As Gellner strongly puts it, the question as to whether a given religious tradition is syncretic is a 'waste of time' (1997: 277). The only valid questions are in his opinion 'when, where, how, and why do *other people* become concerned about, and fight over, the concept of syncretism' (1997; emphasis in the original). These questions suggest that syncretism is rarely an emic category. According to McIntosh (2009: 185), even when syncretism appears to be quite evident to the outsider, it may not be so to the insiders who insist on the authenticity of their religious practice. Indeed, syncretism may appear as anti-syncretism – defined by Shaw and Stewart (1994) as 'the antagonism to religious synthesis shown by agents concerned with the defence of religious boundaries' (7) – in the eyes of the religious practitioners themselves.[20] In this spirit, what to the scholar of religion may look like the combination of incommensurable religious elements into a syncretic synthesis is for Chrislamists not conflictual at all.

That Chrislamists do not pursue internal consistency in their religious practice was highlighted by a university student. She told me that her father is a Muslim who prays in the mosque, while her mother is a Christian who worships in *Oke Tude*. She herself attends the *Oke Tude* services during the holidays that she spends with her family in Lagos. At university she attends a Pentecostal church. Nevertheless, she considers *Oke Tude* more efficacious because she recovered from tuberculosis after running *Tude*. Yet, when I asked her which religious affiliation she fills in on a university form, she responded, 'Muslim, of course, since my father is a Muslim'. The relativism implied in this young woman's narrative

---

[20] An example of anti-syncretism is found in the *Aladura* churches. Peel (1968: 129, 133–4) criticized studies that analyse them as syncretic churches; according to the church members, their forms of prayer healing and possession are not syncretic since they have Western Christian rather than Yoruba origins.

(she remains Muslim while attending Chrislam and Pentecostal services) stands in marked contrast to the essentialist notion of religion that the framework of syncretism reinforces.

That Chrislamists do not necessarily recognize contradictions between Christian and Muslim theologies became clear to me during an interview with a dedicated *Ifeoluwa* member who responded to my question as to whether he worshipped Jesus as the son of God (as in Christianity) or as a prophet (as in Islam) that 'he is both'. Highlighting their similarity, Tella preached, 'Jesus Christ is on my right-hand side, the Prophet Muhammad is on my left-hand side; they are two of my best friends.' Although Chrislamists put Christianity and Islam on the same footing as prophetic traditions, the most fundamental doctrine in Islam is *tawhid*, which holds that God is One. The Islamic principle that God is Unitarian differs from the Christian doctrine of the Trinity. However, Tella's first wife did not see a clash between these doctrines. She exclaimed, 'God is not three but just one. Both Christians and Muslims believe in the same God and they believe that He is one. We aren't idol worshippers!' A minister in *Oke Tude* reacted angrily when I asked him about the differences between Christian and Muslim doctrines,

Whether God is one or three and whether Jesus is the son of God or a prophet doesn't matter to us. Christianity and Islam differ only 5%; they have 95% in common. So what's your argument about? The Ten Commandments can be reduced to two: 1) God is God, nobody is like Him – that's *La ilaha illa Allah* in Islam; and 2) Love your neighbour as you love yourself, as the Christians say. That's what religion is about. Do you get what I'm saying?

Again, this narrative illustrates that Chrislamists perceive Christianity and Islam as similar rather than opposing faiths.

I had expected that Chrislamists would have problems with the notion of the Holy Spirit, because unlike the figure of Jesus this is a notion predominant in Christianity while absent in Islam, but I was proved wrong again. When expressing my confusion about how the notion of the Holy Spirit had become firmly integrated within Chrislam, a female *Ifeoluwa* member lectured me, 'The Holy Spirit is the Holy Spirit, whether it touches a Christian or a Muslim.' Tella added, 'The Holy Spirit is not reserved to Christians – God doesn't discriminate. He revealed himself to humanity through the Holy Spirit. Muslims call him Jibril; Christians call him Gabriel – it's all the same.' These narratives suggest that, for Chrislamists, religion is not centrally about the truth of one religious tradition and the falsehood of others. Instead of embodying competing sets of truth claims, both Christianity and Islam are believed to represent distinct powers for achieving a state of deliverance and therefore may well be combined. A male *Oke Tude* member of long standing put it clearly, 'Unlike what most people think, Chrislam is not about mixing Christianity and Islam in a new religion. We gain the good things from both.'

Because Christianity and Islam are not considered to be contradictory but rather are seen as complementary, most Chrislamists do not feel the need to give up the faith in which they were born upon joining *Ifeoluwa* or *Oke Tude*. During *Oke Tude* programmes, I noticed that several women wore a *hijab*. To prove to a new member from a Muslim background that *Oke Tude* embraces Islam, Saka asked his followers from a Christian background to step forward, followed by those from a Muslim background, during a Sunday service. I observed that like Saka, around 80 per cent of his congregation, and almost all choristers, were born Muslim. Although Muslims are known in Yoruba as *Imale*, meaning 'hard knowledge', Chrislam's Muslim-majority congregation suggests that Islam is 'softer', in the sense of more accommodating, than Christianity.

That differences between Christianity and Islam are not erased but rather upheld by Chrislamists is manifested in their worship. Many Chrislamists told me that in addition to praying in the Chrislam style in *Ifeoluwa*'s temple or *Oke Tude*'s worship centre, they continued praying in either the Muslim or Christian way at home, in the hope of receiving dual blessings. Besides fasting on Fridays (in the case of *Ifeoluwa* initiates) or when running *Tude* (in the case of *Oke Tude* members), it is common practice among Chrislamists from a Muslim background to fast during Ramadan, while many Chrislamists from a Christian background fast during Lent. Furthermore, instead of running around the replica of the Ka'aba during *Tude*, several *Oke Tude* members told me that they were dreaming of going on *hajj* and worshipping at the Ka'aba. Thus Chrislamists remain, to some extent, loyal to the religious tradition in which they were born (mostly Islam), while making use of and interacting with another religious tradition (in most cases Christianity). This openness to religious pluralism is not only a factor in drawing Lagosians to Chrislam; it also explains why membership of Chrislam is not accompanied by a formal conversion ritual such as a baptism or sacramental communion. Rather than rejecting previous identities, as in the conversion from one religious tradition to another, Chrislamists' religious behaviour resembles what Travisano (1981; cited in Kirsch 2004: 707) calls 'alterations', whereby religious practitioners switch between different identities.

From the above, it may be concluded that Chrislam's mode of religious mixing is not just about assimilating Christianity and Islam in a syncretic synthesis, but about drawing on both religious traditions simultaneously while marking them as distinct. That distinctions between Christianity and Islam are preserved rather than assimilated in Chrislam's religious practice was also demonstrated during the naming ceremony of Saka's granddaughter. The ceremony was led by an *Oke Tude* minister and opened with Christian and Muslim prayers for the week-old baby girl and her parents' well-being. Afterwards the *Oke Tude* members sang Christian hymns, followed by *dhikr* whereby Allah was remembered by recalling His names. Some of the guests seemed confused by this mix of Christian and Muslim elements. To enlighten them about Chrislam, the minister preached, 'Our Ministry is called *Oke Tude*. Religion is more than just Christianity or Islam. In our Ministry we preach about love between Christians and Muslims. Love is the fundamental religious principle.' After reciting verses from the Bible and the Qur'an, the three names of the baby were announced: she received a Christian, Muslim, and Yoruba name. As in a Christian naming ceremony, the baby and her parents were then anointed. Donations were collected from the guests and the minister encouraged the baby's mother to spend the money on a Bible and Qur'an for her daughter. After praying the Lord's Prayer and the *Al-Fatiha*,[21] the ceremony was closed with a joint meal composed of rice and *halal* meat, with added lustre from drumming.

Because of the preservation of religious difference through religious mixing, assemblage – which, according to McFarlane and Anderson (2011), functions as 'a name for unity across difference' (162) – seems a more fine-grained analytical tool for analysing Chrislam than syncretism. Whereas syncretism assumes an essence and presupposes the distinctness of religious traditions, the concept of assemblage does not take religious boundaries for granted. As such, it is more in line with the ways in which Chrislamists experience their religiosity. And while syncretism focuses on the mixing of religious elements into a new organic whole that assimilates its component parts, assemblage leaves room for the juxtaposition of divergent religious elements. As the case studies illustrate, Chrislam's mixing of Christian and Muslim beliefs and practices is not about reconciling Christianity and Islam into a comprehensive system; contradictions between Christianity and Islam are not reasoned away, but rather embraced as part of the multitude of spiritual gifts bestowed by God upon humanity – gifts that deliver Chrislamists from hardship in

---

[21] The Lord's Prayer (also called the 'Our Father', *Pater Noster*, or the 'Model Prayer') is a prayer which, according to the New Testament, Jesus taught as the way to pray. The *Al-Fatiha* is the opening prayer in the Qur'an.

their lives. The rationale behind Chrislamists' assemblage of Christianity and Islam is that by appropriating the divergent powers of Christianity *and* Islam, one's chances of having success in this world and the hereafter are accumulated.

To sum up, as part of my wider project of understanding religious pluralism in Lagos and my broader aim of providing an emic stance on religious mixing, we stand to benefit from a more refined analytical tool than syncretism. Assemblage may help us in this endeavour because it challenges the fundamental assumptions about unified theologies in the Abrahamic religions. But while the assemblage of Christian and Muslim beliefs and practices is immanent in the way Chrislamists practise and experience their religiosity, the resulting boundary crossing is sometimes interpreted as trespassing by those in power, as illustrated by Jamiu Yusuf's Chrislam movement outlined in the next section.

From Assemblage to Heresy: Yusuf's Banned Chrislam Movement

Ultimately, in the search for what the Yoruba call *alafia*, that is general well-being, the appropriation of diverse religious elements is permitted as long as it helps them achieve health and wealth. The appropriation of diverse religious elements can be interpreted as a 'hermeneutic procedure' (Schneider 2003: 224–6) whereby symbols and artefacts from one religious tradition are translated into another. As Meyer (1994) illustrates in her study of the translation of the Bible into the Ghanaian Ewe language, translation is both a creative and a risky enterprise in that it may result in the subversion of missionary ideas. As a result of translation, a form of Christianity came into being in Ghana that partly evaded missionary control (63).[22] In a similar vein, the translation process in which Chrislamists are engaged is precarious in that the appropriation of elements from divergent religious traditions may result in their reinterpretation (or misinterpretation): they no longer signify what they signified in the tradition from which they were appropriated, and, as such, translation may open the way for alleged heresy.[23]

---

[22] According to Meyer (1994: 58–9), the widely held belief among the Ewe in the continued existence of witches and evil spirits was an unintended (and undesired) result of the translation of the Bible. Although the Protestant missionaries condemned this belief as a superstitious 'heathen' survival, by using the Ewe term for evil spirits for the Devil they unwittingly encouraged witchcraft beliefs.

[23] As Asad (1993: 39) points out, religion requires authorized practice and authorizing doctrine. Heresy refers to unauthorized religious practice.

Tella and Saka both met with opposition because of their assemblage of Christian and Muslim beliefs and practices. Tella recalled how at the beginning of his mission, he sought publicity for *Ifeoluwa* by writing letters to Gaddafi and Mandela. Since he was jeered at in the local press, he decided to avoid the spotlight and lead a secluded life on the Mountain of Power, until he received a divine message that summoned him to come out to the world. Saka also faced several setbacks: initially, he did not get permission from the government to register his movement as 'Chrislamherb', and more recently, his plans to expand his mission have been thwarted. During a business trip to London in 2008, Saka's auditorium was bulldozed on local government's orders. According to several state authorities, this had nothing to do with Saka's ideology but with his grabbing of land that belonged to the Lagos State Government. Saka's congregation, however, did not buy this explanation; for them the auditorium's demolishment was the sign that the government was 'against Chrislam'. Their scepticism is not ungrounded: land allocation constitutes a form of government control of minority religious groups in Nigeria.[24] The problems that Tella and Saka encountered in running their Chrislam missions are minor compared to what Jamiu Yusuf, the leader of yet another Chrislam movement, had to put up with.[25]

Upon his return from *hajj* in 2010, Yusuf founded a movement called 'The Chosen Kingdom of God' in Abule Egba – a poor neighbourhood in Lagos – where he lived in a rented compound with his three wives, eight children, and thirteen disciples, who were all formally trained in Islam. Earlier he had founded his own Sufi group (Yusuf was a follower of the late Senegalese Tijani leader Ibrahim Niass), but after he had visions in which Jesus appeared to him[26] he started mixing Islam and Christianity. For example, when performing *dhikr* he added 'In Jesus' name'. Yusuf and his disciples met every Sunday to read the Bible and pray together. They attended naming ceremonies, weddings, and

---

[24] For example, in the mid-1990s the governor of Oyo State tried to acquire the property of Guru Maharaj Ji's Divine Love Mission, an Eastern-inspired religious group with a prominently situated prayer camp along the Lagos–Ibadan Expressway. Although Guru Maharaj Ji was able to prove legal ownership of the land in court, he has been accused of engaging in illegal activities ever since.

[25] During my field research in Lagos, Yusuf's Chrislam movement was already banned. The case study in this section is therefore based not on participant observation, but on interviews that I conducted with Jamiu Adegunwa who exposed Yusuf, the chairman of the Muslim Lawyers' Association of Nigeria (MULAN) who brought charges against Yusuf, the lawyer who defended Yusuf, three of his disciples, a police report, court records, and the DVD that Adegunwa recorded of Yusuf's worship.

[26] Yusuf's complainants referred to these visions as 'hallucinations' and questioned his sanity. Yusuf refused to take part in an examination of his mental health, the outcome of which might have shortened his imprisonment.

funerals to preach that the Prophet Muhammad was succeeded by Jesus Christ to save the world. Through proselytization, Yusuf assembled a congregation of around a hundred.

Ustadh Adegunwa[27] – who is popularly known as 'Nigeria's Ahmet Deedat' because like the late South African Muslim missionary he uses Christian styles of preaching and the Bible to strengthen the Muslim defence against Christian evangelism – brought Yusuf's movement to public attention. In an interview, Adegunwa told me that he first heard about Yusuf via one of his 'boys', who lived in the same compound as a follower of Yusuf. What he heard about Yusuf's style of worship alarmed him and he visited him in 2010 to interrogate him about his faith. The DVD that he recorded at this occasion – with the consent of Yusuf, who had hoped for publicity for his movement – starts with songs. We hear Yusuf's disciples singing in Yoruba,

> Take all the glory, Muhammad take all the glory
> Take all the glory, Jesus take all the glory
> Don't let our enemies mock us
> Jesus Christ is our Lord
> Ameen

When they finished singing, Yusuf introduced himself to Adegunwa, 'It's the Prophet Muhammad standing in front of you. Don't think I'm mad. The Prophet said that a *Mahdi* would be coming to the world and that Redeemer is me. … I have been sent to do the work of God; this is my mission.' After reciting a Qur'anic verse in Arabic, Yusuf proceeded, 'The Qur'an is the word of God, but He didn't write it. The Qur'an is an ordinary book; it has been compiled by the Arabs as a reference book.' In disbelief, Adegunwa asked, 'Do you really think that the Qur'an is a mere book?' Yusuf confirmed this by saying, 'God didn't bring the Qur'an to us. What you want to know about the Prophet, you can ask me. I'm here to clarify things.' Before Adegunwa could fire another question at Yusuf, the latter announced that it was time to pray.

We see the camera zooming in on Yusuf's disciples performing ablution (*wudu*). Unlike mainstream Muslims, they washed only their hands and feet and they used water from the same bowl. A disciple explained to Adegunwa that his 'master', Yusuf, had tried to make the Muslim ritual of *wudu* 'less cumbersome'. To simplify the Muslim mode of worship, Yusuf and his disciples prayed once instead of five times a day. After *wudu*, a young disciple dressed in jeans opened the prayer in Yoruba,

---

[27] *Ustadh* is a title for an Islamic scholar.

In the name of Jesus
Praise be to God
The Lord of the heaven and earth
Holy is your name
Yours is all glory and praise
Your mercy is ever lasting
Because you have guided us on your path
The path that you love dearly
Holy is the Judge of the heaven and earth [2x]

The prayer concluded with the congregation kneeling and repeating after the disciple,

God has mercy on His Prophet
Because He has blessed him
He taught him the knowledge of the Bible
We will seek for God's mercy on him
So that he will take us to Jesus our Lord
Alafia

After the prayer, Adegunwa, who had refused to pray with Yusuf and his disciples, enquired, 'I have never seen a prayer like this before. What kind of prayer is this?', to which Yusuf responded, 'This is the most important prayer that is mentioned in the Qur'an: *Salatul wusto*.'[28] The interview closed with both scholars accusing one another of misleading Nigerians. While they shook hands in front of the camera, each prophesied that the one who was telling lies would die within seven days. Penning this some seven years later, both scholars are still alive: Adegunwa is heading *Izhar-ul-Haqq Da'wa Movement*, which is involved in what he calls 'comparative religion', and since his release from prison in 2013, Yusuf is wandering around waiting for a revelation to come to him.

At first sight, Yusuf's mode of worship does not differ that much from the prayers that I observed in *Ifeoluwa* and *Oke Tude* because they all combine Christian and Muslim elements. But while Tella and Saka have not raised much upheaval, when the DVD featuring Yusuf's worship was broadcast on national television protests broke out by Muslim groups based both in- and outside Lagos. The DVD eventually landed on the desk of the director of the State Security Service (SSS) – Nigeria's intelligence agency – who sent out a warrant for Yusuf's arrest in January 2011. A house search did not produce much of a case against Yusuf, except for a booklet he had authored, titled *Falsafatul-Ikhiwa* or

---

[28] *As-Salat Al-Wusta* is believed to be the superior prayer in Islam. It translates as 'the middle prayer' and Islamic scholars disagree among themselves about which of the mandatory five prayers it is.

'The Philosophy of Brotherhood' (2005). In this booklet, written in Arabic, Yusuf acknowledged the brotherhood of all Muslims. Although NASFAT propagates a similar message (see Chapter 4), several Islamic scholars made a fuss about Yusuf's booklet because the cover showed a picture of a romantic *tête-à-tête* between a Western man dressed in a suit and an unveiled woman holding a rose. In the complaint against Yusuf, it was stated that his booklet 'provoked and brought into disaffection a section of the Muslim community'.

In February 2011, Yusuf and his disciples were brought before the Magistrate Court of Lagos State, whose verdict was that Yusuf managed an 'unlawful society' by 'making public utterances designed to disturb peace and promoting animosity between persons of different religious faiths', thereby committing an offence against Sections 63 and 88 of the Criminal Code of Lagos State.[29] Because Yusuf's congregation was not in the position to put up bail for their leader, a group of concerned Muslim intellectuals from Lagos offered support on condition that Yusuf would convert to Islam. Yusuf declined their offer, arguing that he already was a Muslim. Together with his disciples, he spent fifteen months in prison. One of the prosecutors confided to me that while he believed the imprisonment of Yusuf and his disciples was justified, the prison was not just an institution to 'punish them for their act of heresy' but also a 'place of shelter' to protect them against angry mobs of Muslims wanting to lynch them. When the bail conditions were lowered, Yusuf and his disciples were finally bailed out in 2013. Since Yusuf had no place to go to (during his detention his landlord had confiscated his apartment and had driven his wives and children out), he went back to his birthplace, where, I was told, he still lives with his relatives waiting for Jesus to re-appear to him. During an interview with three of Yusuf's former disciples in 2017, they told me that they had converted to Christianity and were attending Pentecostal churches.

The question remains why Tella and Saka, who engage in similar practices of religious pluralism as Yusuf, get away with Chrislam, while Yusuf had to pay the price for it? I believe that the answer lies not so much in Yusuf's assemblage of Christianity and Islam per se, but rather in his public statements that falsified the prophecy of Muhammad and the authenticity of the Qur'an. Based on his ideology, the Magistrate Court of Lagos State accused Yusuf of being an 'extremist' who ran an 'unlawful society' with the aim of 'creating animosity' between Christians and Muslims. The DVD of Yusuf's worship was broadcast on television

---

[29] According to Section 63 of the Criminal Code Law Cap. C17, the charge against managing an unlawful society is seven years of imprisonment.

at a time when the threat of Boko Haram's insurgencies was at its height.[30] The accusation against Yusuf and his disciples therefore needs to be seen in light of the government's pressing need to maintain the security of the public order.

Of overriding importance in Yusuf's verdict was his formal training as an Islamic scholar: he claimed to have graduated from the prestigious *Markaz* Institute of Arabic and Islamic Training Centre in Agege (Lagos).[31] Tella and Saka's religious credentials are such that they are regarded by most of the religious authorities whom I interviewed as 'ignorant' and therefore 'harmless'. Both Tella and Saka emphasized in their sermons, quite strategically I would say, that they were not well versed in religion. While Tella claimed to be illiterate (his *Ifeoluwa* Book was revealed to him by God and he claimed not to have written it himself), Saka introduced himself during our first interview as follows, 'I don't know anything; I'm just an ordinary person,' and he referred me to his personal assistant. Yusuf, on the other hand, publicly presented himself as an Islamic scholar and to underline his reputation of being well-versed in Islam he published in Arabic. Like Yusuf, Saka calls himself a 'prophet' but not in the sense of Muhammad's reincarnation but of a religious intermediary as is also common in the *Aladura* churches. Tella, who considers himself a messenger of God, is working on the *Ifeoluwa* Book that complements the Bible and Qur'an. But unlike Yusuf, he does not claim that the Qur'an is 'inauthentic': according to Tella, the religious scriptures are 'incomplete'. Remarkably, Saka's religious pamphlets contain disclaimers that (1) *Oke Tude* neither adds to nor removes from the Holy Books; and (2) *Oke Tude*'s mission is not to convert Christians to Islam or Muslims to Christianity; its faith is 'Abraham's faith'. By means of these disclaimers, Saka seems to counteract possible accusations of heresy.

A further dilemma that Yusuf's Chrislam movement presents us with is why the secular Nigerian government got involved in determining Chrislam's legal status. As Larkin (2016) observes, the study of religion in Africa has been organized around a binary logic, 'Animist movements

---

[30] While initially attacking 'soft targets', Boko Haram insurgencies in 2011 included the suicide bombing of the United Nations office in Abuja. This led into a state of emergency at the beginning of 2012 – the time of the detainment of Yusuf and his disciples.

[31] This private training centre was founded by Sheikh Adam Abdullah al-Ilory, a graduate from Al-Azhar University in Egypt, in 1952. On its website the centre prides itself for having formalized Islamic training: for the first time in Nigeria's history blackboard and chalk, rather than a wooden slate and reed pen, were used in Qur'anic education (http://morkaz.tripod.com/instituteofarabicandislamictrainingcentermorkaz/id1.html). The rector negated that Yusuf was a *Markaz* graduate.

are opposed to mission Christianity; traditional (often Sufi) Muslims are opposed to Salafis; mainline Christian churches to the Born-Again movement; Islam to Christianity; both of them to animism; and finally, religion to secularism' (633). Whereas *Ifeoluwa* and *Oke Tude* challenge the Christianity–Islam binary, Yusuf's movement further impeaches the dichotomy between religion and secularism. Although Nigeria is officially a secular republic, the latter shows that the Nigerian state regulates religious life and politicizes religion through the law on 'unlawful societies'. As a result, the majority religions, Christianity and Islam, are privileged and linked with the legal and political order.

The aforementioned suggests that religious pluralism is not just a social phenomenon; it is also a political imperative. While Christians embrace secularism as furnishing a minimum degree of church–state separation, which allows them to practise their religion without state interference, Muslims, who believe that a clear separation between religion and politics is impossible, often regard it as a Christian dogma (Obadare 2018: 47). Thus, in a context of religious pluralism, secularism may serve, somewhat paradoxically, as both the reconciler and the instigator of religious clashes. Many Nigerians whom I met during my field research complained that the secular Nigerian state has intensified religious conflicts by converging politics and religion, thereby endorsing what Casanova (1994) calls the 'myth of secularization' (11). Not only has religion become increasingly politicized in Nigeria; Nigerian politics has also obtained a religious veneer. Under the influence of Nigeria's 'Pentecostal presidency' (Obadare 2006), in which politicians are pastors and vice versa, religion has become so deeply entrenched in Nigeria's public domain that the conventional binary of religion and secularism has become defunct. For instance, shortly before the presidential election in 2015, a photograph of Goodluck Jonathan kneeling down for RCCG pastor Enoch Adeboye while seeking blessings went viral. This photograph epitomizes the 'theology of engagement' (Kalu 2004: 59) between religion and politics in Nigeria. Or, in the words of Marshall (2009), 'the terms in which power, redemption, sovereignty, and other political themes are staged in its [Nigeria's] practices and professions of faith, stubbornly resist the distinction between sacred and secular we have come to take for granted in Western society and the categories of analysis we deploy to understand them' (3). Rather than two opposing trends, studying religion and secularism as part of an assemblage is more accurate and provides a better understanding of the operation of religious pluralism in Nigeria's secular political field.

From the above, it could be concluded that the Nigerian state upholds an essentialized conception of religion to create rules about the proper place of religion in society. If we want to gain a better understanding of religion as part of Nigerians' lifeworld, we should therefore move beyond politically entrenched notions of religions as mutually exclusive entities and the conventional religious–secular divide. Rather than separating religious traditions from each other, and the religious sphere from the secular domain, I agree with Casanova (2008) that in the case of pluriform religious settings 'it is not clear where religion begins and the secular ends' (105). What have long been studied as antithetical ideologies and immutable essences are actually interdependent concepts that are necessarily linked in their mutual co-constitution and transformation. From this view, to rethink the notion of 'religion' is also to rethink the 'secular' (Asad 2003; Taylor 2007).

Conclusion

This chapter analysed Chrislam's emergence within Nigeria's secular political field and Lagos's socio-economic setting. Urban dwellers such as Peter, whom we met in this chapter, not only engage in hustling for their survival in Lagos; they also engage in religious shopping with the hope of increasing their chances of having a better life. This aspiration explains the expansion of the Chrislam movement in Lagos, of which the underlying idea is that because Chrislam is an assemblage of Christianity and Islam it offers a greater range of opportunities for improving one's life than each of these traditions on their own.

Studying Chrislam in terms of an assemblage ties in with Lambek's (2008) call for replacing the exclusive 'either/or' binary logic that characterizes Western scholarship on religion with the pluralist logic of 'both/and' to mark local religious practice. For the Malagasy in Mayotte and north-west Madagascar, religion has long been inclusive. They argue that God is the same everywhere and hence it matters little which avenue one uses to approach Him. For example, a devout Malagasy Muslim told Lambek that when he served as a rural policeman in a region without mosques, he simply took part in Christian observances (125). This resembles Chrislam's inclusive religious practice, in which, instead of making absolute choices between bounded alternatives, Chrislamists engage in Christian and Muslim rituals simultaneously. Thus, a both/and perspective may help us in overcoming essentialist conceptions of religion as upheld in theories on syncretism, as well as reductive binaries whereby phenomena are labelled as either Christian or Muslim, religious or secular.

Chrislam affirms culturalist images of Lagos's pluriform religious landscape as tolerant. However, Yusuf's banned Chrislam movement shows that there are restrictions to religious pluralism. Nigeria's secular state determined Yusuf's Chrislam movement illegal; not only was it banned but Yusuf and his disciples were detained for over a year. From this it may be concluded that the state management of religious pluralism tends to reify a normative, monotheistic model of religion. As such, the case of Chrislam shows that religious practitioners' crossing of religious boundaries goes hand in hand with boundary making by the state. A similar ambiguity between boundary crossing and boundary making we see in the case of NASFAT, which I present in the next chapter. Also here the assemblage of Islam and Christianity should not be equated with dissolving religious difference, and religious difference cannot be interpreted as synonymous with religious conflict.

4   Pentecostalizing Islam?

Nasrul-Lahi-il Fathi Society of Nigeria (NASFAT)

> Pluralism takes the reality of difference as its starting point. The challenge of pluralism is not to obliterate or erase difference, nor to smooth out differences under a universalizing canopy, but rather to discover ways of living, connecting, relating, arguing, and disagreeing in a society of differences   (Eck 2007: 745).

The previous chapter showed that Nigerian society is characterized by interwoven religious and political strands. A wave of Pentecostal movements, mushrooming in the 1970s, transformed the political field in Nigeria. As many scholars have demonstrated, the explosion of Pentecostalism was religion's response to the crisis of the nation-state in Nigeria. In an environment marked by economic insecurity and uncertainty, Pentecostalism's health and wealth gospel could gain momentum, attracting millions of disillusioned Nigerian Christians. Indeed, the Pentecostal movement has become so vibrant in Nigeria today that many mainline Christian churches appear to be increasingly 'Pentecostalised' (Gifford 1998: 306). For example, the Nigerian Catholic Church increasingly emphasizes healing and deliverance, and Zink (2012) went as far as coining the term 'Anglocostalism' to describe the influence of Pentecostalism on the Anglican Church.

That Nigeria's Pentecostalisation is not limited to Christian movements is exemplified by *Nasrul-Lahi-il Fathi* Society of Nigeria, or NASFAT for short – the largest Muslim organization in present-day Yorubaland – that has appropriated Pentecostal prayer styles and organizational techniques. In its assemblage of Muslim and Christian elements, NASFAT resembles Chrislam. In fact, NASFAT is popularly known as 'Pentecostal Islam' among both lay Nigerians and scholars alike (Sanni 2004; Soares 2009, 2016; Peel 2016a). Although appealing, such an appellation has limited utility in shedding light on NASFAT's particular mode of religious assemblage. Whereas Chrislamists mix Christian and Muslim beliefs and practices to multiply their chances of achieving a good life, NASFAT's leadership appropriates Pentecostal prayer rituals in order to emphasize its Muslim distinctness. Rather than aiming to 'mirror' (Larkin and Meyer 2006) Pentecostalism, as the label 'Pentecostal Islam' suggests, NASFAT underlines its divergence. In this chapter,[1] I seek to understand NASFAT's assemblage of Muslim and Christian styles and strategies within the larger context of the religious marketplace. The case study of NASFAT illustrates that Muslims copy Pentecostals, while simulatenously drawing boundaries with Christianity, in an effort to increase their competitiveness on the market-place that is Lagos (see also Soares 2016: 687). Based on its appropri-ation of Pentecostal elements, NASFAT points to a new style of Islamic reform that, unlike Salafism, does not advocate the rejection of the West, but combines Islamic ethics and Western capitalist business manage-ment to simultaneously enhance Muslims' competitiveness not only on Lagos's religious marketplace but also on the transnational religious market.

Nigerian Muslims are concerned that Pentecostalism, with its lively worship, its flashy health and wealth gospel, its extensive use of modern media, and its policies of offering leadership positions to young people, will lure their children away from Islam (Soares 2009). In an attempt to curb Muslim parents' anxiety about the exodus of youth, a group of Western-educated Yoruba professionals founded NASFAT in Lagos in 1995. Targeted at Muslim youth, NASFAT is fashioned as a 'pacesetting Islamic organization' aspiring to achieve 'conformity to modernity'.[2] In consonance with neoliberal consumer capitalism and a lifestyle associ-ated with modernity, it offers management courses taking the Prophet Muhammad as an exemplar businessman,[3] employability training work-shops, professional network meetings, and a dating service called 'Dating the *Halal* [lawful in Islam] Way'. These are also the kinds of services that Pentecostal churches offer, which explain their appeal to a youthful, upwardly mobile middle-class. Consequently, NASFAT can be inter-preted as a direct response to Pentecostalism.

---

[1] This chapter is a longer and revised version of my article in a special issue of *Social Anthropology* (Janson 2020). Whereas the latter focuses on NASFAT's appropriation of Pentecostal elements, here I also pay attention to the dialectic between belief and practice.

[2] The citations in this chapter are from NASFAT's Constitution (NASFAT Society 2011), Prayer Book (NASFAT Society 2006), Code of Conduct (NASFAT Society 2005), and website (www.nasfat.org/).

[3] Drawing on the example of the Pentecostal churches that promise 'business breakthrough' and offer 'business clinics', NASFAT member Mudathir Abdul-Ganiyu published a booklet titled *Timeless Wisdom for Modern Managers: Leadership Strategies of Prophet Muhammad* (2006), in which he elaborates on how being a good businessman and a pious believer reinforce each other (in Peel 2016a: 188).

Although I focus here on Pentecostalism's influence on reformist Islam, the influence goes in two directions, as was highlighted during an interview with a Pentecostal woman married to a Muslim. She told me that while Christian funerals normally last several days, many Nigerian Christians nowadays bury their dead the same day, which she explained as a Muslim influence,

> It's cheaper to bury one's beloved ones immediately like the Muslims do: you don't need to pay the bill of the mortuary and you don't need to entertain your guests with food and drinks. Moreover, it's safer: if you keep the body in the mortuary, strangers could enter and do all kinds of evil things [i.e. witchcraft] to the body.

Not only in their ritual performance but also in other religious practices, Christians are influenced by Muslims. For example, copying from NASFAT's travel packages to Mecca, several Pentecostal churches organize pilgrimages to Jerusalem. It has become increasingly popular in Yorubaland for Christians to go on pilgrimage and return from their journey with an elevated status similar to *Alhajis* or *Alhajas*, which they mark with the abbreviation JP – Jerusalem Pilgrim – after their name (Nolte et al. 2010: 104).[4]

The study of religion is at its core a comparative exercise, such as in the conversion from one faith to another and in the interaction between religions (Chidester 1996; van der Veer 2016). This becomes even more pressing in the study of religiously pluriform movements such as NASFAT. While the previous chapter addressed the question of how we can compare Christianity and Islam in one analytical frame, this chapter asks: what are we actually comparing in a comparative study of religion? According to Loimeier (2016), comparison usually involves reduction. We compare what we can observe, such as ritual, prayer, sacrifice, saint veneration, pilgrimage, and other material manifestations of religion, while leaving out what is not manifest: beliefs, meanings, and doctrines. Indeed, Peel's (2016a) argument in his masterpiece *Christianity, Islam, and Oriṣa Religion* is that similarities rest on formal characteristics at the expense of content. The common distinction between 'outward' forms and 'inward' beliefs or content – which is dictated by what Asad (1993) calls a 'Protestant legacy' in which beliefs are privileged above rituals – underpins theorizing about religion. The shortcomings of such an approach have been demonstrated by Asad

---

[4] In this context, Asamoah-Gyadu (2016) speaks of the 'Meccanization of Jerusalem'. Remarkably, the Redeemed Christian Church of God (RCCG) advertises its prayer camp as 'a *Pentecostal Mecca* where Christians of all denominations come to seek the face of God and get their miracles' (Ukah 2013: 191; my emphasis).

(1983) in his sharp critique of Geertz's (1973) study of religion in terms of inner belief, confined to the level of doctrine. In practice, there is no such thing as an 'immaterial religion'; religious traditions are character-ized by diverse practices that blur any clear distinction between outward form and inward substance (Keane 2007; Vásquez 2011; Meyer 2012; Chidester 2018). If we want to gain a better grasp of what I defined in Chapter 1 as lived religion, we need an expanded definition of religion that sheds light on the dialectics between belief and practice or content and form, and NASFAT's religious assemblage may help us in this exercise.

I begin with a historical overview of NASFAT and its mission and vision, before presenting a case study of NASFAT's key ritual, the Sunday prayer assembly or *asalatu*. Although *asalatu* is premised on a Pentecostal prayer form – the crusade – the analysis shows that 'Pentecostal Islam', a concept that has gained currency in the recent upsurge of studies on NASFAT[5] and that implies syncretism, is misleading. I argue that Keane's (2007) notion of 'entextualization' is better suited to analyse NASFAT's religious assemblage in that it pro-vides a window into the process whereby a religious form that emerged within the Pentecostal tradition has become severed from its original context and is inserted into a Muslim context, thereby acquiring a new meaning. Entextualization points to how religions operate in a pluriform setting: as assemblages drawing on practices (form) and beliefs (content) from divergent religious traditions, which they carefully incorporate into their own (Larkin 2016: 637). The urban-religious assemblages that emerge in this process are, I conclude, premised on the skills of religious entrepreneurship; skills that NASFAT's leadership has mastered in its attempt to occupy a niche on the religious market.

NASFAT's Mission and Vision

Concerned about the lack of religious awareness among Muslim young-sters, a group of seven young professional Yoruba men – university graduates who were working in banking and other modern sectors of the Nigerian economy – assembled in Lagos in 1995 to establish a prayer or *asalatu* group. The driving force behind the group was Alhaji Abdul-Lateef Olasupo, now retired as a senior manager with one of Nigeria's largest banks and chairman of NASFAT's Board of Trustees. He and his fellows named the prayer group NASFAT, an acronym of *Nasrul-Lahi-il*

---

[5] See Soares (2009, 2016); Peel (2011, 2016a); Adetona (2012); Sanni (2012); Adeniyi (2013); Obadare (2016); Ibrahim (2017a, b); Janson (2018, 2020).

Fathi Society of Nigeria, which translates as 'There is no help except from Allah', and whose aim was to cater to the spiritual needs of the urban higher-class Muslim youngsters. Muslim youth were a group that had largely been neglected by the established Muslim scholars but who demographically and politically speaking had become a force to contend with.

The establishment of the Muslim Students Society of Nigeria (MSSN) in Lagos in 1954 indicated that Muslim youth had grown into a political force. In its early years MSSN was mainly concerned with giving social support to Muslim students in educational institutions where they were massively outnumbered by Christians, but over time it became more involved in political matters (Loimeier 2007: 55–9). From the late 1970s, students at Ahmadu Bello University, located in Zaria in northern Nigeria, began to radicalize MSSN, holding street demonstrations to support their call for 'Islam only', burning copies of the Nigerian constitution to protest the secularization of the Nigerian state, and voicing strong support for the then ongoing Iranian Islamic revolution (Umar 2001: 138). Unlike MSSN, NASFAT presents itself as a non-political movement, targeting moderate Muslim youth. The differences between both youth movements are most obvious in their perceptions of shariʿa law: whereas MSSN advocates the implementation of 'full shariʿa', NASFAT does not wish for an institutionalization of shariʿa but calls for a 'shariʿa of the soul', whereby members develop themselves spiritually so as to become 'perfect Muslims' (Peel 2016a: 167).

Although NASFAT keeps aloof from politics, it can be interpreted as an emancipatory movement by Yoruba Muslims. Soares (2009: 190) claims that although NASFAT has spread rapidly and widely since its foundation in 1995, it can be regarded as a form of Yoruba Muslim cultural nationalism. Adeniyi (2013) similarly describes NASFAT in ethnic terms. This may explain why NASFAT's spread to northern Nigeria was originally resisted: northerners read an ethnic motive by Yoruba Muslims into the movement's growth (331). Islam in the south-west is often described by northerners as having been subject to a process of 'Yorubacisation' (Danmole 2008: 205–6). This appellation is, as Nolte and Ogen (2017: 14–15) note, problematic because it suggests that there exists a 'pure Islam' from which Yoruba Islam, which is considered less 'orthodox' and more prone to 'syncretic' mixing with traditional elements than Islam in the north, is derived. To counter this image, Muslim groups in Yorubaland have been at the forefront of efforts to reform the practice of Islam from within their own communities. One of the earliest examples was *Ansar-ud-Deen* ('Helpers of the Religion Society of Nigeria'), which was founded in Lagos in 1923 with the aim of reforming Islamic practice through promoting modern, Western-style education (Reichmuth 1996). Along similar lines, NASFAT provides Yoruba Muslims with an organizational framework for a reformed religious community, thereby underlining that Yoruba Islamic practice is 'modern' and 'enlightened'[6] – both terms are being widely used in NASFAT's Mission Statement.

In just over two decades, NASFAT has become hugely successful. It now claims to have over 300 branches, not only in Nigeria but also in other African countries, Europe, the United Kingdom,[7] and the United States, and a membership exceeding 1.2 million. To become a NASFAT member, one must have attended at least five *asalatu* sessions and completed a registration form including the names of two NASFAT members who can act as referees. A registered member signs to comply with NASFAT's Code of Conduct, which aims at 'upholding the tenets of the Holy Qur'an and Sunnah of the Prophet'. This means that s/he agrees to observe NASFAT's moral imperatives of being truthful, steadfast, honest, caring towards her/his fellow Muslims, and moderate in her/his apparel and lifestyle. In case of misconduct, members are referred to NASFAT's Disciplinary Committee, who can impose sanctions such as suspension or termination of membership.[8]

NASFAT's expansion is to be explained by the appeal of its spectacular prayer gatherings or *asalatu*, which take place on Sunday mornings from 8.30 am to 12.30 pm and attract a larger audience than the Friday congregational prayer (*jumat*). Indeed, according to NASFAT's previous president Kamil 'Yomi Bolarinwa, *asalatu* is NASFAT's 'best-selling product', which has inspired other Muslim groups to set up their own

---

[6] While Peel (2016a: 136) claimed that the Yoruba notion of *olaju* – which is generally translated as 'enlightenment' (see Chapter 2) – was distinctly Christian, reformist Muslim groups such as NASFAT have invested heavily in enlightening the Yoruba Muslim community through education. We could thus say that the Yoruba value of *olaju* points to the commonalities between Christian and Muslim proselytizers in their attempts to offer their followers new ways of becoming 'modern'.

[7] During a Sunday *asalatu* that I attended in one of NASFAT's branches in London, the chairman explained to me that NASFAT offers a platform for mainly Yoruba immigrants, not only to acquire in-depth knowledge of Islam but also to socialize. Indeed, after the *asalatu* a group of young male members played table tennis, while the women – separated from the male section by a screen – chatted, ate together, and applied henna tattoos. Underlining NASFAT's social function in the diaspora, the chairman said, 'In London I don't have many relatives; NASFAT is my family.'

[8] As far as I am aware, only two officials have been reported to the Disciplinary Committee for adding supererogatory prayers to NASFAT's Prayer Book and for accepting monetary rewards from members. They were suspended, but when they repented to Allah they were reposted to other branches.

asalatu.[9] Explaining the choice for Sunday – the most important day in the Christian calendar – for *asalatu*, one of NASFAT's founding fathers told me,

We noticed that Muslim youths were useless on Sundays, sleeping late, watching television, doing nothing, while Christians went to church. Friday is the most blessed day for Muslims, but we don't have the same kind of privileges on Fridays as the Christians have on Sundays. That's how the idea of Sunday *asalatu* came up.

Several Muslim youths told me that no matter how long they have been partying on Saturday night, they make sure not to miss NASFAT's *asalatu*. According to a university student, 'My week doesn't start well if I don't attend *asalatu* on Sunday.'

When the number of NASFAT members increased from a few dozen in the mid-1990s to a few thousand in the late 1990s, *asalatu* was decentralized from NASFAT's headquarters in the Lagos Secretariat Central Mosque in Ikeja (the seat of Lagos State Government) to local branches spread all over Yorubaland. Here it should be noted that the mosque in Ikeja does not belong to NASFAT but is rented from the Lagos State Government. Rather than constructing its own mosques, NASFAT's leadership decided to invest in proselytization and education. Now that NASFAT has established hundreds of branches in Nigeria and beyond and its university is operating (see below), a fundraising campaign has been launched for a 2.5 billion Naira proposed mosque, the foundation laying ceremony of which I attended on 30 April 2017. According to the information brochure that I bought at the ceremony, the mosque is designed not just as a place of worship but as 'a citadel of learning and research', and its architectural features are intended to 'attract tourists, students, Muslims and non-Muslims'. One may read in this an attempt to compete with the Pentecostal megachurches that are dominating public space in Lagos. Another attempt to compete with Pentecostalism is NASFAT's prayer camp, where NASFAT's mosque will eventually arise.

The first Sunday of the month, NASFAT members based in Lagos and its environs assemble in NASFAT's prayer camp, stretching to 100 acres of land along the busy Lagos–Ibadan Expressway (Figure 4.1). Drawing on the examples of RCCG's Redemption City and MFM's Prayer City – massive Pentecostal prayer camps where hundreds of thousands of worshippers flock to attend prayer services

---

[9] Over the last two decades, numerous *asalatu* groups have cropped up in Lagos and beyond, but NASFAT is the most popular and influential (Sanni 2012).

Figure 4.1 NASFAT's prayer camp.
Photographer: Akintunde Akinleye

(see Chapter 2) – NASFAT's prayer camp, called NASFAT Islamic Centre, is being projected as a model city for Muslims. That NASFAT competes with the Pentecostal prayer camps became apparent in 2001, when its celebration of *Laylatul Qadr* or the Night of Power (the night during Ramadan when the first verses of the Qur'an were allegedly revealed to Muhammad) attracted tens of thousands of worshippers, as a result of which the traffic along the Lagos–Ibadan Expressway was blocked for two entire days. Because in the south-west the blocking of streets for prayer is usually associated with Pentecostal churches, NASFAT's flooding of the Expressway can be interpreted as an attempt to assert Muslim presence in what is marked a 'Christian space' (Obadare 2016: 75–76).

A missioner[10] explained NASFAT's enormous success as follows,

NASFAT has a strong mission and vision, which speaks to the Muslim elite. The majority of our members are bankers, business executives, accountants, lawyers,

---

[10] Perhaps in an effort to distinguish themselves from Christian missionaries, many NASFAT officials self-identified as 'missioners'. Their main responsibility is to spread NASFAT's message through *da'wa* (the 'call to Islam'). While all Muslim organizations engage in *da'wa*, within NASFAT this activity also encompasses economic empowerment in the form of business ventures (see later in the chapter).

engineers, doctors, university lecturers, and government officials. Besides elites, we are progressive Muslims who practise Islam in a way that fits today's world. Our social profile distinguishes us from other prayer groups.

The Western suits and ties that are worn during NASFAT's executive meetings are a symbol of the elite status to which NASFAT aspires. The targeting of Muslim professionals needs to be studied in relation to Pentecostalism's theology of the Prosperity Gospel that preaches that God bestows spiritual and material blessings on those He loves, which explains Pentecostalism's popularity among a young, upwardly mobile middle-class. In an attempt to reconcile Islam with the modern society in which urban youth live, NASFAT overtly copies from Pentecostalism. In line with its self-presentation as a modernist movement for the Western-educated elite, NASFAT preaches and publishes mainly in English. It struck me that only a minority of NASFAT leaders and members are literate in Arabic, that is, the language of the religious establishment.

In addition to its appeal among Muslim professionals, another factor behind NASFAT's phenomenal growth is, according to another NASFAT missioner, its inclusivity,

Any Muslim can thrive in NASFAT; we are a liberal movement.[11] Sufis, Izalas, and Salafis assemble on Sundays to pray together. You find here men with beards, clean-shaved men, men wearing their trousers cut at ankle-length, men with long trousers, women with fashionable *hijabs*, and women with body-covering gowns.[12] When you are a Muslim who accepts other Muslims, you are welcome.

NASFAT's non-sectarian character explains why the younger generation feels attracted to it. A university student told me: 'Other Muslim movements are strict on their members; they don't want women to wear fashionable clothes. But when I attend *asalatu* in jeans with a small shawl to cover my hair, nobody will complain. That's why I feel at home in NASFAT.' In line with its moral imperatives not to discriminate against Muslims and to recognize the equality of all Muslims for the sake of promoting Muslim brotherhood, NASFAT – unlike many other reformist Muslim movements in Nigeria – does not openly propagate an anti-Sufi position. Still, NASFAT's motto 'There is no help except from

---

[11] Underlining NASFAT's liberal character, I was told that the headquarters have employed seven Christians in (paid) secretarial functions.

[12] The style of Muslim dressing and the beard are seen as signs for sectarian distinctions between Muslim men. Following a well-known *hadith* (account of what the Prophet said or did), adherents of the Tablighi Jama'at and Izala – popular reformist Muslim movements in Nigeria – cut their trousers at ankle length and grow beards. For women, the length of the *hijab* is a marker of Muslim identity.

Allah' could be interpreted as a veiled criticism of the Sufi sheikhs who act as intermediaries between individual believers and God, and who in return for their spiritual services demand material rewards (Adeniyi 2013: 325). It may therefore be argued that, despite its open character,[13] NASFAT is preoccupied with the development of a reformed Muslim society that condemns the way Islam has long been practised locally.

To draw in more youth, NASFAT has set up a Youth Wing that is actively involved in organizing activities for youngsters, such as vocational and employability training, a platform for professional networking, a dating service, and an annual Youth Conference. Like youth, children have their own programmes. In addition to providing Qur'anic education, NASFAT's Children's Wing organizes holiday camps. The camp in 2012 took place in Mecca and Medina. That hundreds of parents were in a position to send their children on camp demonstrates NASFAT members' affluence. While NASFAT's mission is to cater for the spiritual needs of young people, the social aspect of its missionary activities should not be neglected. Indeed, NASFAT prides itself that its activities produce social bonding. According to a missioner, 'During our network meetings, like-minded Muslims can meet and learn from each other.' This social function, and not simply the provision of religious services, has contributed to NASFAT's popularity, especially in an anonymous megacity such as Lagos where many urban dwellers do not have a strong social safety net.

NASFAT targets not only the younger generation as the instrument of Islamic reform but also women. NASFAT's Women's Wing has been successful in raising the religious status of Muslim women and in bringing them together for educational purposes, such as vocational training, *tafsir* (Qur'anic exegesis) classes, and Arabic lessons. The latter take place on Sundays, as part of what NASFAT calls its 'Sunday School'. Since NASFAT's executive body opened up leadership positions to women, female representatives have become members of the National Executive Council and operate at the senior-most level of NASFAT, taking decisions on strategy, planning, policy, and investment. A female representative explained women's leadership roles in NASFAT as follows,

---

[13] This open character, which provides Muslims a platform to interact without being hampered by sectarianism, explains not only NASFAT's popularity but could, according to some critics, also herald its downfall. Frustrated by NASFAT's lack of theological foundation, a number of leading members have established splinter groups (Adetona 2012).

Women are the main pillar of support for NASFAT. They are more effective in raising funds and they are more committed to their faith than their male counterparts. Men are a bit funny you know. If you want to draw them in, you need to pamper them like babies. Women aren't like that.

Recently, NASFAT has started sending female delegates to the Da'wah Institute of Nigeria (DIN) for training so that they will be better able to proselytize. Because NASFAT is negotiating new roles for women, some established Muslim scholars accused its leadership of implementing *bid'a* or unlawful innovations (Adeniyi 2013: 332). A self-identified Salafi exclaimed,

Look at the women in NASFAT! They don't veil properly. They are just nominal Muslims: they don't observe the Islamic principles and they mix different religious ingredients, like in a soup. *Asalatu* groups such as NASFAT are like *Olobeyoo* [derived from *obe yoo*: a kind of soup that is popular among the Yoruba]; they are not pure Muslims.

NASFAT's leadership defended itself against such accusations by arguing that they strictly obey the Islamic principle of gender segregation. Women and men sit separately during *asalatu*, and security patrols to make sure that this rule is observed. Furthermore, female missioners are not allowed to preach among a male audience.

Criticism is coming not only from outside of NASFAT but also from within. Although the copying of Pentecostal organizational structures contributed to NASFAT's success, its spiritual leader, Chief Missioner Alhaji Abdullah Akinbode, criticized the way NASFAT is run as a business and demanded the merging of its administrative and spiritual leadership. When Akinbode's call for greater spirituality fell on deaf ears, he resigned in April 2017, taking many NASFAT members with him. Ironically, the solution to NASFAT's leadership crisis lies, according to a NASFAT representative, in its willingness to learn from Pentecostal leadership styles, 'If we do not want to lose our grip on the Society [NASFAT], we must copy Christian management structures. Only then can we deliver on our mandate of providing strong leadership to the Muslim *umma* in combating the onslaught of Pentecostalism.' NASFAT's modernist message of Islamic reform is disseminated during Sunday *asalatu*, which, copying Pentecostal discourse, are referred to as prayer crusades and the timing of which coincides with that of church services. Next I describe the course of events during *asalatu*.

NASFAT's Prayer Crusade

After another sleepless night caused by the loud night vigil in the Pentecostal church next to the compound where I was staying, my alarm clock rang at some ungodly hour. Dressed in a body-covering dress and a *hijab* I rushed to the gate, where my driver – whose car window sported a NASFAT sticker – was waiting. Along the way, we picked up my research collaborator Mustapha Bello, who at that time was NASFAT's Assistant General Secretary. Although it was Sunday, we got stuck in a 'go-slow'. From the stationary car, I observed Lagosians heading to their various religious programmes. In the cars next to us, I spotted men wearing smart suits accompanied by dressed-up women wearing hats or towering headdresses, with a Bible on the back shelf. In other cars, with prayer beads (*tasbih*) attached to the rear-view mirror, men dressed in caftans with matching caps were accompanied by women wearing colourful headscarves or more distinguished black *hijabs*. Bumper stickers propagated a variety of religious messages, ranging from 'I've found a friend in Jesus' to 'Proud to be a Muslim'. A group of young evangelists ran along the motorway, accompanied by a brass band, while shouting 'Hallelujah' in an attempt to combine their early-morning workout with proselytization. Hoping for alms from drivers stuck in the traffic, beggars reciting Qur'anic verses knocked on car windows. Young men manoeuvred between the cars recommending their merchandise, including religious paraphernalia. Loudspeakers set up in the recording studios along the highway sounded Christian hymns and Muslim sermons. Mustapha did not seem to be disturbed by this cacophony of religious sounds and symbols: 'This is Lagos for you,' was his dry remark.

We finally reached NASFAT's headquarters. At the gate – with separate entrances for women and men – a young woman and man, wearing vests with the caption 'usher', distributed envelopes for members' prayer requests – a practice that is common in Pentecostal churches, but that I had never observed among Muslim groups. In the stall next to the gate, I bought Alhaji Akinbode's CDs with what Mustapha called 'Islamic gospel music'. I knew Akinbode as NASFAT's Chief Missioner, but it turned out that in a previous career he had been the renowned lead vocalist of 'Voice of Islamic Ummah'. To my surprise, the CDs did not contain the solemn Qur'anic recitation that I was used to, but upbeat songs – resembling Christian gospel music – praising God and the Prophet. In another stall I bought NASFAT literature, including a booklet subtitled *Believers' Sword* – a collection of Muslim prayers for 'protection and for shielding against evil' (Shekoni 2012) – which resembled the booklets with special prayer formulas or prayer points that are sold in Pentecostal bookstores.

After shopping, we entered what Mustapha called the 'extension ground', where several tents had been put up promoting NASFAT's strategic objectives. According to its Mission Statement, which addresses

NASFAT members as stakeholders, it is NASFAT's mission to 'empower Muslims spiritually as well as economically'.[14] With this aim, it has invested heavily in business ventures, of which TAFSAN (NASFAT spelled backwards) Beverages is the oldest. TAFSAN produces and markets the non-alcoholic malt beverage Nasmalt,[15] fruit juice Nasita, and table water Fasan, which are sold during *asalatu*. Ten per cent of TAFSAN's profits go to NASFAT's university, Fountain University, which was founded in Osogbo (Osun State) in 2007. Explaining the university's foundation, a missioner told me,

Because of the Pentecostal syndrome that keeps Nigeria firmly in its grasp, we decided to establish our own university.[16] All big Pentecostal churches have a university, so we thought we also needed one. You can compare our mutual competition to that between MTN and Glo,[17] or Coca Cola and Pepsi.

That the foundation of Fountain University has not been a very lucrative business I noticed when I visited the university in 2017 and was welcomed by a dried-up fountain (the emblem of the university, representing a pool of knowledge) at the university gate. The dried-up fountain symbolized the state in which the university found itself, with a lack of funds to invest in infrastructure and with difficulties recruiting students and qualified staff. Somewhat ironically for a faith-based university, Fountain University does not teach Islamic Studies and Arabic. Several NASFAT members with the financial means to send their children to a private university opted for the established Pentecostal universities, rather than the relatively new and needy Fountain University. For most parents whom I interviewed, their children's perspectives of finding a good job on graduation had the upper hand over religious motivations (Dilger and Janson f.c.). In addition to a university, NASFAT runs nursery, primary, and secondary schools, combining Western subjects with moral values.

Also TAFSAN Tours and Travels and TAFSAN Investment were represented at the extension ground. To facilitate the increasing number

---

[14] NASFAT's use of a managerial language recalls that of Pentecostal churches, which from their American sources are well saturated with the idioms of corporate business (Peel 2016a: 188).

[15] Nasmalt tastes like Maltina, a non-alcoholic drink popular at Pentecostal social events (Peel 2016a: 277n.53).

[16] While NASFAT copied its university from Pentecostal churches, other Muslim organizations copied from NASFAT. For instance, *Ansar-ud-Deen* opened Summit University in 2017, and the *Ahmadiyya Muslim Jama'at*, which was involved in education long before NASFAT, intends to open its proposed Minaret International University soon.

[17] These are two competing telecommunication companies in Nigeria.

of Nigerian pilgrims to Mecca, NASFAT launched its own travel agency in 2006, which arranges travel to and accommodation in Mecca.[18] TAFSAN Investment is the name of NASFAT's community bank, which operates in accordance with the ban in Islamic jurisprudence on charging interest on loans. It offers microcredit for small businesses and vocational training for women and youth. NAZAS (NASFAT Agency for *Zakat* and *Sadaqat*) is a relatively new agency, responsible for the collection and distribution of alms and the provision of scholarships and empowerment grants. Since its foundation in 2014, NAZAS has collected *zakat*[19] worth 87 million Naira, which it has distributed among thousands of beneficiaries. In addition, NAZAS has donated clothes, shoes, and toiletries to the IDPs (internally displaced people) who suffered from Boko Haram insurgencies in the north-east, and has provided free medical services to those in need. Although most beneficiaries are Muslims, when a Christian family lost its house due to a mudslide in Lagos, NAZAS was the first religious organization to assist them. Another tent at the extension ground was occupied by NASHHIN (NASFAT Health and HIV Initiative), which provides medical services and raises awareness about HIV/AIDS and sickle-cell disease.[20] During the *asalatu*, members walked in to have their blood pressure checked. According to NASHHIN's health coordinator, health is a primary concern of NASFAT because 'only a healthy mind in a healthy body can serve God'.

These business ventures, which fill the vacuum left by the Nigerian state and generate income and publicity for NASFAT, put the movement on a par with Pentecostal churches running elaborate marketing plans that have turned them into known 'brands' on the heavily contested religious marketplace that is Lagos (Ukah 2013: 189). Unlike many other Nigerian Muslim organizations, NASFAT is not patronized by Islamic scholars but is organized as a corporate business composed of an Executive Council, Management Council, Board of Trustees, Business Secretary, Treasurer, and a Strategic Committee that is responsible for developing the corporate strategy of the organization. Similar to Pentecostal churches, over the past two decades NASFAT has turned into a known brand that is recognizable by its stylized logo composed of

---

[18] A 'Budget *Hajj* Package' costs roughly 1,525,000 Naira (approximately 3,000 GBP).

[19] *Zakat* – the third pillar of Islam – is the compulsory giving of 2.5 per cent of an affluent Muslim's total savings to charity.

[20] Sickle-cell disease, which causes people to die young, is common in Nigeria. Subscribers to the 'Dating the *Halal* Way' programme are advised to do a blood test in order to find out their genotype. The coordinators of the dating programme make sure to match couples with matching genotypes.

Figure 4.2 NASFAT's merchandise.
Photographer: Akintunde Akinleye

the Islamic star and crescent, which has gained both national and international recognition. Cars with a bumper sticker with the NASFAT logo
have become a common sight in the Nigerian traffic. NASFAT's former
vice-president told me laughingly that even his Christian friends drive
cars with a NASFAT bumper sticker, 'NASFAT has become a household name in Nigeria. Because NASFAT members are known to be
trustworthy, my friends believe the police will not stop them at road-
blocks when they see the sticker with the NASFAT logo.'

In addition to bumper stickers, the NASFAT logo is printed on the
promotional materials merchandized on NASFAT's website and sold at
asalatu, such as prayer mats, wall hangings, T-Shirts with the text
'Islam – my brand', veils, key rings, and the like (Figure 4.2). Another
way in which NASFAT has turned into a known brand is through its
media campaigns (Ibrahim 2017b). With a mixture of both awe and
disdain, a media-savvy Muslim preacher told me, 'The Nigerian media
have been overtaken by Pentecostals. Similar to the advertisements on
television for Coca Cola, Omo, and the like, the Pentecostal television
shows sink in. They enter your heart and you are affected by them,
irrespective of whether you are a Christian or a Muslim.' Drawing on
the example of the Pentecostal churches, NASFAT runs a public

relations office that negotiates airtime for missioners on radio and television, sends out press releases, and posts on Facebook and Twitter. Making use of new media technologies to help further its objective to develop an enlightened Muslim community, in 2005 NASFAT partnered with MTN to launch its Daily *Ayaat* service, enabling subscribers to receive the teachings of the Prophet on their mobile phones. Because of its active involvement in media and marketing – domains that have long been dominated by Christians – some mainstream Muslim organizations categorized NASFAT as not 'truly Muslim'. NASFAT's leadership responded to this criticism by arguing that their involvement in business-related activities is the only effective way in which Islam can survive the onslaught of rival faiths (Adeniyi 2013: 336).

When the sound of thousands of voices reciting Qur'anic verses was elevated to ear-splitting volume, we hurried to the prayer ground where I seated myself with a group of young women on a prayer mat at the rear, while Mustapha joined the missioners at the front. As with Pentecostal services, the *asalatu* began with praise worship, that is, praise of God and the invocation of blessings on Muhammad.[21] Similar to the hymn book in Pentecostal churches, NASFAT uses a Prayer Book for its praise worship. The Prayer Book, which is available in print, on CD, and as e-book, contains selected Qur'anic verses, supererogatory prayers (*du'a*) from the Qur'an, and prayers for the Prophet Muhammad. The verses, prayers, and supplications are in Arabic, presented in Latin transliteration alongside English and Yoruba translations.

The praise worship was followed by Qur'anic recitation or *tankara*.[22] Afterwards, the congregation was encouraged to donate money to the sponsoring of Fountain University. A NASFAT missioner explained the collection of donations in a way similar to how Pentecostal pastors legitimize donations in their churches, 'By giving money during *tankara*, Allah will reward us and make us prosperous.' Mustapha Bello added, 'We don't force members to donate; all contributions are voluntarily, but by donating our members can more easily relate with Allah.' In other words, donating is encouraged as a means of entering into a relationship with God (see below). Some members donated via credit-card to ushers with POS machines. NASFAT's funding is largely based

---

[21] Here it should be noted that the praise worship at *asalatu* parallels not only Pentecostal practices but also the Sufi invocations of blessings on the Prophet Muhammad, and the notion that there is special power in verbal formulas of praise of God (Peel 2016a: 190).

[22] This term is derived from the Arabic *iqra*, meaning 'read' or 'recite'. It is believed to be the first word of the Qur'an to be revealed through the angel Jibril, who commanded the Prophet '*Iqra*'. NASFAT coined the term *tankara* for the practice of reciting the Qur'an during *asalatu* and teaching the verses' lessons.

on contributions and collections at *asalatu*, which seems to have grown into a fund-raising event. To indicate NASFAT's popularity: the donations collected during a single *asalatu* sometimes exceed half a million Naira (about 1,000 GBP) (Adetona 2012).

After *tankara* an Islamic scholar delivered a lecture. Parallel to the trend in Pentecostalism towards a higher level of intellectualization, the sermons delivered at *asalatu* are referred to as lectures, during which the congregation takes notes. During a lecture that I attended, an invited Islamic scholar preached in English about prayer as the key to success,

Do not engage only in *salat* [the obligatory prayer five times a day] but also perform *du'a* [supereragatory prayer]. Only then you can develop yourself spiritually, and only then you will meet success in life. ... Pray ceaselessly and your problems will be solved. If you want to be successful in life, then raise your hands.

After being responded to by a mass of outstretched arms, the scholar concluded his lecture by preaching, 'May we all *insha'Allah* ("God willing") reap the full benefits of our praying and may *Allah Subhanahu wa ta'ala* ("The Most Glorious, the Most High") reward us.' At the end of the lecture, male members asked questions, while female members – whose voices are believed to be a part of the body that needs to be concealed – wrote down their questions on a piece of paper, which ushers passed on to the lecturer. Most questions were about the observance of Islamic principles in daily life.

As with Pentecostal services, the *asalatu* concluded with prayer requests. A missioner read out the requests that members had scribbled down at the gate, followed by a long prayer session during which the prayer requests would be answered. Several members then gave testimonies. Like in Pentecostal services, members testified that they were healed, found employment, or had a baby upon praying during *asalatu*. A young man testified that he survived a car accident because he carried the Qur'an and NASFAT's Prayer Book with him, to which the audience responded with *Allah Akbar* ('God is great'). Members like him, who encounter 'miracles' in their lives, often make generous donations to NASFAT. After the concluding prayer, thanksgiving was collected with the aim of – as the ushers explained to me – 'being spiritually and economically uplifted'. NASFAT holds out the promise to its members that individual ethical reform and economic empowerment go hand in hand (Soares 2009: 192). Again, this is in line with Pentecostalism's Property Gospel that emphasizes the achievement of success and wealth by worshippers as the mark of salvation. Indeed, according to NASFAT's leadership, the essence of *asalatu* is to be determined to please Allah in order to be granted prosperity by Him (see also Adetona 2012: 103).

After the recitation of blessings, most middle-aged members left for Sunday lunch with their families. Mustapha and I stayed to attend the monthly programme organized by NASFAT's Youth Wing, called 'Dating the *Halal* Way'. With the neoliberal reforms in the 1990s, many Nigerian youths find it hard to achieve adulthood. SAPs affected their access to economic opportunities, as a result of which they lack the financial means to marry and set up their own households. Recognizing the profound social consequences of stalled adulthood, Pentecostal churches have become involved in matchmaking events and marriage counselling (e.g. Marshall-Fratani 1993; van Dijk 2013). Sharing similar concerns as Pentecostal churches, NASFAT founded a dating service in 2000, with the aim of matching young Muslim women and men in a *halal* way and teaching them about matrimony as a divinely ordained institution. A Youth Coordinator sighed, 'Our Muslim sisters have been snatched by Christian men.' Indeed, several single Muslim women confided to me that they preferred marrying a Christian man, since Christians are known to 'take better care of their wives'. A divorced Muslim woman, who had given up on Muslim men, said, 'Christian men give you presents and take you out, whereas the only gift to expect from a Muslim man is prayer.' Christian men were not only believed to be more chivalrous but also better educated. NASFAT therefore promotes Fountain University among its male congregants in the hope of making them potential marriage material.

The 'Dating the *Halal* Way' programme that I attended started with Qur'anic recitation and praises of the Prophet. A university lecturer then took the floor to preach in English about the importance of avoiding pre-marital sex,

In Saudi Arabia one is stoned to death for *zina* [unlawful sexual intercourse]. Since we can't implement shariʿa all over Nigeria, make sure that you lower your gaze among people of the opposite sex. Don't meet with a person of the opposite sex in a secluded place; meet at public programmes like this one, but don't go behind doors. ... Don't engage in the sin of the hand. That means, don't shake hands with persons of the opposite sex. Shaking the hand of a girl you are not married to is like holding burning charcoal. One misstep easily leads to another one. Eye contact sends a signal to the heart and then the hand follows the heart and the doctor will tell you the result [i.e. pregnancy] of your misstep. Many youngsters believe that kissing is allowed before marriage. My brothers and sisters don't kiss. When you kiss, you have already done it [i.e. engaged in pre-marital sex]. ... Don't think that you are modern when you enter into a pre-marital sexual relationship; if you engage in pre-marital sex, you are a loser.

After the lecture and a round of questions, the moderator, in line with NASFAT's goal to economically uplift Nigerian youths, announced two vacancies in companies run by NASFAT members. The Youth Coordinators then distributed registration forms among new members. In addition to their personal details, including blood group and genotype, the form asked for new members' preferences in their spouse-to-be, such as skin complexion ('light, dark, anyone'), height ('tall, short, average'), weight ('plump, slender, average'), and beauty ('very beautiful, good-looking, average-looking'). The form also asked for preferences in educational qualifications ('must be a university graduate, could be a secondary school graduate, could be uneducated'), and finally level of faith and social status ('should be a *hijabite* [veiled] sister/an *alfa* [Muslim cleric, but in this context used in the sense of a man well-versed in Islam], could be wearing *hijab*, should be devout and sociable'). After a joint prayer for the well-being of Nigerian youth, the participants went home.[23]

Following a calendar similar to that of Pentecostal churches, NASFAT organizes not only weekly prayer crusades and a monthly dating service but also conducts bi-monthly night vigils or *tahajjud*, that is, all-night prayer meetings. When I asked a NASFAT missioner about the origins of *tahajjud*, he responded, 'We might say that Pentecostalism encouraged the congregational *tahajjud* as we do it in NASFAT every first and third Friday of the month.'[24] *Tahajjud* is an intense spiritual experience, in the course of which NASFAT members pray collectively. The proceedings of *tahajjud* resemble that of *asalatu* with as the main difference that there is more room for prayer that is ascribed an ecstatic quality (Peel 2016a: 187) (Figure 4.3).[25] Enhancing the ecstatic quality of communal prayers, the congregation chants in English and Yoruba during *tahajjud*,

---

[23] For a more detailed description of NASFAT's dating programme, see Janson (2018).

[24] The question of whether night vigils originated in either Christianity or Islam is hotly debated among religious scholars in Nigeria. According to Peel (2016a: 176–7), night vigils were not part of the evangelical missionary tradition, but originated with the *Aladura* church Cherubim and Seraphim. Realizing the benefits of communal prayer, the first modernist Muslim group, Ahmadiyya, copied from Cherubim and Seraphim. Ahmadi missioners went around in a group to members' houses to wake them up to pray, thus giving *tahajjud* – which of old has been an individual form of prayer in Islam – a communal dimension. Nowadays, most religious denominations, excluding Salafis who consider it to be an unlawful innovation (*bid'a*), hold night vigils. Most of my interlocutors (Christians and Muslims alike) agreed that in present-day discourse night vigil has a strong Pentecostal connotation.

[25] Here it should be noted that the ecstatic quality of *tahajjud* resembles not only Pentecostal night vigils but also bears similarities with long-established Sufi practices, the ultimate goal of which is to draw near to God.

Figure 4.3 Ecstatic prayer at *tahajjud*.
Photographer: Akintunde Akinleye

He has solved it for me (2x)
Allah
All the problems that I face
In my family
All the problems that I'm afraid of
Don't let me encounter them
Ameen

The resemblance with Pentecostal songs, which assign primacy to maximizing one's success in life, is striking. Highlighting the similarities, Mustapha referred to NASFAT's chants as hymns, 'The hymns spice up the *tahajjud* and give instant relief from tiredness. It has the same effect as drinking Nasmalt or Nescafé, which are sold during *tahajjud*.' According to Adetona (2012: 105–6), *tahajjud*'s aim is to provide NASFAT members with problem-solving or healing means: an aim that is close to Pentecostals' motivations to attend night vigils. Because of the prospect of encountering health and wealth, NASFAT's *tahajjud* often attracts thousands of worshippers, including Christians, waiting for miracles to happen in their lives.

This case study illustrates that there are many overlaps between NASFAT and Pentecostalism, especially in the style of worship during prayer crusades and night vigils. Remarkably, these overlaps are dictated not by NASFAT's wish to be similar to Pentecostalism so much as by the need to be different and enhance its competitiveness on Lagos's marketplace.

Developing Common Ground between Islam and Christianity

Established at a time when the Pentecostal presence in the public domain was increasingly pronounced, NASFAT is probably the most effective response to the Pentecostal movement. Somewhat paradoxically, while Islam and Christianity compete to win souls and secure urban space in Lagos, the very act of competition has led NASFAT to copy from Pentecostalism to a significant extent. Like producers commanding market share, NASFAT is engaged in competition with Pentecostalism by copying effective elements from it in order to win customers – a competition that is specific to the pluriform religious landscape in Lagos. Within this market analogy, NASFAT is an outstanding example of what Lanz and Oosterbaan (2016) call 'entrepreneurial religion', in which religion is regarded as a constitutive force of contemporary capitalism and therefore needs to be placed at the heart of the neoliberal construction of urban space. Indeed, NASFAT reformed Islam to be able to respond to new modes of urban living. For example, its executive body is engaged in business ventures, professionalization activities, network events, and dating programmes with a goal to empower Yoruba Muslims, a group that has long felt discriminated by northern Muslims.

What struck me most during my field research was that NASFAT's leadership openly acknowledged that they were influenced by Pentecostalism and drew parallels between its own practices and Pentecostal ones. This begs the question of how Muslim leaders learn Pentecostal practices and teachings. The answer lies in Lagos's oversaturation with Pentecostalism. Pentecostalism is present on every street corner in the form of churches or parishes, and in the streets renamed after Pentecostal megachurches and its leaders. Indeed, the mission of the RCCG, Nigeria's largest Pentecostal church, is to plant parishes within five minutes' walking distance in every city and town in Nigeria, and it seems to have attained this mission at least in Lagos. Pentecostalism's omnipresence makes Lagos, paraphrasing Anderson (2004), arguably 'the most Pentecostal city in the world' (4). Pentecostalism's public presence in Lagos is not just visible; it is also highly audible in the loudspeakers with amplified sermons. Pentecostal leaders buy airtime on radio and television and spaces in newspapers to propagate their message to the extent that, as noted by

Onuoha (2011: 222), the Nigerian media is almost synonymous with Pentecostalism. When I interviewed the previously cited media-savvy Muslim preacher who complained that the Nigerian media have been overtaken by Pentecostals, I also sensed awe for Pentecostals' media strategies. After the interview, the preacher gave me a tour in his private library, containing several books written by Nigerian and American Pentecostal pastors. When I asked him whether he had read these books, he admitted proudly,

Of course I have; these books inspire me in my sermons and motivational talks. I'm not conservative; I'm open to change, that's why I read the books written by Pentecostal pastors and watch Pentecostal shows on television. If you want to make a name for yourself as a religious scholar in this country, you must be competitive.

Although the public reputation of NASFAT's leadership does not allow them to attend Pentecostal programmes, it is common knowledge that lay Muslims in search of 'miracles' attend Pentecostal night vigils.[26] Since night vigils take place late at night, they can attend them unnoticed. This made Mustapha complain that 'many Nigerians are Muslims during the day, but at night they are somebody else'.

The case study of *asalatu* suggests that NASFAT's copying of Pentecostalism occurs especially in formal aspects. An example is NASFAT's prayer style: homilies and litanies play an important role in *asalatu*. In addition to prayer as the battleground of NASFAT's competition with Pentecostalism (Obadare 2016), NASFAT has copied proselytization strategies from Pentecostalism. It is actively involved in evangelism through the guided leadership of a body of missioners, who, as part of social service provision, pay regular visits to hospitals, prisons, and orphanages. These extra-ritual activities underline NASFAT's self-conscious modernity. In building up a portfolio of welfare and development activities, NASFAT follows a trail that Pentecostal churches have blazed in Nigeria in the past three decades (Peel 2016a: 188–9). Besides missioners, NASFAT uses marketing strategies to recruit new members and proselytizes via (social) media.[27] Like Pentecostal pastors, NASFAT's missioners appear in religious talk shows on radio and

---

[26] Mustapha Bello was not pleased when he noticed that some NASFAT members attended Chrislam night vigils. The opposite also occurred: Sanni (2012) states that 'membership of the [Muslim] prayer groups is not denomination specific, and there are even reports of non-Muslims partaking in the prayer sessions of the Muslim prayer groups from time to time, as long as they believe in the efficacy of prayer, whatever the source or agency' (162).

[27] NASFAT is active on Facebook (www.facebook.com/NASFAT.WORLDWIDE/) and Twitter (https://twitter.com/hashtag/nasfat).

television. In an attempt to challenge Pentecostals' digital hegemony, NASFAT recently launched its own live TV. Another overlap concerns NASFAT's use of space and institutional framework: in an effort to inscribe itself in the Pentecostal-dominated public space, NASFAT has opened a prayer camp along the Lagos–Ibadan Expressway, where it plans to build a mega-mosque. Finally, NASFAT's organizational structure resembles that of Pentecostal churches that operate as corporate businesses, whose primary goals are to produce and market religion and to generate profit. Underlining that religion has turned into a business in Nigeria, a middle-aged Muslim man noted, 'These days you don't know whether you are entering a mosque, church, or bank: they all look the same with their glass facades and high-tech architecture.'

Irrespective of these formal similarities, NASFAT preaches a strictly Muslim message that aims, according to NASFAT's Mission Statement, to 'develop an enlightened Muslim society nurtured by a true understanding of Islam for the spiritual upliftment and welfare of mankind'. Nonetheless, the effect of this mission resembles the message preached by Pentecostalism: if members lead a pious life that is in accord with religious principles, they will be granted health and wealth. This suggests that NASFAT has, to some extent, appropriated the Pentecostal theology of the Prosperity Gospel as part of its doctrine. Thus, although NASFAT's copying of Pentecostal elements concerns primarily formal features rather than substance, form and content cannot easily be separated.

The conventional form–content dichotomy in the study of religion is reminiscent of a typically Protestant distinction – emphasized by Weber (1930) – between inward substance and outward shape, or spirit and matter, in which the material manifestations of religion are subordinated to the immaterial meanings (Keane 2007: 67–8; Meyer 2012: 8–9). Meyer's (2009: 6–11) notion of the 'sensational form' challenges the taken-for-granted understanding of religion as being an 'inward' phenomenon. To grasp why and how religious doctrines convince and bind believers, she explores religious communities as 'aesthetic formations', in which the aesthetic is not limited to the Kantian notion of beauty, but encompasses Aristotle's much older notion of *aisthesis*, referring to the sensory experience of the world and our sensitive knowledge of it. Through the notion of the sensational form, Meyer pleads for an awareness that the emergence and sustenance of Pentecostal communities depends on styles that form and bind subjects not only through doctrines but first and foremost through moulding the senses and building bodies. Contrary to what the Protestant bias suggests, the notion of the sensational form thus shows that meaning in religion is not produced through abstract substance alone, but always in interaction with sensorial and material processes.

The ethnographic examples outlined in this section illustrate that the notion of the sensational form is a useful heuristic device to bring together the mentalistic dimension of religion with the material one not only in the study of Pentecostalism but also in Islam. In the case of NASFAT, I observed three modalities of assembling Muslim and Christian beliefs and practices, resulting in Pentecostal forms either being appropriated and inscribed with Muslim content, or both Pentecostal forms and content being transposed into a Muslim idiom, or existing Muslim forms being transformed to express new content. Whatever modality is highlighted, these three examples illustrate that the ingrained form–content dichotomy is untenable.

To analyse how form and content are conjoined in NASFAT's prayer assemblies, I propose employing Keane's (2007) notion of 'entextualiza-tion'. Linguistic anthropologists developed this notion to describe how chunks of discourse came to be extracted from its particular context and were made portable (Silverstein and Urban 1996). These chunks of discourse – or 'texts' as Keane (2007) calls them – can thereby circulate and be 'recontextualized', that is, inserted in new contexts. According to Keane, the movement of language through decontextualization and recontextualization is a condition for all cultural circulation, including religion (15). For instance, entextualization practices have facilitated the spread of Christianity: certain parts of the scripture, such as Christ's Sermon on the Mount or the Lord's Prayer, are taken by many believers to reproduce words that were originally spoken in a particular context. As they circulate, the entextualized words in the scripture are subject to recontextualization, as they are performed, read out aloud, or made the objects of silent meditation (Keane 2004: 439). From this Keane concludes that linguistic forms are not fully deterministic but are subject to reinterpretation within particular social and historical circumstances, 'form may persist while function or interpretation changes' (444). If we translate Keane's example of religious texts to our NASFAT case, what looks like a syncretic form of 'Pentecostal Islam' is actually the outcome of a semiotic form in motion. The semiotic form stands here for the prayer crusade – an intense, bodily form of worship that cultivates piety – which in the process of entextualization has become decontextual-ized from its specific Christian origin and recontextualized in a shared Yoruba setting, thereby inscribed with new meaning. What we thus see here is that form and content mutually constitute each other. Below I apply Keane's entextualization theory to three specific ethnographic examples.

Example 1: Possession

My first ethnographic example is that of possession. Possession, or rather deliverance because possession has in Pentecostal discourse the negative connotation of 'exorcism', is a practice of mediation between individual worshippers and God. In Pentecostal doctrine, deliverance is conceptualized as a 'spiritual fight' between God and Satan, which aims at a person's liberation from 'occultic bondage' (Meyer 1998: 321). During deliverance rituals, gifted prayer leaders attend, by intense prayer and laying hands, to the 'afflicted' person. At the heart of the deliverance ritual is the phase when the spirits dwelling in the afflicted person express themselves. They do so at the very moment when the Holy Spirit is supposed to enter the person who seeks deliverance. The Holy Spirit is perceived as a force that fights evil powers by making them leave the body. Successful deliverance from these demonic powers is expressed in trance-like possession, during which the possessed gesticulates dramatically, swivels around, shouts, and finally falls on the floor (337–9). The notion of the Holy Spirit that is predominant in Pentecostalism is absent in NASFAT, whose fundamental doctrine is *tawhid* – the idea that God is One. Still, NASFAT members believe in possession (*egun*) and they use an idiom that is close to Pentecostal deliverance ideology.

During *tahajjud*, I heard a female NASFAT member shouting 'Allah, Allah', waving her arms before falling down unconsciously. She was being attended by a group of ambulance officers, who put her in such a position that she could not harm herself, but for the rest did not intervene. When I asked the woman sitting next to me what had happened, she told me that the woman was 'possessed by God', which she explained in terms of an extreme spiritual experience. Ibrahim (2017a) encountered a similar phenomenon during his research on NASFAT in Nigeria's capital Abuja. According to him this was a rare instance of *jazabu*, interpreted by his interlocutors as when 'the spirit of the *zikr* [*dhikr*] or invocation of God ... descended on them' (160). A more common form of possession in Islam involves evil spirits or *jinns*, known as *alujonu n lo* in Yoruba, and is manifested through 'madness' (*janun*) and seizures. Since *jinns* are believed to be active especially at night, several NASFAT members confided to me that they attended *tahajjud* in the hope of being 'delivered from spiritual bondage'; a phrase that is reminiscent of Pentecostal discourse.[28] According to them, prayer at

---

[28] Although there is an Islamic ritual for the exorcism of *jinns*, called *al-Ruqyah*, I did not witness this ritual performed at NASFAT programmes. I was told that it is normally performed by 'traditional' Muslim healers in the privacy of the home of the possessed. It

tahajjud is a more effective tool for deliverance than at *asalatu*. What we thus see here is that both a Pentecostal form (the night vigil as a medium for deliverance) and Pentecostal content (deliverance ideology) is being appropriated and translated into a Muslim form (*tahajjud*). In the translation process, not only the form of the ritual changes but the meaning as well. Possession no longer refers only to the more common possession by *jinns*; the outpouring of devotion during *tahajjud* may also result in NASFAT members becoming possessed by God.

Based on the personal experiences of his first wife, who was allegedly possessed by a *jinn* for many years, my research collaborator Mustapha Bello (2007) wrote a booklet titled *Meeting Heart Desires: A Concise Discourse on Faith and Spiritual Consultancy.*[29] Mustapha's heart's desire was to heal his wife from her 'diabolically induced madness' (40). After undergoing the ritual of *jalbu*, defined by Mustapha as 'the process of offering spiritual guidance and counselling to distressed and troubled clientele on multifarious issues requiring more than physical/medical attention' (39), his wife was finally cured. Mustapha's interpretation differs from the conventional meaning of *jalbu*: the preparation of amulets by Muslim clerics. According to Mustapha, whereas *jalbu* in the sense of 'spiritual consultancy' is allowed in Islam, the fabrication and wearing of amulets is 'unorthodox' and borders on 'magic' (42, 61). Although described as an Islamic ritual, the Pentecostal influence is – as also Peel (2016a: 189–90), who got hold of Mustapha's booklet during his field research, has remarked – unmistakably present in Mustapha's description of *jalbu*, not only in the language of counselling and consultancy but also in his '12 points Faith Enhancement Tips' that are meant to 'assist the distressed and afflicted to weather the storm of afflictions' (Bello 2007: iii).

The aforementioned suggests that NASFAT not only appropriates a Pentecostal form (the night vigil) to fill it with Muslim content, and uses an existing Muslim form (*jalbu*) to express a new meaning ('spiritual consultancy') but that it also appropriates Pentecostal content (deliverance ideology) and transposes it into a Muslim form (*jalbu*). Hence, these instances of the form–content assemblage complement the rather one-sided focus by scholars of religion preaching a 'material turn' on the

---

consists of the invocation of certain Qur'anic verses, *dhikr*, and the recitation of the Qur'an over water that the possessed then drinks or washes with.

[29] Mustapha Bello is a prolific writer. Reminiscent of Pentecostal pastors' writing style, he has also written two booklets with tips for Muslims for 'conquering your enemy' (2010a) and having a 'blissful married life' (2010b). Bello's publications were officially launched by NASFAT and are for sale during NASFAT programmes. I therefore take what Bello writes as representative of NASFAT's vision.

sensational form (e.g. Meyer 2009; Morgan 2010; Vásquez 2011), and show the importance of studying religion through the intertwinement of form and content.

Example 2: Maintaining a Personal Relationship with God

Based on his experiences in NASFAT, Mustapha Bello (2007) writes in *Meeting Heart Desires*,

> The God that we serve – Allah – is an Ever-Present, Ever-Living, Ever-Listening, Ever-Willing and Omnipotent God. Unlike the god of the Old Testament of the Bible who rested on the seventh day after the laborious task of creating the world in six days, our God – Allah – neither slumbers nor sleeps and feels no fatigue in the creation, guarding, supervision and preservation of the entire creation. ... He is not an absentee God because He is Ever-Present (102–3).

To experience the 'supremacy of the One-Living God', Mustapha admonishes his readership to invest in a 'personal relationship' with Him through prayer (87). Like Mustapha, several NASFAT leaders and members asserted that, in order to cultivate piety, a Muslim needs to enter into a personal relationship with God, interpreted by Peel (2016a) as 'the hallmark evangelical phrase' (190). For Pentecostals, God is no longer a remote entity but a 'pal' (Luhrmann 2004, 2012). Along similar lines, NASFAT members do not imagine God as distant but rather as a companion. A dedicated NASFAT member put it aptly, 'Allah is my helper, my protector, and my friend.'

During interviews, Pentecostals – often described in terms of 'prayer addicts' in local discourse – as well as NASFAT members emphasized prayer as the practice on which their personal relationship with God was built.[30] In a language redolent of Pentecostal discourse, Mustapha Bello (2010a) writes in his other booklet, titled *Conquering Your Enemy*, 'Prayer is the sword of the Muslims' (102). For many NASFAT members prayer is both a weapon to seek protection from God and a tool through which to communicate with God. For instance, a NASFAT missioner described prayer as 'the means to get close to my Allah'. The frequent use of 'my Allah' by NASFAT leaders and members alike underlines their notion of a personalized relationship with God. The wish to enter

---

[30] In this, NASFAT members resemble Chrislamists who consider prayer a means to communicate with God (see Chapter 3). But whereas Chrislamists believe that they can influence God through their ritual actions, NASFAT members do not believe in God's manipulability and emphasize His omnipotence.

into an intimate relationship with God explains the fervent and ecstatic quality of the prayers performed at *asalatu* and *tahajjud*. Members shut their eyes, hold out their hands, sway back and forth, and sometimes get so overwhelmed by God's greatness that they enter into trance, as became clear in the previous example.

It was not uncommon to see NASFAT members cry during *tahajjud*. For my interlocutors tears are necessary for reaching what they called a higher level of spirituality. This makes weeping an example of what Luhrmann (2004: 519) calls metakinesis, through which worshippers identify bodily and emotional states as signs of God's presence in their life. As pointed out by NASHHIN's health coordinator cited earlier, NASFAT epitomizes the centrality of the body as a harbinger of piety. Through specific disciplinary techniques of the body, such as intense prayer (including weeping), group recitations, chanting, and fasting, *asalatu* and *tahajjud* enact a particular moral state in their congregation (see also Mahmood 2005; Hirschkind 2006). Underlining the corporeal dimension of piety, several NASFAT members told me that their body transformed when they joined NASFAT by growing healthier, which they interpreted as a sign that they had been blessed by God. Like among Pentecostals, illness is considered evidence of sin; health and beauty the blessing of divine approval (Griffith 2004).

Meyer (2012) stresses the role of the body in Pentecostal rituals, which acts as a 'producer, transmitter and receiver of the transcendent', to the extent that it actually 'makes belief' (28). In a similar vein, NASFAT members experience religiosity in intense, bodily ways, and they use these experiences to build intimate relationships with God and to culti- vate piety. As a result, faith comes alive for them in a way it was never before. What this pattern of sensational devotional practices suggests is that rituals (forms) are not ancillary, but rather central to doctrine (see also Luhrmann 2004: 518–19). Through ritual forms such as *asalatu* and *tahajjud*, NASFAT members embody Islamic principles and transform themselves into 'true believers'. We may thus conclude that corporeal modes of worship are effective because they are affective (Morgan 2010: 59).

Here it should be noted that the ritual forms that make up NASFAT's worship do not merely signify belief: in fact, they 'host belief' (Morgan 2010). Put differently, by participating in NASFAT's ecstatic modes of worship, members internalize piety to such an extent that they become pious Muslims who embody the Prophetic traditions in all their under- takings. Opposing the Protestant bias, form is then not subordinated to content (belief); instead, it is the necessary condition for expressing and embodying it.

Example 3: The Changed Substance of Prayer

Finally, NASFAT has not only appropriated Pentecostal devotional forms such as the prayer crusade and night vigil but these forms have also changed the very content of prayer. Inspired by Pentecostalism's obsession with affluence, satanic forces, and spiritual warfare (Bastian 1993; Hackett 2011; Butticci 2013), *asalatu* dictates prayers for achieving health, wealth, and success in life, as well as for protection against evil. Mustapha Bello, who in his scarce leisure time acts as what he calls a 'spiritual counsellor', sends his followers text messages containing 'prayers to conquer their enemies'. Copying Pentecostal idiom, I heard NASFAT missioners introducing themselves during *tahajjud* as 'prayer warriors', ordaining prayers for women seeking 'the fruit of the womb', and for youths looking for 'protection against enemies who block one's ways to achieve success'.

Remarkably, NASFAT has translated the Arabic term for evil in the Qur'anic verse *Sura Al-Falaq* – a verse recited during *asalatu* and *tahajjud* for spiritual protection – into 'witchcraft'[31] – thereby copying the promise of many Pentecostal pastors to offer protection against witchcraft attacks. Furthermore, I witnessed that the participants in *asalatu* were encouraged to place their right hand on their head while praying, 'I seek refuge in Allah and in His Power from the evil and of what I guard against'. This is in line with a practice that I observed in Pentecostal churches where pastors prompted their congregations to hold body parts with the aim of 'casting out the evil' and 'experiencing breakthrough'. In a similar vein, the aspiration for health and wealth has changed not only the form but also the content of prayer in NASFAT. A focus on prayer thus allows a restoration of the balance between form and content that was lost with the rise of Protestantism, and opens up new possibilities for understanding form 'not as a vehicle but as a generator of meaning and experience, in all religious practice' (Meyer 2012: 11–12).

Conquering the Market

NASFAT's appropriation of Pentecostal styles and strategies has, as I mentioned earlier, invoked descriptions in terms of 'Pentecostal Islam' (Sanni 2004; Soares 2009, 2016), 'Born-Again Islam' (Peel 2016a), and 'Charismatic Islam' (Obadare 2016). Although openly

---

[31] NASFAT's translation of the verse reads, 'I seek refuge with (Allaah) the Lord of the daybreak, from the evil of what He has created, and from the evil of the darkening (night) as it comes with its darkness, and from the evil of the witchcraft when they blow in the knots, and from the evil of the envier when he envies' (Shekoni 2012: 27).

acknowledging that they copied certain elements from Pentecostalism, NASFAT leaders strongly disagreed with these portmanteau terms. During interviews, they dissociated themselves wholeheartedly from Pentecostal worship, which they considered a form of 'hero-worship'. The founders of the Pentecostal megachurches, or General Overseers (GOs) as they are called, have become celebrities in Nigeria, dressing conspicuously, driving posh cars, and travelling in private jets.[32] NASFAT, on the other hand, has a strong aversion to this kind of personality cult that envelops prominent Pentecostal GOs and to the flashy and noisy quality of Pentecostal worship. Countering Pentecostalism's mode of worship, NASFAT's leadership described NASFAT as a 'pious movement that preaches humbleness rather than clapping and dancing'. But despite their preaching of sobriety, I noticed that NASFAT leaders' lifestyle did not necessarily reflect sobriety. Many of them lived in luxury apartments in the upscale districts of Lagos and they arrived at NASFAT programmes in expensive cars, sometimes with their private drivers. Still, NASFAT's leadership underlined that their appropriation of Pentecostal prayer forms and styles does not in any way affect the fundamentals of Islam; in fact, it only strengthens them. In their opinion, Pentecostal devotional practices and styles help NASFAT to preach a theology that strictly adheres to the Qur'an and *Sunna* (the Prophetic traditions), the overriding ethos of which is to develop a Muslim society nurtured by 'a true understanding of Islam'. Elucidating this mission, NASFAT's previous president Kamil 'Yomi Bolarinwa told me, 'NASFAT is about Islamic knowledge: we aim to increase our members' knowledge of Islam and to make them into total Muslims.'

By engaging in *asalatu* and *tahajjud*, NASFAT members can transform themselves into 'total Muslims' who appreciate 'the beauty of Islam' and strive for 'moral perfection' by living in accordance with the Islamic principles – phrases that were frequently used in interviews with NASFAT members and leaders and in NASFAT publications. In this spirit, NASFAT is not a mere response to Pentecostalism; it, at the same time, is part of a reformist trend within the wider Muslim world where Muslims have been increasingly concerned with questions about ethics and moral self-transformation. Looking for a new expression of their Muslim identity, Nigerian Muslim leaders aiming to reform Islam have stepped into the vacuum that was created by the shrinking ranks of the

---

[32] In 2015, five of the ten richest pastors in the world were Nigerians (Obadare 2018: 132). For an example of Pentecostalism's 'showbiz' (Peel 2016a: 87), see http://citifmonline. com/2014/09/nigerias-superstar-men-of-god/.

Sufi orders in the 1980s (Loimeier 2007). Rather than attaching themselves to a Sufi sheikh, they insisted that Muslims must seek direct access
to the sources of the faith without an intermediary, which explains their
preoccupation with prayer. Their newly founded prayer groups, including NASFAT, identified prayer as key to cultivating a virtuous self and
effecting moral reform, which would lead into the social advancement of
the global Muslim community or *umma*, thereby echoing the aims of
Islamic reform movements in other parts of Africa and elsewhere in the
Muslim world.[33]

Here I would like to draw attention to a new trend of Islamic reform as
represented by the Indonesian self-styled spiritual reform movement,
eloquently described by Rudnyckyj (2010). Although I am referring to
a different ethnographic setting, the similarities between this movement
and NASFAT are striking in that they both conceive of economic reform
and neoliberal restructuring as matters of piety and spiritual virtue. Like
NASFAT propagates a modernist Islam, for the Indonesian reformers
Islam is compatible with neoliberal reforms. This compatibility involves
the creation of a set of equivalences between Islam and business management strategies, which Rudnyckyj refers to as 'engineering Islam'
(112–17). Engineering Islam alerts us to novel articulations between
religious and economic practices – practices that have long been studied
separately by anthropologists – whereby global economic developments
become linked to the cultivation of ethical dispositions. Along similar
lines, NASFAT recasts Islamic reform as development in a neoliberal
economy, thereby making faith conducive to both personal spiritual
growth and business success.

Besides the fact that they are considered to be pejorative and ignore
that NASFAT identifies with a global trend of Muslim piety movements,
another reason why I think that popular appellations such as 'Pentecostal
Islam' are somewhat misleading is that they suggest that NASFAT is a
syncretic movement, which mixes Pentecostalism and Islam in a new
configuration. However, NASFAT's leadership regards the copying of
Pentecostal styles and strategies not as an attempt to Pentecostalise
Islam, but rather as a means to consolidate what it calls 'true Islam'.
Here it should be noted that some NASFAT officials used the concept of
syncretism, but never in relation to the Islam that they propagated. For
instance, Mustapha opposed the 'true Islam' propagated by NASFAT to
the Islam practised by *malams* who 'bastardise Islam'. Examples of the
'bastardisation of Islam' were in his opinion *hantu* (verses of the Qur'an

---

[33] See e.g. Kane (2003); Mahmood (2005); Deeb (2006); Hirschkind (2006); Masquelier
(2009); Schulz (2012); Janson (2014).

written with ink on a wooden slate and then washed off with water for consumption) and *tira* (Qur'anic verses written on slips of paper folded and wrapped in leather, carried on the body). Although NASFAT feels strongly about tolerance towards all Muslims, irrespective of their denomination, Mustapha condemned these practices as syncretic. In his booklet *Meeting Heart Desires*, he writes that the 'rank and file [of committed Muslims] is corrupted by syncretic Muslims whose activities constitute an aberration to Islam' (Bello 2007: 3).

What we thus see in NASFAT is that its copying of Pentecostalism is founded on religious divergence rather than on convergence. This echoes Nolte and Ogen's (2017) argument that religious appropriation is premised on religious boundaries,

The drawing of clear religious boundaries is not a denial but a recognition of the religious agency of others, and transgression or transcendence do not imply that religious boundaries do no matter: in fact, the agency that derives from such practices is only meaningful as long as religious differences exist (13–14).

Rather than synthesizing Muslim and Christian beliefs and practices in a syncretic configuration, NASFAT copies Christian prayer forms to emphasize its Muslim credentials. It is this unique ability to appropriate the form of Pentecostal worship and entextualize it in a Muslim idiom that explains NASFAT's appeal among a young, upwardly mobile middle-class, aspiring to success. For them, NASFAT offers a platform to negotiate their, at times conflicting, ambitions to be pious and modern Muslims, and to put themselves on a par with their Pentecostal peers. By participating in NASFAT's professionalization activities, network events, and dating programmes, Lagosian Muslim youths have refashioned themselves from a generation in 'waithood' (Honwana 2012), excluded from salaried jobs and social adulthood, into enlightened Muslims who are continuously on the lookout for new prospects and in the process cultivate a modernist form of piety.

Conclusion

In their influential article *Pentecostalism, Islam and Culture: New Religious Movements in West Africa*, Larkin and Meyer (2006) study reformist Islam and Pentecostal Christianity as mirror images of one another. This chapter has pointed out that NASFAT does more than just mirror Pentecostalism. While openly copying from Pentecostalism in its prayer styles, missionary techniques, media practices, and organizational strategies, NASFAT simultaneously draws religious boundaries with Christianity (Soares 2016: 687). Hence, NASFAT offers a strong

analytical case for conducting comparison not just by stressing similarities but also by taking into account religious differences (see also Peel
2016b). Complementing the typical image of Nigeria as being torn by
religious conflict, the intricate religious assemblage of Islam and
Christianity showcased by NASFAT demonstrates that religious difference does not necessarily result in violence. This is not to say, however,
that this mode of assemblage is automatically conducive to religio-
political cohesion. As we have seen in the previous chapters, the
Nigerian political field is increasingly being marked by a cleavage along
religious lines, and reformist Muslim movements such as NASFAT
regard local Islamic traditions as 'un-Islamic'.

NASFAT emphasizes its distinctness from other Muslim movements
as well as from Pentecostalism in an attempt to expand itself into a
modernist Muslim movement that can compete with the Pentecostal
mega-churches. By raising Muslim awareness among Yoruba youths, it
wants them to take pride in Islam so that they will not desert to
Pentecostalism. To attain this mission, NASFAT constantly reinvents
itself by developing new business ventures and media strategies. Through
investing in an extensive marketing plan that links economic development with spiritual growth, NASFAT's leadership has mastered the skills
of religious entrepreneurship with the aim of conquering the competitive
religious marketplace that is Lagos. It remains to be seen, however, how
much further NASFAT can grow. The recent crisis that was caused by
the resignation of its spiritual leader, Alhaji Akinbode, shows that there
are limits to NASFAT's success. The inauguration of a new spiritual
leader in 2017, and a new president in 2019, heralded a new era in the
history of NASFAT – an era that will focus, in line with its entrepreneurial approach to Islam, on interventions in four areas: Health, Education,
Livelihood, and Da'wa (with the acronym HELD).[34]

To provide a window into NASFAT's particular mode of religious
assemblage, I employed Keane's (2007) entextualization theory. It can
be concluded that what goes for assemblage also goes for entextualization. In the entextualization process Christian rituals and Muslim beliefs
are assembled in ways that illustrate that their mapping on a hierarchized
form–content dichotomy is mistaken. One way to conceive of religion,
then, is precisely as a sphere of human activity and creativity concerned
with articulating the relationship between form and content, or practice
and belief. Such a conception is more beneficial than the one-sided
equation of religion with belief in religious studies. That ritual forms

[34] See http://nasfat.org/acceptance-speech-by-president-niyi-yusuf-sunday-oct-20-2019/.

are appropriated and invested with new signification is also illustrated by the case of The Indigenous Faith of Africa (IFA), *Ijo Orunmila Ato*, which, as I will discuss in the next chapter, has framed 'Yoruba religion' in a Christian, biblical format. Like NASFAT, this is another example of religious cultural nationalism in which the Yoruba appropriated Christian forms in order to compete with the rival faith, Christianity.

5   Reviving 'Yoruba Religion'

The Indigenous Faith of Africa (IFA), *Ijo Orunmila Ato*

> A theistic religion need be neither monotheistic nor polytheistic. It may be both. It is the question of the level, or situation, of thought, rather than of exclusive types of thought   (Evans-Pritchard 1956: 316).

Although reformist Islam and, especially, Pentecostalism have dominated Lagos's religious marketplace since the 1970s, 'Yoruba religion' did not wither away. At the heart of Yoruba religious practice is the search for well-being and protection against misfortune through establishing relations with the unseen, but personalized, deities called *orisas*, who control everything that happens in the physical world. *Babalawos*, or divination priests, mediate the power of the *orisas* to lay practitioners. Olodumara, also known as Olorun ('Almighty'), is the ultimate source of power in the Yoruba pantheon and the creator of all other forces of the universe. Yoruba's belief in a Supreme Being indicates an opening to monotheism. This explains why, with the expansion of the monotheistic religions, 'Yoruba religion' was able to transform itself according to the new socio-religious context (Peel 2016a: 217–19). In its transformation, 'Yoruba religion' adopted elements of both Islam and Christianity. To conceptualize religious pluralism in a setting where 'Yoruba religion' does not exist as an ossified tradition but is part and parcel of Islam and Christianity, I use the term 'Yoruba religion' enclosed within inverted commas (see also Brenner 1989).[1] I agree with Chidester (2018) that, while it may not be possible to get rid of terms like 'traditional religion' and 'world religion', we need to become more aware of the genealogies and asymmetrical power relations that constitute our

---

[1] Acknowledging the limitations of 'Yoruba religion' as a category, several authors have suggested alternatives. For example, Peel (2016a) spoke in his last book of '*Orişa* religion', while others used terms such as 'Yoruba religious culture' (Olupona and Rey 2008), 'Yoruba cosmology' (Barber 1981), or 'Yoruba philosophy' (Mbiti 1969; Gbadegesin 1991). While the former reduces 'Yoruba religion' to the belief in *orisas*, Yoruba 'cosmology' and 'philosophy' question its very status as a 'religion'.

religious categorizations. My use of 'Yoruba religion' within inverted commas is a – rather half-hearted, I must admit – measure to come to terms with these complexities and to put so-called traditional religion on a par with the 'modern' world religions, Islam and Christianity.

This chapter presents the case study of the Indigenous Faith of Africa (IFA), *Ijo Orunmila Ato* (hereafter referred to as *Ijo Orunmila*), which, in its attempt to revive 'Yoruba religion' as a response to the surging Christianity, assembled elements from 'traditional' religion and the newly adopted religion. The movement, which is located in Ebute-Metta – one of the oldest Yoruba neighbourhoods in Lagos, inhabited by predominantly lower middle-class people – was founded by an Anglican Yoruba named Olorunfumi Oshiga, after he had a vision in which the *orisa* Orunmila appeared to him, in 1920. While *Ijo Orunmila*'s doctrines are based on *Ifa* – a divination cult – the movement's worship is composed of hymns, prayers, and sermons modelled closely on those of the mission church, and, more recently, the Pentecostal church (Barber 1990; Laguda 2010, 2015).[2] As a result of its particular worship style, *Ijo Orunmila* was able to attract a mostly Yoruba congregation, who meets every Saturday in a temple that resembles a church but also contains a shrine, to worship both Orunmila and Jesus.

The project of reframing traditional religious practice within a Christian format that *Ijo Orunmila* embarks on is not new.[3] Still, according to Sanneh (1989), the 'overlap between the Christian revival and the revitalization of indigenous culture remains one of the most undervalued themes in the study of Christian expansion' (185). Indeed, there is a persistent division of labour between scholars studying African Traditional Religion (ATR) and those studying Christianity. Analysing the interaction between 'traditional' religion and the 'world religions', Barnes (1997) writes,

---

[2] The history that I recorded of *Ijo Orunmila* resembles that of Laguda (2010, 2015), who introduced me to the movement. Barber (1990) conducted her research much earlier among a local branch in Ife.

[3] For a notable example in Congo, see MacGaffey's (1983) ethnography of Kimbanguism – a prophet movement – which he sets at the intersection of the 'traditional' world of customary institutions and the 'bureaucratic' world of Christian missionaries and colonial officers. According to Meyer (2004: 450), the realization by Africanists such as MacGaffey that it was fruitful to focus on Christianity in Africa as a dynamic field, in which indigenous religion and Christian movements were in ongoing exchange, conflict, and dialogue with each other, changed the ways in which anthropologists and other scholars of religion constructed their very research object. In a similar vein, scholars of 'African Islam' have investigated the continuities between 'traditional' and Muslim beliefs and practices (e.g. Parkin 1970; Fisher 1985; Brenner 2000; Masquelier 2001; Launay 2004; Soares 2005; McIntosh 2009).

Because these categories were grounded in an evolutionary perspective, the tendency when the two types of system were studied in the same frame of reference was – and here is where the legacy persists – to give the great traditions, such as Islam or Christianity, a central position and the little traditions a peripheral one (21).

The reason for the dominance of the 'great traditions' is that they are institutionalized and have standardized and written doctrines. In comparison, the 'little traditions' are characterized as localized and are largely associated with illiteracy (Barnes 1997). This chapter contends that it is more fruitful to analyse the 'great traditions', as represented by Christianity, and the 'little traditions', as represented by 'Yoruba religion', within a single comparative frame that transcends the shortcomings imposed by an approach that studies religions as separate, self-contained systems. Challenging the evolutionary perspective that underpins the study of religion in Africa, I take 'Yoruba religion' and Christianity as contemporaries, thereby opening conceptual space for rethinking the anthropological trope of 'tradition', as well as the ingrained tradition–modernity schism.

Placing 'Yoruba religion' and Christianity within one comparative framework offers a fresh perspective on issues around conversion. In line with Horton's (1975a, b) influential conversion theory, conversion has long been conceived as a teleological shift from 'traditional' religion to the 'world religions'. Horton understood conversion as a response to changes in the scale of converts' social experience. African 'traditional' religions are characterized by a belief in the 'lesser spirits', which make sense of living in localized, small-scale communities or 'microcosms'. When people move into a wider field of social relations or 'macrocosms' – through migration, long-distance trade, conquest, and/or colonization – they are drawn to the 'world religions', marked by a belief in the Supreme Being. Horton's proposition was that widening social experience encourages a cosmological shift towards the High God of Christianity or Islam, leading to a gradual abandoning, or even demonization, of the 'lesser spirits'.

The contrast between microcosmic and macrocosmic cosmologies in Horton's conversion theory is consistent with the two sets of dichotomies that have been much employed in the study of religion in Africa (and beyond): first, between 'traditional' religion and the 'world religions'; and second, between 'non-literate religions' and 'religions of the Book' (e.g. Shaw 1990; Ranger 2002; Kirsch 2008). The case of *Ijo Orunmila* prompts us to revisit these analytical oppositions. Contrary to the conventional approach to analysing 'Yoruba religion' in terms of a traditional religion, Peel (2016a) studied it as a flexible and dynamic entity, which never existed in isolation from the so-called world religions. Underlining the dynamic nature of 'Yoruba religion', *Ijo Orunmila*'s current acting High Priest (*Oluwo*), Ademola Ifabunmi, said, 'According to Ifa, the only constant factor in the universe is change.' Like 'Yoruba religion' and the 'world religions' are not mutually exclusive categories, *Ijo Orunmila*'s scriptures – composed of the oral Ifa corpus reconfigured in a biblical format – illustrate that rather than oppositions, orality and literacy are mutually determining processes.

Because of its tendency to be simultaneously engaged in traditional ritual practices, such as divination, and Christian rituals, *Ijo Orunmila* has been described in the literature as a 'syncretic church' (Bascom 1969; Laguda 2015; Peel 2016a). This description reflects the anxiety of colonial missionaries that Christianity would become corrupted by indigenous elements. While a notion of syncretism as 'contamination' sits easily with the missionaries' doctrinally grounded faith, it is hard to see how it can be applied plausibly to *Ijo Orunmila*, which was accommodative to Christianity. Drawing on Barber (1990), I argue that *Ijo Orunmila*'s simultaneous engagement in divination and Christian rituals needs to be seen against the backdrop of Yoruba cultural nationalism: a movement that flourished between the late nineteenth and early twentieth centuries, which aimed at validating African 'tradition' while at the same time promoting the incorporation of European 'modernity'. Cultural nationalists such as *Ijo Orunmila*'s founder, Oshiga, demonstrated that 'traditional' religion was a mode of worship that was capable of development along lines parallel and equal to European Christianity, which was taken as a pathway to modernity. In this context, *Ijo Orunmila* is more than a syncretic church; it is a complex process of the assembling of heterogeneous elements while claiming authenticity, recreating Yoruba culture in the name of preserving it, and forging new identities through affirming old ones (199–200).

I begin with a historical overview of *Ijo Orunmila* as it originated in the Yoruba movement of cultural nationalism. After describing the complex divination system of Ifa, from which *Ijo Orunmila* derived its name, I proceed with an ethnographic case study of a Saturday service that I attended in *Ijo Orunmila*'s temple. To analyse this case study, I draw inspiration from Peel's (2016a) apt phrase 'the past in the present': '... the past is not just an objectively given anterior state to the present, the baseline on which change works, but is often regarded as something of such intrinsic positive value that serious attempts are made to download it for contemporary application' (114). Rather than studying 'Yoruba religion' as part of an outmoded past and hence ultimately opposed to modernity, I conclude that the past is reflected in the present and therefore an essential part of discourses and practices of modernity.

Ijo Orunmila's Cultural-Nationalist Mission

Anthropologists and other scholars of religion have long tried to conceive of 'Yoruba religion' as both an ATR and a coherent entity.[4] Although it can be seen as a major strand in Yoruba religious culture, *Ijo Orunmila* is neither a 'traditional' religion nor does it form a unified and bounded religion. Instead, it is an assemblage of 'Yoruba religion' and Christianity that revives indigenous religion in a new form that is relevant to the context of Christianization. Rather than 'Yoruba religion' and Christianity forming two distinct entities with *Ijo Orunmila* being the syncretic synthesis of their contradictions, *Ijo Orunmila* emerged within their interaction (see also Peel 1990). This section goes more deeply into the interaction between 'Yoruba religion' and Christianity, which I study against the backdrop of the twentieth-century Yoruba movement of cultural nationalism.

The 1920s and 1930s saw the birth of *Aladura* or 'praying' churches that distanced themselves from the historical mission churches with the aim of 'Africanizing' Christianity. While *Aladura*'s theological content was Christian, its ritual forms owed much to the indigenous religious background, recalling aspects of 'Yoruba religion' (Peel 1968). *Ijo Orunmila* was founded around the time of the emergence of the *Aladura* churches. Just as the *Aladura* churches rejected the mission churches as being 'cold' and not in line with African modes of worship, *Ijo Orunmila* rejected mainline Christianity as being 'too rigid' and it drew on 'Yoruba religion' in order to, quoting the High Priest Chief Ifabunmi, 'spice up Christianity'.

Ijo Orunmila's origins can be traced to 1920 when the late Olorunfumi Oshiga – a Yoruba member of the Anglican Church who was born in Ijebu Ode in south-west Nigeria – had a vision in which the *orisa* Orunmila appeared to him. He was instructed by the deity to assemble a group of Ifa devotees. In 1932, he had mobilized a substantial number of devotees and he built a church at Freeman Street in Ebute-Metta, an old part of Lagos, where the first service was held (Laguda 2010: 195–6). Whereas Oshiga, who worked as a civil servant, belonged to the Yoruba

---

[4] This applies not only to Western scholars but also to African intellectuals. While Parrinder (1954) gave ATR its hegemony within African religious studies, the writings of African scholars such as the Kenyan theologian Mbiti (1969) and the Nigerian cultural nationalist Idowu (1973) constructed an authorized version of ATR as a single African belief system comparable to Christianity (Shaw 1990: 343–5).

higher class, most of the present-day *Ijo Orunmila* members are from a lower class background, as became clear when I visited them at home. Although he has gained prestige as a *babalawo*, Chief Ifabunmi lived in very modest one-room accommodation in a slum settlement in Lagos. Since the slum was built on swampland, mosquitoes, and thus malaria, were a major problem. Chief Ifabunmi complained that he was not able to sleep at night because of the mosquitoes and therefore he spent most of the night studying his notebooks with Ifa divination verses.

Initially, Oshiga's group was called *Ijo Akoda* ('the first church'). Because this name suggested that this church was more 'authentic' than the mission churches, it was considered offensive by the colonial rulers. Upon the latter's decree that the group's name had to reflect its belief in Ifa, Oshiga renamed his group the Indigenous Faith of Africa (IFA), *Ijo Orunmila Ato* (Laguda 2010). Initially, the group met for Sunday service, but because several members were Christian and wanted to attend the Sunday services in their churches, the weekly service shifted to Saturday. Chief Ifabunmi recalled that when he was initiated in 1967, worshippers had started referring to the church as a temple to underline its distinctness from mainline Christianity.

Elucidating *Ijo Orunmila*'s origins, Chief Ifabunmi recounted,

The Bible says: 'In the beginning was the word, and the word was with God'. That word was Ifa. We serve Orunmila in this temple. Orunmila is the name of the prophet who brought down Ifa. Ifa is the foundation of the Yoruba culture. Christians have Jesus; Muslims have Muhammad; we have Orunmila.

This narrative points to the cultural-nationalist ideals of *Ijo Orunmila*: validating Yoruba culture, as represented by Ifa, by placing it on an equal footing with the so-called world religions and its associated discourses of enlightenment, development, and civilization as encapsulated in the Yoruba value of *olaju*. The 1920s were a time when Yoruba cultural nationalism burgeoned in Lagos and Abeokuta – the strongholds of the Anglican Church Missionary Society (CMS). Barber (1990) defines Yoruba cultural nationalism as a project of 'cultural brokerage' aimed to 'extract from a vast, dynamic and heterogeneous indigenous culture a set of values, exemplary texts, cultural monuments and touchstones, that could stand in opposition to, as an alternative to, or in combination with, the European culture' (196). In line with the cultural-nationalist ideology at the time, Oshiga searched for a cultural tradition to place alongside the Christianity of the British rulers and the CMS missionaries. To him, Ifa offered itself as the best candidate because of its embeddedness in Yoruba culture. Underscoring the cultural-nationalist mission of *Ijo Orunmila*, a long-standing male member told me,

The missionaries wanted to wash [i.e. purify] Africans like babies. But instead of throwing the bathwater away after washing the baby, they threw the baby [Ifa] out with the bathwater. Our task was to revive the baby. Because we have redressed it, it looks different but it is still our baby.

This quote illustrates well that *Ijo Orunmila* has been constructed on the Yoruba agenda of restoring the indigenous mode of worship. In this spirit, Peel (2000: 304) labels *Ijo Orunmila* an unambiguous case of cultural nationalism.

While *Ijo Orunmila* was an early example of cultural nationalism, which was moulded in the religious field, the cultural nationalism that came to fruition in the period prior to Nigeria's independence in 1960 was more politically oriented. Still, it coincided with developments in the religious field. The symbolic apex of cultural nationalism was FESTAC '77, the Second World Black and African Festival of Arts and Culture, which took place in Lagos in 1977, when Nigeria had built itself up after the civil war and the growth in oil revenues raised hopes for Nigeria's national development. FESTAC was funded with oil money by the Nigerian state, whose aim it was to provide black people in Africa and the diaspora a platform to identify with their roots and cultural heritage (Apter 2005). While it was intended to celebrate traditional cultural and religious life, FESTAC evoked protests by Pentecostals and reformist Muslims who saw in it a revival of 'paganism' (45). While Christian-influenced practitioners of 'Yoruba religion' like Oshiga had played an instrumental role in shaping Yoruba cultural nationalism in the early twentieth century, after independence Pentecostals and politicized reformist Muslims abandoned the cultural-nationalist project for a post-nationalist agenda aimed at promoting universalizing rather than Africanizing idioms (Peel 2016a: 155, 221).[5] Instead of associating themselves with Yoruba culture, they considered themselves part of a larger whole, in the sense of World Christianity and the global community of Muslims, the *umma*.

In line with the cultural-nationalist ideals at the time of *Ijo Orunmila*, the Oodua People's Progress (OPC)[6] – a Yoruba militia that was founded by medical doctor and pro-democracy activist Dr Frederick Fasehun in 1994 – attempted to reassert the dignity of the Yoruba by reviving Yoruba culture. When Fasehun was arrested by the Abacha

---

[5] An exception is the moderate reformist Muslim movement NASFAT, which, as we have seen in Chapter 4, can be interpreted in terms of a Yoruba Muslim emancipation movement. Still, the Islamic message that NASFAT propagates is in line with the aims of Islamic reform movements in other parts of the Muslim world.

[6] Oodua or Oduduwa is the name of the mythical founder of human civilization in Yorubaland.

regime in 1996, his deputy, Gani Adams, took over leadership of the OPC (Nolte 2007: 220–2). In an interview with Adams, he highlighted the ways in which Yoruba culture plays into present-day Yoruba identity politics,

I'm a freedom fighter; I fight for the cause of the Yoruba people. Yoruba culture is a very rich and deep culture. We want to make our members aware of the richness of our culture; that being Yoruba is something to be proud of. Yoruba culture should not fade away under the onslaught of Western civilization. When the British arrived here, they tried to impose their culture onto us. But our culture is so much richer. While the Britons knew only one style of dressing – the suit and tie – the Yoruba had fifteen different styles of dressing. Still, the colonial rulers frowned upon our culture. Because we are proud of our culture, we want to revive it.

OPC's revival of Yoruba culture is undertaken within a discourse of democracy and human rights. In this sense, 'tradition' is not just a site of Yoruba cultural and religious identity but also a political resource.

Although *Ijo Orunmila* is premised on 'Yoruba religion', it should be noted here that unlike contemporary forms of Yoruba cultural nationalism as represented by the OPC, it is not restricted by ethnicity. *Ijo Orunmila*'s temple is located near the market in Ebute-Metta, a cosmopolitan area inhabited by Yoruba, as well as Hausa and Igbo traders. Although the majority of the congregation is Yoruba, some Hausa and Igbo worship in *Ijo Orunmila*. Besides ethnicity, *Ijo Orunmila*'s congregation is not restricted by religious affiliation. Several members told me that they also worshipped in churches. Given that the history of *Ijo Orunmila* is closely interwoven with the Anglican Church, they did not consider worshipping in churches contradictory with their membership of *Ijo Orunmila*. According to a long-standing member, 'Unlike human beings, God doesn't know jealousy. He doesn't mind if we worship Him in different places.' I also met Muslims in *Ijo Orunmila*'s temple, who consulted Ifa for divination and healing purposes. Contrary to Chrislam (see Chapter 3), where membership is not accompanied by a ritual, several worshippers told me that they had been initiated into *Ijo Orunmila*. Because of its secretive nature, they were unwilling to elaborate on their initiation ritual. Unlike the ordinary members, the initiates worship only in *Ijo Orunmila*. Both categories of worshippers pay 100 Naira (approximately 20 pence) membership fees per month (although they are encouraged to give more for the maintenance of the temple).

In addition to ethnicity and religious affiliation, membership of *Ijo Orunmila* cuts across gender and age. I observed more women than men worshipping in the temple. This gender imbalance is not surprising since the great bulk of regular worshippers in the *orisa* cults have been women (Peel 2000: 103). Whereas women are actively involved in *Ijo Orunmila*, the leadership is male. There is a strict hierarchy in the temple: the *Oluwo* (High Priest) is assisted by the *Akoda Awo* (second in command), *Aseda Awo* (third in command), and *Abese Awo* who acts as a warden. While Chief Ifabunmi was the *Aseda Awo* when I first met him, after the passing of the *Oluwo* he was appointed to act as the High Priest. The priests, who are all practising *babalawos* or divination priests, attained their position owing to their knowledge of the Ifa corpus and their seniority (Laguda 2010: 197).

Chief Ifabunmi told me that *Ijo Orunmila* has several branches in Lagos and the wider Yorubaland region, as well as in other parts of West Africa, and among the Nigerian diaspora in Europe, the United Kingdom, and the United States. He estimated that the Lagos branch, which is the largest, has 2,000 members. Although a feature of 'Yoruba religion' is that it is secretive, *Ijo Orunmila* seeks to reach out through the media. It used to have a sponsored programme, *Iroke Orunmila* ('The Voice of Orunmila'), on Radio Lagos. Nowadays, it attracts new members especially via Facebook.[7] Members are encouraged to spread the message of Ifa in their communities. According to Chief Ifabunmi, the congregation should try to reach out more, 'It's not a sin to be ambitious. The temple is looking old now. We must give it a modern look.' Before going more deeply into how *Ijo Orunmila* tries to modernize 'Yoruba religion', we first need to discuss what makes it 'traditional'.

In the Beginning There Was *Ifa*

Although 'Yoruba religion' has been on the decline since the 1950s – the time that Islam and Christianity claimed a majority of nearly 90 per cent in Yorubaland – its memory and ethos still exert a large influence today, and some of its cosmological framework informs the present-day practice of Islam and Christianity (Peel 2016a: 220). Many practising Yoruba Muslims and Christians consult *babalawos* when they are ill, and participation in traditional festivals commemorating the ancestors is considered a part of Yoruba cultural life. Moreover, the expansion of *Ijo Orunmila* illustrates that 'Yoruba religion' is alive.

'Yoruba religion', which is indigenous to Yorubaland, is premised on the belief that the material world is continuously affected by unseen

[7] See   www.facebook.com/ademola.ifabunmi?__tn__=%2CdK-R-R&eid=ARAZqkYQrAzFb X6BPdSNES0duNnUGOoj45pG7EWq_iDFlXnkLtrBHPgtfzH2Tw2CQ3FTTgeb s2yx0A4m&fref=mentions.

powers of various kinds. These powers are represented by the remote supreme God called Olodumare; a vast range of subordinate gods or *orisas*, that is, personalized deities, sometimes associated with natural forces (such as rivers, mountains, and trees) or with human activities linked to them (farming, rainmaking, ironmaking, healing);[8] ancestors (*babanla*) of relatively minor importance; other forms of power embodied in a human form, such as witches (*aje*); and an oracular cult called Ifa (Peel 2000: 93–101). Practitioners of 'Yoruba religion' worship Olodumare through the *orisas*. They communicate with the *orisas* via prayers and sacrifices offered at shrines. In return, the *orisas* are asked to give blessings in the form of children, health, protection against enemies and witches, and long life. Barber (1981) has shown the reciprocity of the relationship between devotees and their *orisa*. While devotees make the name of their *orisas* by sacrificing and singing their praises (*oriki*), the latter give health and wealth in return. If the deities fail to give to their devotees what they desire, they will devote themselves to another *orisa*.

Ifa was, and to some extent still is, at the apex of 'Yoruba religion'. Ifa is the name of both an *orisa* and an oracular cult,[9] which is based on a vast corpus of oral traditions. Ifa as a deity came to the world, founded the system of divination, taught his followers the technique and the verses, and then departed (Barber 1990: 209). According to Peel (2000: 98), Ifa as a divination system provides answers to two basic questions: (1) Who is the source of trouble clients of the oracular cult are struggling with?; and (2) What needs to be done to solve this problem? To answer these questions, the *babalawo* needs to find out, through divination, which unseen power lies behind his client's misfortune, and how this power's anger or ill-will can be assuaged.

But Ifa is more than a spiritual being and a divination system: it also refers to the very essence of Yorubaness, that what makes the Yoruba distinctive as a people. In Yoruba studies, Ifa is considered the summation of Yoruba culture and thought (Abimbola 1976). Reverend Onadele Epega insisted in 1932 that Ifa was 'the embodiment of the soul of the Yoruba nation and the repository of their knowledge, religious, historical, and medical' (cited in Peel 2000: 304). This outlook continues in the work of contemporary Yoruba scholars. Today, Ifa is widely accepted

---

[8] For example, *orisa* Oko is the god of farming, Sango the god of thunder, Ogun the god of war and iron, and Osanyin the god of medicine.

[9] Ifa is not the only system of divination practised by the Yoruba, but it is certainly the most salient one.

by practitioners and scholars alike as the undisputed source of every aspect of Yoruba culture.

Ifa as a comprehensive philosophy is based on a large oral corpus of verses (*ese*), which are organized under the 256 divination figures (*odu*) that the *babalawo* may cast with his divination apparatus: a chain (*opele*) that consists of eight half palm nuts linked together. Noticing my difficulty in understanding Ifa, which for me resembled mathematics, Chief Ifabunmi explained,

> Ifa can be compared to a television. Like a television has channels, Ifa has 256 (16x16) channels. Some channels are more popular than others. In Ifa, the most popular channels are sixteen: the principal *Odu*.[10] All these channels have different names and different stories attached to them. These stories are derived from our vast Yoruba cosmology. The instrument that is used to 'watch' these channels is the *opele*. Those with the knowledge to handle this instrument are called *Baba Alawos*: 'Fathers who know the secrets of the world'. That's how the term *babalawo* came into being. A *babalawo* has the knowledge to interpret the channels' different stories and based on this, he advises his clients which sacrifices to make for their problems to be solved.

As this narrative suggests, Ifa stresses pragmatism: it dwells on predicting and explaining clients' problems such as illness, infertility, poverty, or 'bad luck', and offering a solution.

A divination session begins with the *babalawo* casting the *opele* or, less frequently because more time-consuming, manipulating the sacred palm nuts (*ikin*) and announcing the resulting signs, that is, the patterns produced by the configuration of the palm nuts, convex or concave side facing upwards. He then recites the *ese* appropriate to the figure cast, which will give a key to the client's problem. The divination outcome is narrated to the client in the form of a parable or proverb (*odu Ifa*). These divinatory narratives express the mythical worldview of the Yoruba: they are verbal manifestations of divine power. In short, the *babalawo*'s role is to interpret his client's situation through the events and meanings the Ifa corpus conveys and to prescribe which ritual actions need to be taken to improve his client's condition (Olupona 2011: 173–84).

The solution to the client's problem is most often found in sacrifice. Sacrifice is at the heart of the devotional relationship in 'Yoruba religion': to worship an *orisa* is to sacrifice (*bo*) to it – the generic word for 'sacrifice' (*ebo*) being formed from this relationship (Peel 2000: 99).[11] In 'Yoruba

---

[10] Sixteen is a mystical number in Ifa divination (Bascom 1969: 121).

[11] While Yoruba Muslims and Christians say they *sin* ('worship') God, the term *sin* is usually not used by practitioners of 'Yoruba religion' in their relations with the *orisas*. Rather, they use *bo* (meaning 'sacrifice', 'propitiate', or 'appease'). Therefore, many

religion' humans cannot sacrifice directly to Olodumare. The latter is assisted by two intermediaries: Esu (the ambivalent trickster) and Orunmila (literally, 'heaven's reconciliation'), who reveals Olodumare's will to humans through divination (Ifa). There is a close relationship between Ifa and Esu, who receives a portion of all the sacrifices made through Ifa to any of the *orisas* (Abimbola 1976: 9). Because Orunmila is the god of Ifa, he is seen as being above the *orisa* pantheon. His name alludes to God's abode (*orun* means 'heaven') and he is considered God's special messenger: his official title is *Igbakeji Olodumare*, that is, Deputy of Olodumare (Peel 2000: 121, 303).

The Ifa corpus is transmitted from generation to generation of *babalawos*, who master it by a rigorous method of rote-learning (Barber 1990: 197). Chief Ifabunmi was trained by a renowned *babalawo*, Chief Agboola, who was among the pioneer members of *Ijo Orunmila*. His training lasted twelve years. Besides his training as a *babalawo*, he attended a mission school. As a result, Chief Ifabunmi is well versed in both Ifa and the Bible. He emphasized that learning the sacred knowledge of Ifa is a long and difficult process in which one is initiated as a novice and gradually qualifies for initiation into the highest order, *Awo Olodu*. To facilitate and abridge the learning process, Chief Ifabunmi opened the International Ifa Training Institute in 1997. Here he trains apprentices from all over the world in Ifa and herbalism by means of both oral traditions and a written handbook. In the words of Chief Ifabunmi, the training takes approximately one year, 'depending on the apprentice's intelligence'.[12] On his graduation from the International Ifa Training Institute, the apprentice receives a plasticized diploma. This diploma allows the graduate to call himself an 'Ifa consultant'. Besides providing Ifa training, Chief Ifabunmi's institute also organizes seminars to enlighten people about 'Yoruba religion', and collaborates with national and international researchers (like me) who want to know more about 'Yoruba religion'.[13] Chief Ifabunmi's wish for the future is to 'establish libraries and museums for the preservation of the Yoruba cultural heritage.'

---

practitioners of 'Yoruba religion' refer to themselves as *Aborisa* (meaning, 'the one who propitiates *orisa*') (personal communication with Adeyemi Balogun, September 2018).

[12] According to Abimbola (1976: 18), the training of Ifa priests normally lasts between ten and twelve years. One year of training in the International Ifa Training Institute is thus a record time to become a *babalawo*.

[13] There is an increasing interest in learning about Ifa from outside Nigeria. During my interview with OPC's leader Gani Adams, I met with a group of Brazilian tourists who introduced themselves as Candomblé practitioners who had travelled to Nigeria in search of 'authentic' Yoruba culture. Candomblé is a religion that is derived from Yoruba beliefs that were brought to Brazil by the enslaved (van de Port 2011).

As is common among *babalawos*, Chief Ifabunmi added medical practice to his divination knowledge. A poster on the wall of his office in the temple shows that he has served as the vice-chairman of the National Association of Nigerian Traditional Medicine Practitioners (NANTMP), which was founded by the Federal Ministry of Health in 2006. According to Chief Ifabunmi, certain herbal medicines are useful if infused with the power of the *orisas* to cure a variety of diseases and 'spiritual inflictions'. Another of Chief Ifabunmi's sideline activities has been acting in Nollywood films. Now that he is getting older, he is acting less himself and devoting more time to training Nollywood actors. According to Haynes (2007: 145), Nollywood films portray Nigeria as a dangerous landscape permeated by occult forces, which appear in many guises including computer-generated demons. Among the Nollywood actors are *babalawos*, who use their powers to eliminate these occult forces. Chief Ifabunmi trains *babalawo* actors so that their actions look 'authentic',

> I'm not only a *babalawo*, but also an artist. As an Ifa priest, my specialization is Yoruba history. Many people who watch Nollywood films consider 'Yoruba religion' to be idol worshipping. They associate it with fetishism. As an artist, I see it as my duty to tell the true story of our religion.

Troubled by the demonization of ATR by Pentecostals and reformist Muslims, Chief Ifabunmi tries to counter the images of 'Yoruba religion' as 'backward' and 'fetishistic' with its 'true story'.[14] In this sense, his involvement in the Nollywood film industry can be seen as a new proselytization method. This had some effect: a number of people who had seen him on screen came to *Ijo Orunmila* and they now count among its regular worshippers.

The aforementioned suggests that *Ijo Orunmila* embarks on mixing 'traditional' religious elements with 'modern' strategies to seek publicity, including a radio show and social media, the International Ifa Training Institute, and even the Nollywood film industry. These strategies are inspired by the priesthood's wish to retain the authenticity and competitiveness of 'Yoruba religion' in Lagos's competitive religious marketplace, which is increasingly being dominated by Pentecostalism and reformist Islam. According to many Pentecostal Christians and reformist Muslims, 'Yoruba religion' resembles a 'cult' involved in 'occult practices' such as ritual murder. Labelling a religious movement that is not

---

[14] Like in Nigeria, the prominent depiction of *juju* in Ghana's booming video film industry is a recurrent bone of contention between video filmmakers who want to educate their audiences about the nation's cultural heritage, and Pentecostals who claim that these depictions reinforce 'pagan superstitions' (Meyer 2015).

aligned to Christianity or Islam a 'cult' is a popular way of abusing rival congregations in Nigeria (Hackett 1989, 2001). To counteract this tendency, *Ijo Orunmila* has started appropriating Pentecostal elements. The case study in the next section illustrates how *Ijo Orunmila* mixes 'Yoruba religion' with (Pentecostal) Christianity in an assemblage that could best be described as a neo-traditionalist religion (de Witte 2012), because it strives to revive indigenous religion in a new form that is relevant to Lagos's contemporary religious landscape.

Seaman's Schnapps and Kola Nuts: *Ijo Orunmila*'s Worship

Early in the morning, my research collaborator Mustapha Bello and I took a taxi to *Ijo Orunmila*'s temple on Freeman Street, a busy commercial street near Oyingbo market in Ebute-Metta. The taxi driver, who had recently, what he called, 'switched churches' after his brother told him about the miracles he encountered in his Pentecostal church, had never heard of *Ijo Orunmila* and wanted to know more about it. From what we told him, he concluded that this was a 'handy' faith because it combines religious elements. A banner on top of the gate showed that we had reached our destination. On the banner the Ifa symbol was portrayed: a divination tray with eight kola nuts. From the outside the temple looked like a church with its large windows and old wooden doors. Empty Seaman's Schnapps bottles in the front yard revealed that this was not an ordinary church. Seaman's Schnapps is used by practitioners of 'Yoruba religion' to pour libations to the *orisas*. The interior of the temple, composed of pews, a choir stall, and a pulpit, did not show any signs of the *orisas* being worshipped here. Although Mustapha's Muslim apparel was incongruous with both the temple's exterior and interior, his presence did not raise any questions. In the temple we met several Christians and a couple of Muslims who presented themselves as 'liberal', 'Here we treat everyone equally; we don't discriminate.'

We were given a warm reception by Chief Ifabunmi and his wife, whom we presented a bag of kola nuts. Chief Ifabunmi invited us to his office on the first floor, a large space that was almost empty except for a desk and some plastic chairs, where we were introduced to his assistants and attended a divination session. A young woman, whose name revealed that she was a Muslim, consulted Chief Ifabunmi because she was suffering from 'bad dreams'. Chief Ifabunmi told her to bring out some money. She took out a 100 Naira note from her wrapper, held it together with Chief Ifabunmi's divination chain (*opele*) in her right hand, and whispered a prayer request on it. Chief Ifabunmi then threw the *opele* on his desk and wrote down the cast figures in a notebook. After reciting the corresponding divination verses (*ese*), he made a calculation in his notebook and told the woman that she needed to sacrifice three chickens that very day and bring a number of items to the temple with a total value of 5,410 Naira (approximately 11 GBP) if she wanted to have a 'peaceful mind'.

Chief Ifabunmi then excused himself to prepare for the service, while his assistants made arrangements for the client's sacrifice. Mustapha and I went downstairs where we met with a congregation of about forty people. Because we had to wait for nearly an hour for the service to start, Mustapha complained that while NASFAT 'respects time' *Ijo Orunmila* observes 'African time'.[15] Finally, the female choristers, barefooted and dressed in white, entered the temple, followed by male drummers, who were also dressed in white.[16] A young man rang a bell (*iro*) to attract Ifa's attention. The drummers were followed by three priests, with Chief Ifabunmi at the back holding a cow-tail whisk (*irukere*). Also, the priests were barefooted and dressed in white, wearing chains and bracelets made of beads (*ide*).[17] The choristers, drummers, and priests kneeled on the ground to pray, before seating themselves. While the choristers were seated in the choir stall, the priests sat separately from the choir and the congregation in an open room behind the pulpit. The congregation was divided according to gender: women were seated on pews to the left of the pulpit and men on the right side. Most congregants were dressed in local apparel, and all female congregants had covered their head. Despite the small number of congregants attending the service, a loud-speaker system was used.

Like in a Christian order of service, the service in *Ijo Orunmila* started with praise worship but in Yoruba,

> *The Great King*
> *Praise be to God*
> *We praise you today*
> *We exalt you*

Chief Ifabunmi opened the service by offering invocations to Ifa and the other *orisas*. He prayed for Nigeria, the temple, and the congregation.

---

[15] Mustapha, a NASFAT official, criticized the perceived tendency of Africans toward a more relaxed attitude to time, running late for meetings.

[16] Similar to the white garments worn in the *Aladura* churches, *Ifeoluwa*, and NASFAT, white represents purity in *Ijo Orunmila*.

[17] *Babalawos* are distinguished by a beaded bracelet worn on the left wrist known as *ide Ifa* or 'beads of Ifa'. Copying Orunmila, they sometimes also wear beads around their neck. The cow-tail whisk (*irukere*) is another insignia of *babalawos* (Bascom 1969: 84).

Whereas in a church the congregation responds to prayers with 'Amen', here the congregation said '*Ase*' – a Yoruba word that is believed to invoke divine forces. After the prayers, *Ijo Orunmila*'s creed was recited in Yoruba,

> *I believe in God, the Almighty*
> *Maker of heaven and earth*
> *I believe in Orunmila*
> *The first prophet of Olodumare*

After the creed, the choir sang hymns from *Ijo Orunmila*'s hymn book. While some of the choristers and the three priests had their own copy of the hymn book, most congregants did not have a copy. Still, they memorized the hymns.

A junior priest took the floor to recite blessings for the barren and pregnant women in the congregation, the children, unemployed men, and new members. These blessings were followed by another hymn in which the congregation was encouraged to 'serve God with humility'. The atmosphere was exuberant and several congregants danced. Then it was time for announcements, including upcoming naming ceremonies and other life-cycle rituals. The priest mentioned that attendance was low this week, which he explained by the fact that one of the priests was burying his mother-in-law in Ogun State. Many members were attending the funeral. His fellow priest had intended to attend the funeral, but after consulting Ifa he decided to stay in Lagos because it was not 'safe' for him to travel on this particular day. Upon hearing this testimony, the congregation responded with a loud '*Ase*'. The priest encouraged the congregation to attend services regularly, to make donations, and to pay their monthly membership fees. He then prayed for the relatives of the deceased woman and for the members who had travelled to Ogun State so that they would return safely. These prayers were followed by prayers for protection against witchcraft and illness, and for good leadership, 'Gaddafi ruled for a long time, before he was removed because of poor leadership. We are not even enjoying half of what the Libyans were enjoying under Gaddafi. God should help us getting better leaders, so that we can live in peace and affluence.' During the prayers, a chorister walked between the pews to distribute kola nuts among the congregants in return for an offering in the form of a small amount of money.

After the singing of hymns, Chief Ifabunmi delivered a sermon in both Yoruba and English in the form of an Ifa lesson. An old man had three sons. He visited a *babalawo* because he was getting feeble and wanted to know what he could do to postpone his death. After consulting Ifa, the *babalawo* told him to sacrifice fresh fish. The old man asked his sons to get him fish from the sea. The first two sons did not consult Ifa before embarking on the long journey to the sea. They did not catch any fish. In fact, their bait killed all the fish in the sea. Only the youngest son consulted Ifa and sacrificed before he left for the sea. His journey was successful: he caught a lot of fish and brought it home. Eating the fish rejuvenated his father. The moral of the story, Chief Ifabunmi explained, was that the congregation must always consult Ifa before undertaking anything,[18]

Consulting Ifa is very important. Ifa is the word of God. My father died when he was very, very old. Today even children are dying. Why? Because they have abandoned their traditions. Today some people don't want to speak Yoruba with their children; they speak only English because they think it's civilized. This shows that they have turned their back on their culture. My children go to school, but I still train them to become *babalawos*. May God inspire us to learn more about our ancestral religion and cultural history.

While criticizing the congregation for not following their traditions, Chief Ifabunmi was also critical of 'fake *babalawos*' who tell lies and do anything to make 'cheap money'. He concluded his sermon with a lesson, 'Always speak the truth and don't talk about things you don't have knowledge of. Truthfulness will make Nigeria prosper', to which the congregation responded with '*Ase*'.

After the sermon, the choir sang hymns in Yoruba praising Orunmila, backed by the drummers. This woke up some of the worshippers who had fallen asleep. Mustapha, whose mother was a Christian before she married his father and converted to Islam, recognized a hymn as Christian and noted that the choir had replaced Jesus Christ by Orunmila,

> *I will worship you*
> *All the worship in the world is yours*
> *All the wealth belongs to you*
> *Orunmila did his part and the world became successful*
> *All the worship in the world is yours*
> *All the wealth belongs to you*
> *Hear our prayers*
> *And protect the black race*

In another hymn the choir had replaced 'God the father' by 'Orunmila the father',

> *Orunmila is the one I have as a father* (2x)
> *Help me shout his name* (3x)

---

[18] The Ifa corpus is composed of an enormous stock of stories, each of which makes the same point through the same structural form: they constitute a precedent for the present and a model for the future. The moral is always the same: Ifa knows best; do what Ifa tells you and you will prosper; disobey Ifa and disaster will ensue (Barber 1990: 208).

Figure 5.1 *Obi pipa*.
Photographer: Akintunde Akinleye

During the singing of hymns, a chorister collected 'thanksgiving' among the congregation. Similar to a Pentecostal service, two members were called forward to give a testimony. They testified how through consulting Ifa they managed to escape from a car accident and prayed to Orunmila to thank him. The service ended with a ritual called *obi pipa*, 'casting the lots' (Figure 5.1). While the choir sang, accompanied by the drummers, the junior priest brought in a tray with kola nuts and unrolled a prayer mat. He was joined by the other priests who prayed on the kola nuts. The junior priest placed the kola nuts on his colleagues' forehead, before breaking them into two. He then called the congregation – first male congregants, followed by female ones, the choristers, and children – to come forward. The congregants took out a 50 Naira banknote, touched their forehead with it, and whispered their prayer request on it, begging Ifa to reveal the secret behind their problems and to find an appropriate solution. They placed the banknote in front of the priest, who invoked Ifa. The lots were used to answer questions with 'yes' or 'no'.[19] By the

---

[19] Questions to Ifa are posed in terms of two statements, the first affirmative and the second negative, such as 'The venture which I'm considering will be good for me', and 'The venture which I'm considering will not be good for me' (Bascom 1969: 51).

way the lots landed on the mat (with convex or concave side facing upwards), the priest determined the steps the worshippers needed to take to solve their problems. I was also asked to come forward but when I presented, like the congregants, a 50 Naira banknote, the priest reprimanded me that this amount was 'too small' to consult Ifa. When I took out more money, the priest prayed for the success of my research. Before he closed the session, he said, 'May this not be the last *obi pipa* in your life; may your prayers be answered – *Ase*.'

Chief Ifabunmi closed the service with a prayer and a hymn after nearly two hours. The choristers first left the temple, followed by the drummers and finally the priests, while the congregation knelt down to pray. Afterwards male congregants shook hands, while the female congregants socialized among themselves. Some congregants went home, while others took the stairs to the first floor for a private divination session with Chief Ifabunmi. The other priests had already left to visit an ill *Ijo Orunmila* member in hospital. Mustapha and I joined the congregants in Chief Ifabunmi's office, where we were invited to enter the shrine (*ile Ifa*: 'house of Ifa'). Mustapha declined the invitation, but I happily accepted it. Before entering the shrine, I removed my shoes. Behind a white cloth I saw numerous bowls and pots with sacrifices (cooked and raw food items, leaves and roots of plants, and meat from sacrificial animals) and a chunk of laterite covered with oil and blood of sacrificial animals. Chief Ifabunmi asked me to kneel down on a mat and to whisper my prayer request on a kola nut while his assistants recited incantations. He poured half a glass of Seaman's Schnapps over the kola nut and ordered me to drink the remainder of it. After touching the kola nut with my forehead and chest, I was instructed to eat it while Chief Ifabunmi prayed for the success of my research. Because of the heavy rain, we spent – to Mustapha's dissatisfaction who was displeased about spending so much time near a shrine – the entire afternoon in Chief Ifabunmi's office, chatting with his clients and observing several divination sessions. A great number of glasses of Seaman's Schnapps later, the rain stopped and Chief Ifabunmi and his assistants, all a bit tipsy, saw us off.

Reframing 'Yoruba Religion'

The aforementioned illustrates that *Ijo Orunmila*'s worship is modelled on that of Christianity, with its standardized liturgy, hymn book, sermons, and strict hierarchy of priests. At the same time, it draws from 'Yoruba religion' in its use of traditional symbols like beads, the invocation of the *orisas*, the recitation from the Ifa corpus, and the casting of kola nuts. The latter ritual is performed every five days in the temple.[20] In addition to the casting of the kola nuts and the weekly worship service, a couple of years ago *Ijo Orunmila* introduced monthly night vigils. However, these all-night prayer meetings did not attract a large congregation: for safety reasons worshippers, most of whom do not own a private car, did not want to travel by public transportation at night – the time when both evil powers and armed robbers are believed to be active – and were discontinued. Another programme that is borrowed from the Pentecostal church is the annual Convention to publicize Ifa among a larger audience. Besides, every August the New Yam Festival is celebrated to restore the cosmic order. During this festival the High Priest offers sacrifices on behalf of the congregation to thank the *orisas* for the previous year and to pray for more years ahead. This illustrates that *Ijo Orunmila*'s religious calendar is a mixture of traditional and (Pentecostal) Christian rituals.

Because of the mixing of Yoruba and Christian elements, *Ijo Orunmila* has been labelled under the banner of 'syncretism' in the literature. According to Bascom, who first mentioned *Ijo Orunmila* in his voluminous work on Ifa, the 'church' represents 'one of the most striking religious syncretisms resulting from European contact' (1969: 12). In the words of Barber, *Ijo Orunmila* is a 'revamped, syncretic Ifá' (1990: 221). Peel, who mentions *Ijo Orunmila* in passing, describes it as a syncretic movement in Sundkler's sense of 'new wine [i.e. meeting religious demand from non-Yoruba] in old wineskins [i.e. Yoruba cultural forms]' (2016a: 228–9). However, while syncretism underlines assimilation, *Ijo Orunmila*'s founding father Oshiga struggled to maintain Yoruba cultural authenticity with the onslaught of Christianization. For Oshiga, religious independence, that is, the freedom to worship traditionally, equated political independence. From such a cultural nationalist perspective, compromising one's religious 'authenticity' as in syncretism would be tantamount to political submission to the colonial missionaries. Thus rather than assimilating 'Yoruba religion' and mission Christianity, Oshiga maintained religious boundaries. That religious boundaries are upheld also today is apparent in the layout of *Ijo Orunmila*'s temple, where traditional practices and Christian rituals are largely separated in space. Whereas the ground floor resembles a church, the shrine is located on the first floor (Figures 5.2 and 5.3). Again this demonstrates that assemblage, which foregrounds coeval religious traditions and allows for their mixing to be more than simply an aggregate of its component parts, is better suited to analyse *Ijo Orunmila* than syncretism.

---

[20] Of old, Ifa priests make sacrifices to their *orisa* every five days (Abimbola 1976: 11).

Figure 5.2 Ground floor of *Ijo Orunmila*'s temple.
Photographer: Akintunde Akinleye

Figure 5.3 *Ijo Orunmila*'s shrine.
Photographer: Akintunde Akinleye

Ijo Orunmila's mission of reframing 'Yoruba religion' in a Christian format calls not only for a reconsideration of anthropologists' conceptual frame of syncretism but also for a reflection on anthropology's legacy of debates on 'tradition'. According to Hobsbawm and Ranger (1983), many African 'customs', including chieftaincy, ethnicity, and ATR, were actually inventions of colonial authorities and their missionary accomplices. Hobsbawm and Ranger's emphasis on 'invention' challenged the alleged timelessness of 'tradition'. The anthropological trope of 'tradition' received further reconsideration in the 1990s with the renewed interest in witchcraft. Following in Evans-Pritchard's (1937) footsteps, anthropologists argued that witchcraft did not serve as a marker of the 'primitive other' but needed to be understood in relation to contemporary socio-economic transformations, growing inequalities, and imaginations of modernity. For example, Geschiere (1997) demonstrated how in Cameroon 'traditional' witchcraft and 'modern' politics are deeply entwined. In this spirit, the anthropological debates on the invention of tradition and the modernity of witchcraft denounced the long-standing myth of modernization as linear progress.

In a similar vein, neo-traditionalist groups such as *Ijo Orunmila* uproot the evolutionist premise of typologies that oppose 'tradition' to 'modernity' by showing that 'tradition' is contiguous with, or even constitutive of, 'modernity'. Indeed, *Ijo Orunmila* tries to be 'traditional' and 'modern' at the same time by drawing on ancient Yoruba culture and customs, while also affiliating itself with Christianity, which came to signify progress and modernity during the colonial era. Whereas at the time of its foundation in 1920, mission Christianity provided a model for *Ijo Orunmila*, Chief Ifabunmi and his colleagues have lately appropriated innovations from Pentecostalism. For example, they experimented with night vigils and annual conventions. They also introduced new proselytization methods in the form of the mass media and even the Nollywood film industry. In line with Pentecostalism's missionary zeal, *Ijo Orunmila* has opened an Ifa Training Institute where apprentices from all over the world can learn to become modern-type *babalawos* or 'consultants'. Aware that the Ifa Training Institute, where one can graduate as a *babalawo* in just a year, could impair the legitimacy of priesthood, Chief Ifabunmi stressed the importance of 'truthfulness' in his sermon cited in the previous case study: *babalawos* must speak the truth and should not divine with the sole aim of making money. To establish its public presence on Lagos's heavily Pentecostalized religious marketplace, *Ijo Orunmila* – which is located in a bustling market area in Lagos – makes use of a public address system. This had some effect: services now attract not only Yoruba worshippers but also Hausa and Igbo traders, who came to the temple out of curiosity on hearing the amplified services. In competition with the faith healing in Pentecostal churches, Chief Ifabunmi sells herbal medicine, which is popular not only among practitioners of 'Yoruba religion' but also among Christians and Muslims.

What we see here is that *Ijo Orunmila* is caught between ATR and Christianity. In order not to be considered a 'cult', *Ijo Orunmila* framed 'Yoruba religion' in a 'modern' Christian format, but in order to be regarded as 'authentic' it presented itself as the 'traditional' other to Christianity.[21] Hence, *Ijo Orunmila*'s revival of 'Yoruba religion' does not imply a relapse into the temporalizing device that locates tradition in the past but needs to be seen as a mode to respond to developments in the present, such as (Pentecostal) Christianity's inroads in Nigeria. If we want to gain a better understanding of neo-traditionalist groups such as *Ijo Orunmila*, we must therefore eradicate the discursive framework that conceptualizes ATR in opposition to the 'world religions'.

With this goal in mind, let us now take a closer look at the abbreviation 'R' in ATR. Some scholars deny that 'Yoruba religion' was ever a 'religion' (Taiwo 2008: 84–85; Olupona 2011: 87). In their opinion, the Yoruba word for religion, *esin*, was introduced by Muslims and Christians to refer exclusively to their own faiths. Since it was not its practitioners but rather missionaries who first constructed 'traditional' religion as a religion, the label of ATR has been criticized (Shaw 1990). Despite these reservations, under the influence of the Yoruba slave trade to the Americas, 'Yoruba religion' became established in new settings where, eventually, it came to be seen as a world religion in its own right (Olupona and Rey 2008). This then legitimized the 'R' in ATR, but challenged the 'A'. An irony of 'Yoruba religion' today is that whereas it is declining in Nigeria, it is practised overwhelmingly outside Africa by non-Yoruba people (Peel 2016a: 215).[22] As a result, it has become increasingly difficult to define 'Yoruba religion' as an exclusively 'African' religion (Matory 2005).

A related terminological dilemma is raised by the identification of 'Yoruba religion' as 'traditional'. There is plenty of historical evidence

---

[21] A similar tension can be seen in the Afrikania Mission in Ghana, which was founded by a former Catholic priest with the aim of reviving ATR as a modern world religion to serve as a religious base for pan-Africanism in the 1980s (de Witte 2012).

[22] The upsurge of 'Yoruba religion' in the diaspora resulted in a boom of 'heritage tourism' to Nigeria, where the Osun-Osogbo Sacred Grove – a sacred forest famous for its sculptures of *orisas* created by the Austrian artist and priestess Susanne Wenger and her team of local artists along the banks of the Osun river – has grown into a pilgrimage centre for devotees of the river goddess Osun from all over the world. In 2005, the Sacred Grove in Osogbo (Osun State) was declared a UNESCO World Heritage Site (Probst 2011).

that 'Yoruba religion' has always been dynamic and changing and never existed in isolation from Islam and Christianity. For example, it was not uncommon for Ifa to advise its clients that the answer to their problems was to become a Muslim or Christian – that is, to worship God directly, rather than through the *orisas* (Peel 2016a: 78, 218). Because 'Yoruba religion' is distinguished by the variety of its *orisas* and by the reality of personal choice, there is considerable room for gradual adjustment and flexibility in the sense that if one *orisa* fails to answer the devotee's calls, he or she is free to experiment with another *orisa* (Peel 2000: 106). It is this willingness to try something new that conditioned the ways in which first Islam and later Christianity were received in Yorubaland (Barber 1981: 741).

Because of its flexibility, Peel studied 'Yoruba religion' as a dynamic tradition that still has relevance today, composed of 'fluid and malleable deities, less a single religion than a spectrum of local cult complexes' (2016a: 7). From this point of view, it would be unjust to treat 'Yoruba religion', Islam, and Christianity as bounded and distinct traditions. Instead, Taiwo (2018) perceives the three religious traditions in inter-action, as a 'compendium of phenomena' (93–94). Because the Yoruba do not conceive of religion as a coherent belief system, they may go to the mosque and/or church and yet believe in *orisas* and act on these beliefs. This fits the popular conception of 'Yoruba religion' as a stool with three legs or a crossroads (*orita*) between the three faith traditions (Peel 2016a: 220). From this it may be concluded, then, that rather than being a superstitious remnant of the past or an invented tradition, *Ijo Orunmila* stands for a theocentric cosmology in which 'Yoruba religion' is neither believed to precede the 'world religions' nor to have been submerged by them, but to coexist with them.

Orality through Literacy

The tradition–modernity typology is homologous with the conceptual opposition between 'non-literate religions' and 'religions of the Book'. In line with the dominant view of 'religion as text' (Shaw 1990: 339), *Ijo Orunmila* has published the oral Ifa corpus into a written form. Besides, it uses a Christian hymn book in which the name of Jesus has been replaced by Orunmila. Still, *Ijo Orunmila* has many features of a so-called non-literate religion. By means of an analysis of *Ijo Orunmila*'s texts, this section calls the conventional orality–literacy dichotomy into question by showing that orality and literacy do not oppose but mutually consti-tute each other.

A key feature of 'Yoruba religion' is that it lacks written scriptures on which its tenets are based. Instead of scriptures, it relies on the oral *Ifa* corpus. Because Ifa is based on oral modes of transmission it enshrines the principle of secrecy: only the *babalawos* (literally, 'fathers of mysteries') know how to access secrets (*awo*) (Peel 2000: 98). According to Bascom (1969: 120), there used to be strong resistance among *babalawos* against the recording of Ifa verses, which they considered their professional secrets that helped them build a name for themselves. By contrast, the so-called world religions are 'religions of the Book'. In Yoruba, Christians are known as *Onibuko* or 'book people'. The Yoruba term for Muslims is *Imale*, meaning 'hard knowledge': a reference to the arduous practice of Islam with its training in the acquisition of Arabic in order to be able to read the Qur'an in its original language (Olupona 2016: 168–9). Whereas in 'Yoruba religion' the focus was on secrets, for Muslim and Christian missionaries it was vital that the word of God was made openly available, either in the sacred language of Arabic or in the local languages.[23]

Underlining the transforming effect of literate activity on cognitive structures, Goody (1987) equated 'literacy' with 'rationality'. To him, 'cognitively as well as sociologically, writing underpins "civilization"' (300). This ethnocentric idea interlocks with the entrenched tendency to use orality as a shorthand way of setting 'Africa', associated with primitivity and timelessness, apart from 'the West', associated with modernity and progress. In such a view, the orality–literacy binary has evolutionist connotations and functions as a variety of what Mudimbe (1988) calls an 'ideology of otherness'. The divide between orality and literacy has been criticized by Finnegan (2012 [1970]), who argues that African oral literature can be regarded as a type of literature,

the contrast between fully oral forms on the one hand and the impersonal medium of print on the other is clearly only a relative one: we would hardly suggest that works written and, in part, orally transmitted before the advent of printing were therefore not literature, any more than we would be prepared to state dogmatically that the Homeric epics – or an African poem – only became literature on the day they were first written down (21).

This oft-cited quote gave rise to the orality versus literacy debate, which illustrated that the distinction between oral and written forms of literature was not as rigid and profound as had long been taken for granted.

---

[23] As Sanneh (1989) has argued, there are striking differences in Islam's and Christianity's respective approaches to mission. Whereas Muslim missionization has proceeded on the basis of the non-translatability of the Qur'an, for Christians missionization has preeminently come to mean translation.

Since then, many scholars have come to see the contrast at best as a relative and changing continuum, rather than an absolute divide (e.g. Barber 1989; Miller 1990; Engelke 2004; Kirsch 2008).

Indeed, *Ijo Orunmila*'s texts cut across the apparent orality versus literacy divide. Similar to the Tiv elders, living in the central-eastern part of Nigeria, who so valued their past that several of them who were literate were anxious to get their oral traditions down in writing (Fardon 2015), *Ijo Orunmila*'s founding fathers valued Ifa to the extent that opposing the value attached to secrecy, they recorded their divination verses. Chief Ifabunmi explained to me,

> For a long time, the knowledge that we tap from Ifa was not recorded. It was handed down from generation to generation of *babalawos*. That is how I learned it. But traditions that are not written down tend to be forgotten. That is why Pa Oshiga and some other pioneer members of *Ijo Orunmila* wrote their own books, so that people would not forget about Ifa. In their books, they combined Ifa with Christian themes. Still, Ifa is beyond the scriptures. It is a vast body of sacred knowledge that covers the entire universe.

The books to which Chief Ifabunmi alluded are *Iwe Odu Mimo* ('Holy Book of *Odu*') and *Oju Olowo Oriki Ifa* ('The Eulogy of Ifa'). While these books have been printed, other scriptures used by *Ijo Orunmila* are handwritten. For instance, Chief Ifabunmi has written down his knowledge of Ifa by hand in notebooks. He consults these notebooks during Ifa sessions with clients and he reads aloud from them during the Saturday service. Since his notebooks contain the fruits of years of study, which he does not want to 'give away for free', Chief Ifabunmi stores them at home. Every Saturday he carries them in a nylon bag to *Ijo Orunmila*'s temple. As a result of this frequent travelling, the notebooks are falling apart. Because printing is expensive, one of his colleagues has started a fundraising campaign on Facebook. He complained that now that 'ignorant Western scholars' (this might well have been an indirect criticism of my research) claim to have knowledge of Ifa and write books about it, it is high time for Ifa priests to publish their own Ifa books. Although part of the Ifa corpus has been published or has been written down in personal notebooks, similar to the oral Ifa corpus a sense of secrecy surrounds these texts. Under the pretext that he did not have the 'copyright' on *Ijo Orunmila*'s scriptures, Chief Ifabunmi did not allow me to copy his printed Ifa corpus and hymn book nor his handwritten notebooks. Furthermore, my colleague, the photographer Akintunde Akinleye, was not allowed to take pictures of these texts.

All Chief Ifabunmi was willing to tell me was that *Ijo Orunmila*'s scriptures have been modelled on the Bible. According to Barber

(1990: 215–18), who had access to the *Iwe Odu Mimo* during her field-work, its layout copies the Bible, being divided into chapters (corres-ponding to the *Odu* – the sacred Ifa verses) with numbered verses and hymns. There are echoes of the Bible not only in style but also in the narratives that glorify the High God. Irrespective of the similarities with the Bible, *Ijo Orunmila*'s scriptures affirm the authority of Ifa as an infallible divination system and of Orunmila as the god of divination. Because Yoruba and Christian themes alternate, Barber concludes that the *Iwe Odu Mimo* cannot be interpreted as a 'Bible in traditional clothing' (213).

According to Peel (1990: 347), the mission's strategy in Yorubaland depended on the construction of 'paganism' as a system homologous to Christianity, in which some elements would be retained (such as God and the idea of a savior) and others replaced (Orunmila by Jesus, sacrifice by prayer, etc). Such symbolic homologies were not only aids to a more effective evangelization; they would eventually encourage a degree of mutual adaption. But although mission Christianity sought to inscribe itself into Yoruba culture by treating the *orisas* – and above all Orunmila – as a prefiguration of Jesus, *Ijo Orunmila* does not identify Orunmila with Christ but worships him as the god of Ifa. Moreover, while Esu has been translated as 'Satan' in the Bible, *Ijo Orunmila* considers him an *orisa* in his own right. Chief Fabunmi explained, 'Ajayi Crowther [the first indi-genous bishop of the Anglican Church] did a lousy job when he trans-lated the Bible into Yoruba. He translated Esu with Satan, but they are different. Esu is the architect of the universe, of good and bad, of heaven and hell.' This affirms Barnes' (1997: 19) argument that there is a marked contrast between Christian modes of thought and Yoruba beliefs: whereas in Christianity 'good' and 'evil' are seen as opposing categories, symbolized by God and Satan, in 'Yoruba religion' positive and negative power cannot be separated. Again, this shows that despite the overlap between *Ijo Orunmila*'s scriptures and the Bible in both form and content, there are also major differences.

A further difference is that whereas churches offer Bible Studies, these text-based services do not take place in *Ijo Orunmila*, where the emphasis is on the performance of the scriptures. *Ijo Orunmila*'s worshippers believe that only when the Ifa corpus is orally performed by *babalawos* can it develop its spiritually empowering potential, that is, help them find a solution for the problems they encounter in life. That most worshippers did not have their own copy of *Ijo Orunmila*'s hymn book but were still aware of the order of service and joined in the hymns also suggests that the scriptures are in the first instance meant to be performed. Chief Ifabunmi explained to me,

Our founding fathers looked at the way the Christians composed their hymns, but they didn't just copy them; they composed hymns in the Ifa way. These hymns are performed not only during the Saturday worship service, but also at naming ceremonies and weddings. When members are in distress, we sing for them to cheer them up. We distinguish between church songs and Ifa songs.

This narrative suggests that similar to the Masowe apostolic church in Zimbabwe studied by Engelke (2004: 79–80), for whom the Bible is a symbol of the colonial encounter, *Ijo Orunmila* is first and foremost a 'performative faith', in which 'reading' is an act that is oral and collective.

Since performativity outweighs textuality, *Ijo Orunmila*'s scriptures differ from the fashion in which Christians conceive of the Bible as an inerrant, unchanging, primordial transcript of God's word. Unlike the sacred text of the Bible, the way *Ijo Orunmila*'s scriptures are recited varies, depending on the context, the priest's eloquence, and the involvement of the congregation, who serves as an audience, nodding for approval and responding to the Ifa lessons with prayers, singing, and dancing. Moreover, whereas the form of the text in the Bible is linear, that of *Ijo Orunmila*'s scriptures is repetitive. As a result, a sermon in *Ijo Orunmila*'s temple is delivered as an assemblage of overlapping, partly distinguishable pieces, rather than a story narrated from the beginning till the end (Barber 1990: 216–17).

In sum, in *Ijo Orunmila* Ifa remains, to some extent, dependent on oral modes of transmission. Orality and literacy are not absolute categories but rather dialectical ones. Indeed, Chief Ifabunmi uses both oral and written transmission modes in his International Ifa Training Institute. His apprentices say the Ifa verses after him, but to facilitate their learning Chief Ifabunmi has also written an Ifa Handbook. Another instance where oral and written modes of transmission coalesce is when he writes down the outcome of his divination sessions in a notebook. Furthermore, I noticed priests taking notes during the sermons to make sure that the same Ifa lessons are not delivered in each service. The coalescence between orality and literacy informs *Ijo Orunmila*'s religious practice. Hence, by continuing making use of ingrained distinctions such as 'ATR' and 'world religions', and correspondingly, 'non-literate religions' and 'religions of the Book', we are holding on to evolutionary connotations that do not do justice to the dynamics of religious pluralism in *Ijo Orunmila*.

Conclusion

Neo-traditionalist religious movements such as *Ijo Orunmila* challenge not only theological boundaries between monotheistic and polytheistic religions but also spatio-temporal boundaries between local versions of 'traditional' religion versus the modern 'world religions'. Such attempts at boundary making are one of the stumbling blocks in the study of religion in Africa. According to Barnes (1997: 21), the very act of classification had the effect of predetermining the direction of change: devotees of 'Yoruba religion' are converted to, or their beliefs are merged with or replaced by, the 'world religions', as in Horton's (1975a, b) influential conversion theory. The case of *Ijo Orunmila* illustrates that such a teleological approach to conversion obscures the dynamic fluidity of 'Yoruba religion', and is contrary to the religious pluralism that marks Yorubaland. In order to go beyond the teleological inclinations of conversion theory, the Comaroffs (1991) introduced the concept of 'conversation'. That this concept is more accurate than conversion is illustrated by *Ijo Orunmila*: rather than converting from 'Yoruba religion' to Christianity, founding father Oshiga put the two into conversation and within the dialogue a religious assemblage occurred.

This chapter explored the extent to which Christianity has shaped 'Yoruba religion' within the conversation that took place between colonial missionaries and *babalawos* (see also Peel 1990). While *Ijo Orunmila*'s initial appropriation of Christian elements was an attempt to maintain religious independence in a context dominated by mission Christianity, its present copying of Pentecostal techniques can be interpreted as a means to cast off the stigma of 'paganism' that surrounds the practice of 'Yoruba religion' in a setting dominated by reformist types of religion. On President Buhari's return to Nigeria, after having received medical treatment in London, in March 2017, he thanked both Muslims and Christians for their prayers for his recovery. That he did not thank practitioners of 'Yoruba religion' indexed, according to Chief Ifabunmi, its marginal status in present-day Nigeria. By appropriating elements from Pentecostalism, *Ijo Orunmila* tackles its stigmatization as a 'cult'.

Because 'Yoruba religion' and Christianity exist side-by-side in *Ijo Orunmila* – literally as apparent in the layout of the temple, which is divided into a church on the ground floor and a shrine on the first floor, and the layout of *Ijo Orunmila*'s scriptures in which Yoruba and Christian themes alternate – it emerged that syncretism is a much too limited conceptual frame to analyse the group's mode of religious pluralism. Instead of synthesizing 'Yoruba religion' and Christianity in a syncretic configuration, Oshiga maintained the religious boundaries between the two traditions, which he considered to be equal. His notion of equation, rather than synthesis, fits in with the ideology of Yoruba cultural nationalism current at the time of *Ijo Orunmila*'s foundation, which considered 'Yoruba religion' and Christianity to be coterminous.

   Although it is nearly a century old, *Ijo Orunmila* is still alive and kicking in Lagos since it gives a measure of the cultural underpinnings at work in a multi-religious setting where God is believed to work through Islam, Christianity, and Ifa. As we will see in the next chapter, *Ijo Orunmila* shares its openness to religious pluralism with the exogenous religio-spiritual movements the Grail Movement and Eckankar that have cropped up in Lagos since the 1970s. In their attempt to occupy Lagos's religious marketplace, these movements transcended multiple religious boundaries to ensure a broader conception of wellbeing (*alafia*) and enlightenment (*olaju*) than the Yoruba cultural nationalists that founded *Ijo Orunmila* could ever have surmised.

6   Beyond Religion
The Grail Movement and Eckankar

> What if we think of religion, at the individual level, as an ever-changing, multifaceted, often messy – even contradictory – amalgam of beliefs and practices that are not necessarily those religious institutions consider important? (McGuire 2008a: 4).

Flying over Lagos by plane, one sees an enormous patchwork of lagoons, meandering roads, and rusty-roofed compounds with in the north-east all of a sudden a green plain with hills, the Iju Hills. If one presses one's nose against the airplane window, one sees a huge concentric circle in the middle of the plain, as if a UFO had landed there (Figure 6.1). This is Grailland, the 300-acre large settlement of the Grail Movement, a spiritual movement that emerged in Lagos in the 1970s, where Grail members assemble on a weekly basis to engage in meditative exercises. The Grail Movement was founded by the self-proclaimed Messiah Oskar Ernst Bernhardt (1875–1941), better known by his pen-name Abd-Ru-Shin (a name composed of Persian-Arabic elements meaning 'Servant [or Son] of the Light'), in Austria in 1928. Although it has its own scripture, *In the Light of Truth: The Grail Message*,[1] 'religion' does not describe the Grail Movement well. As Abd-Ru-Shin writes in the preface of *The Grail Message*, he did not bring a new religion but a 'Message' that was intended as 'the torch to help all serious listeners or readers find the right path, which leads them to the longed-for height', that is, the Grail. For the Grail members whom I interviewed, the Grail Movement is not a religion but a 'life science' that helps them to advance spiritually.

In its non-denominational character and international outlook, the Grail Movement resembles Eckankar (literally, 'Co-Worker with God'). Unlike the Grail Movement, Eckankar defines itself as a religion, but it stresses its distinctness from institutionalized religion. According to an Eckist (a member of Eckankar) from a Catholic background, 'Eckankar is

---

[1] *The Grail Message* is a compilation of 168 lectures written by Abd-Ru-Shin between 1923 and 1938, combined in three volumes. The work has been translated into 17 languages and is available in more than 90 countries (www.grail-message.com).

154

Figure 6.1 Grailland.
Courtesy of Grailland, Iju Hill: www.grailnet.info/english/grailland.html

the melting pot of all religions: Islam, Christianity, African Traditional Religion, Hinduism are all part of Eckankar.' Founded as a modern-day 'universal religion' by Paul Twitchell (1908–71) in Las Vegas in 1965,[2] Eckankar helps individuals find their own 'custom-made approach to the Kingdom of God'.[3] Whatever their religious background, Eckankar's teachings – premised on esoteric exercises such as out-of-the-body experiences or 'soul travel' – show Eckists how to look and listen to the divine within themselves in order to expand their consciousness and enjoy 'spiritual freedom'.

A study of Lagos's religious marketplace is incomplete without paying attention to the upsurge of religio-spiritual movements such as the Grail

---

[2] Although Twitchell founded Eckankar in 1965, his followers believed that the basis for Eckankar's teachings date back beyond the beginning of human existence. Indeed, Eckankar claims to be the 'root religion', 'the ancient teaching that is the source from which all religions and philosophies sprang' (Barrett 2004a: 178).

[3] See www.eckankar.org and *Eckankar: Ancient Wisdom for Today*.

Movement and Eckankar since the 1970s.[4] These movements are distinguished by their quest for spiritual knowledge and power, higher states of
consciousness and direct spiritual experiences, as well as the use of
certain techniques and practices that draw on hidden forces in order to
manipulate the course of events in the here and now (Hackett 1989:
153–5, 163).[5] More than Chrislam, NASFAT, and *Ijo Orunmila*, they are
eclectic in nature because they mix Islam, Christianity, indigenous traditions, 'Eastern' religions, as well as non-religious sources. This chapter
addresses the question why religio-spiritual movements, which are
exogenous to Nigeria and differ radically from mainstream religion,
could attract an increasing membership in Lagos. I argue that the answer
to this question lies in what van Dijk (2015) calls the 'too-muchness' of
Pentecostalism. As should be clear by now, Pentecostalism has had an
enormous impact on the spatial configuration of Lagos. Indeed, the
material culture of the Pentecostal movement in Lagos is ubiquitous,
ranging from huge billboards advertising 'miracle makers' to megachurches and the prayer camps along the Lagos–Ibadan Expressway.
According to Ukah (2016: 529), the sights and sounds of
Pentecostalism create the atmosphere of Lagos: at any time of day or
night, in some part of the city, a Pentecostal crusade, night vigil, or other
programme is happening. While Chrislam, NASFAT, and *Ijo Orunmila*
have capitalized on Pentecostalism's spatial appropriation of Lagos by
copying Pentecostal styles and strategies, the Grail Movement and
Eckankar expanded because they turned away from Pentecostalism and
offered an alternative that promised individual spiritual liberation in the
here and now. Today their 'otherness' attracts especially the newly
emerging middle class, who are looking for ways to distinguish themselves from 'dogmatic' mainstream believers. This chapter shows that
spirituality is one way of distinguishing oneself in the anonymous megacity that is Lagos.

---

[4] In their only reference to Sub-Saharan Africa, Heelas and Woodhead (2005) claim that
conventional religion is 'flourishing' and that unlike in the United Kingdom and the
United States, the turn to new spiritualities is 'scarcely in evidence' in the region (127).
That this is a sweeping generalization was demonstrated by Jules-Rosette (1989: 147),
who estimated in the late 1980s that there were 7,000 new religious groups in Sub-
Saharan Africa with around 32 million members. Today there are many more religio-
spiritual movements active in Sub-Saharan Africa in general, and in Nigeria in particular.

[5] Other examples of religio-spiritual movements in Lagos are the Ancient Mystical Order
Rosae Crucis (AMORC), the International Society of Krishna Consciousness (ISKCON,
better known as 'Hare Krishna'), and the Baha'i Faith. While these movements originated
outside of Nigeria, a typical example of an indigenous spiritual movement is the Divine
Love Mission, which has a huge prayer camp along the Lagos–Ibadan Expressway. Its
founder, Sat Guru Maharaj Ji, preaches that to be decolonized from the 'foreign
religions', Islam and Christianity, Nigerians should revive 'traditional' religion.

During interviews, several Lagosians from the newly emerging middle class told me that they had become disillusioned with Pentecostalism. In their opinion, Pentecostalism lacked 'spiritual inspiration' and was 'too flashy' and 'too loud'.[6] According to a female Eckist, 'Pentecostal pastors preach about prosperity and their congregations are encouraged to show off. Spirituality, however, is not about such trivialities.' In a similar vein, several highly educated Lagosians from a Muslim background noted that they felt discouraged by reformist Islam, which they considered 'too radical'. According to a male Eckist, 'Unlike in the Prophet's time, Islam has come to stand for war.' For people like them, the Grail Movement and Eckankar, who regard all religions as 'true', are a better alternative than the reformist-oriented types of religion. In this spirit, spiritual belonging lays the foundation for a new middle-class identity, which entails more than socio-economic status and educational background.[7] What we see here is that, echoing the words of van Dijk (2015), a novel class-based spiritual space is emerging in Africa 'after Pentecostalism' and, I would like to add, after reformist Islam, 'an indeterminate and inchoate space that is ideologically intellectual but not necessarily secular in a Taylorian way' (217).[8]

Mapping the expansion of the new religio-spiritual movements in Lagos, I begin by describing the worship services that I attended in the Grail Movement and Eckankar. While based on Christian teachings and drawing inspiration from both 'Yoruba religion' and Islam, the Grail Movement and Eckankar have appropriated elements from the 'Eastern' traditions as well. Because of the diverse mixing in which these movements engage, assemblage – in the sense of the bringing together of heterogeneous beliefs and practices – is a useful heuristic device to analyse them. While the assemblage of religious and spiritual traditions

---

[6] Pentecostal services are usually deafening because the underlying idea is, according to a member of the RCCG, 'the louder you shout the better God will hear you'. In an environment marked by 'noise pollution' (see Chapter 1), the Grail Movement's silent worship – a means of generating spiritual presence and disciplining the self – is a novelty.

[7] 'Middle class' has become an important concept, not only in contemporary international policy discourse but also in the way Africans think and speak about their own position in society (e.g. Spronk 2014; Melber 2016). The African Development Bank, which declared in a 2012 briefing that between 300 and 500 million Africans had entered the middle classes, keeps a daily per capita expenditure of USD 2 as threshold (African Development Bank 2012: 13). Rather than an economic definition, Lentz (2016: 46) defines middle class as a multi-dimensional concept that refers to a socio-economic category, a cultural world, and a political discourse. From this perspective, religio-spiritual affiliation is part of class identity.

[8] According to Taylor (2007), religion and secularism do not oppose but mutually constitute each other (see Chapter 3).

is believed to bring about enlightenment, it may equally result in the hardening of religious boundaries. In present-day Lagos, boundary crossing intensified processes of boundary marking. Ultimately, the Grail Movement and Eckankar's assemblage of religious traditions and non-religious sources calls for a critical investigation of the very notion of 'religion' itself. Although I do not want to go as far as abandoning the concept of religion altogether (de Vries 2008; Chidester 2018), my aim in this chapter is to shed light on the blind spots in the established ways of studying religion in order to develop a new perspective that leaves room for un-institutionalized forms for religion in which religiosity is less a matter of doctrine and more of spiritual practice and personal conviction.

The Grail Movement: In Search of Spiritual Awakening

The Grail Movement originated when businessman Oskar Ernst Bernhardt, alias Abd-Ru-Shin, took up residence in Vomperberg, Tyrol (Austria), in 1928 in order to focus on the writing of his main work *In the Light of Truth: The Grail Message*. When readers of *The Grail Message*, wishing to live and work in Abd-Ru-Shin's vicinity, moved to Vomperberg, a Grail Settlement was established. This development was interrupted in 1938 when the Nazi regime annexed Austria and expropriated the Grail Settlement. Abd-Ru-Shin was arrested and taken to prison. All residents were expelled so that the Settlement could be used as a Nazi training camp. Abd-Ru-Shin was eventually released but kept under house arrest until he died in Kipsdorf, Germany, in 1941. After the war, the Grail Settlement was returned to Abd-Ru-Shin's widow, Maria Bernhardt.[9] Under her direction, the Grail Movement developed as a group designation for readers of *The Grail Message*. Over the years, numerous Grail Centres or 'Circles' have formed in Europe, the United Kingdom, North America, Australia, New Zealand, South America, and Africa.[10]

The first Grail Circle in Africa was founded in Lagos by the late Chief Adeyemi Lawson (1924–93), one of the first major Nigerian industrialists who founded Ecobank. I had arranged an interview with his son, who told me in the lounge of the four-star Sheraton Hotel Lagos about the historical origins of the Grail Movement in Nigeria. Chief Lawson was

---

[9] Maria Bernhardt died in 1957 and was succeeded first by her son Alexander, and later by her daughter Irmgard. When Irmgard died in 1990, a conflict about leadership broke out that divided the Grail Movement. Grail members took sides with either the 'Movement' (Vomperberg, Austria) or the 'Foundation' (Stuttgart, Germany) (Introvigne 2004: 244).

[10] Today's worldwide Grail membership is estimated at between 20,000 and 40,000. The international readership of *The Grail Message* is probably much larger.

baptized in the Anglican Church and came across *The Grail Message* in a bookstore in London, where he studied law, in 1963. His return journey to Lagos by boat took several weeks. This gave him time to read the book. He was so impressed by what he read that on his arrival in Lagos, he ordered a hundred copies of *The Grail Message*, which he sent to his friends in lieu of a Christmas card. Eager to know more about the movement, he travelled to Vomperberg, where he received approval to establish a Grail Circle in Lagos in 1965. Initially, the adherents – mostly members of the elite like Chief Lawson himself – met in his house. When the membership grew, he bought land on the outskirts of Lagos in the Iju Hills, where he established Grailland and built a temple that could host 2,000 Grail members.

Like Chief Lawson's widow, some wealthy Grail members have moved permanently to Grailland, which, similar to the prayer camps along the Lagos–Ibadan Expressway, serves as a model city for those seeking spiritual awakening. Unlike Lagos's overcrowded and polluted cityscape, Grailland is spacious and green. Chief Lawson's son invited me to visit Grailland and during our tour we passed big mansions that were separated by flower gardens. The street names, some of which were in German, referred to flowers. Grailland's event centre advertised flower arrangement lessons. We parked at Grailland's massive farmland, which provides the restaurants in Grailland with vegetables and fruit. Afterwards, we visited Chief Lawson's widow in her huge mansion decorated with pictures of the worldwide Grail Centres, a tiger taxidermy, and other curiosities purchased during her late husband's business trips.

Currently, there are around sixty Grail Circles in Nigeria. According to the national leadership of the Grail Movement, these are most popular in Lagos, where they attract the newly emerging middle class, which has become dissatisfied with the religions in which they were born and want to try something new. An example is Bob, a middle-aged manager of a news agency, who told me that he could not find answers to the questions about life and death he was struggling with in the Anglican Church. After attending a public Grail lecture as a student at the University of Lagos in 1987, his new life started: a life which he described as 'spiritual development and joy'. That he joined the Grail Movement does not mean that Bob no longer worships in the Anglican Church, however,

Many of my friends are Anglicans and if I have time, I still go to church with them on Sundays. Becoming a Grail member made me a better Christian because by reading *The Grail Message*, I understood the Bible better. *The Grail Message* also gave me a better understanding of the Prophet Muhammad's mercy and made me aware of the relationships between the different religions.

Because he wishes others a similar 'all-embracing experience of spiritual awakening', Bob occasionally organizes public lectures on *The Grail Message* in his home in an estate in an upscale part of Lagos. He invited me to one of these Sunday lectures, which was entitled 'The Need for Spiritual Awakening'.

Eager not to miss anything, I arrived early at Bob's villa that Sunday afternoon. Because the security guards would not let me enter (probably because of my driver's old car, which looked incongruous on the posh estate), I had to phone Bob to ask him to open the gate. In an effort to entertain me while she was busy preparing snacks for the guests, Bob's wife – a dedicated Grail member who was close to finishing her PhD in African literature – switched on the television, broadcasting a football match, in their luxurious living room. After the other guests, mostly university students, arrived, Bob turned off the volume of the television and put on a CD. For the next half an hour we watched the football match in silence while listening to Wagner to put us in the right mood for *The Grail Message*. A Grail official, who was introduced as a 'sacral leader', dressed in white, welcomed us. The golden Grail cross around his neck revealed his religious status. There is no formal conversion or initiation ritual in the Grail Movement, but if readers are convinced of the truth of *The Grail Message* they can decide to 'seal' their conviction in a 'covenant' with the Creator. As a symbol of this covenant, the reader receives a Grail cross. This cross differs from the Christian cross in that it is an isosceles cross (a cross with arms of equal length). The Grail Movement refers to the Christian cross as the 'cross of suffering' (the cross on which Jesus was crucified), whereas the roundness of the Grail cross represents the balanced nature of creation. Once a Grail member is 'sealed', he or she is called a 'cross-bearer'.[11]

The sacral leader explained to the guests that *The Grail Message*, which provides answers to the 'most important questions of life: What is the purpose of life?; Who am I?; Where do I come from?; and Where am I going to?', strengthens the awareness of the 'true values of life', and points the way to the 'recognition of the Creator'. He lectured, 'To encounter the love of our Creator, we must be prepared to learn. Buddha, Krishna, Moses, and Muhammad were all sent to help human beings to acquire divine knowledge.' Anticipating confusion among the

---

[11] Although a hierarchical organizational structure is lacking in the Grail Movement, there are three spiritual levels: at the lowest level are the silver cross-bearers, followed by the golden cross-bearers (the called ones, who are full-time workers for the Grail Movement), and disciples (a small portion of whom are appointed as holders of the golden cross with a precious stone). The latter lead the Grail rituals.

guests about what the Grail Movement stands for, he concluded by saying, 'There is nothing cultic about the Grail Movement, which is like a university where you move from one year group to another and grow spiritually.' After the lecture, his colleague delivered Lecture 34 from the first volume of *The Grail Message*, entitled 'The Language of the Lord'. Its message was that people need to learn to understand the 'living language' that the Creator speaks to them in order to be enlightened. Then it was time for questions. Two guests wanted to know more about the position of Jesus in *The Grail Message*. The sacral leader explained that although the Grail Movement does not deny that Jesus is the son of God, they do not believe that he died by crucifixion as a sacrifice for human's sin. Furthermore, *The Grail Message* states that Jesus was 'pro-created physically' and not through virgin birth. At the end of the Q&A, we were encouraged to buy *The Grail Message*.

In addition to public lectures, the Grail Movement organizes Grail Festivals and Sunday worship services. There are three annual festivals: during the Festival of the Holy Dove, which takes place on 30 May, the Event of the Pentecost is commemorated and the power of the Holy Spirit is renewed. The Festival of the Lily, symbolizing purity and beauty, takes place on 7 September. Since women are believed to have a closer relation to beauty and nature, this festival is above all addressed to womanhood. Finally, the Festival of the Radiant Star on 29 December celebrates the birth of Jesus, but not the 'historical Christ' who died on the cross, but the 'living Christ' who spread the message of love. Although these are festive occasions, the Grail Festivals are celebrated in silence. In addition, the Grail Movement organizes the four Grail Acts: blessings of babies and newly-wed couples; blessings of couples who have been married for some time; and blessings at funeral ceremonies. During funerals Grail members are expected to maintain 'absolute decorum', which means that they must try not to cry. Underlining the difference with institutionalized, congregational religion, Grail members are not obliged to take part in the Grail Festivals and Grail Acts; they can also read *The Grail Message* in the privacy of their homes.

Although the Grail worship services are open only to members who have studied at least two volumes of *The Grail Message*, by boasting that I was a fast reader I received an invitation to attend the Sunday worship in the Grail Circle in Ikeja, Lagos's business district. Before the worship started, a middle-aged man dressed in a black suit with a bow tie showed me around the white-washed Grail Circle and its garden. He was pleased to hear that I am Dutch because the flower decorations in the Circle had been imported from the Netherlands. Before the service started, the sacral leader instructed me in the dos and don'ts of Grail worship,

Like Christians, we assemble on Sundays but neither for clapping and dancing, nor for seeking miracles. Worship is too serious to clap and dance. Creation in itself is a miracle. Worship is a means to communicate with our Creator. To have full access to its power,[12] we worship in silence.

After this instruction, I was sent over to the 'lady's room' to 'beautify myself for the Creator'. An embroidery on the door indicated that 'silence is the golden rule'. Inside, a group of women were quietly ironing their clothes, applying make-up, and polishing their high-heeled shoes. One woman showed her new suede shoes, which she recently bought during a trip to Vomperberg in Austria, to her friend. The woman who was appointed as my guide whispered, 'If you go to a party, you dress up. So if you come here to worship, you should also beautify yourself.' She inspected my sober black outfit and because she felt that my high-locked blouse still revealed too much skin, she used a pin to close it up to my neck.

At 8.30am we entered a large white hall, where around 100 Grail members were contemplating in silence, while staring at a flower arrangement displayed on a table in front of the hall. Male and female members were seated separately. Whereas the women were dressed up in native attire, the men were dressed in either simple grey gowns or black suits with a tie. As a sign of 'humility' to the Creator, the head was left uncovered by both women and men. Shortly before 9am a tape with ringing bells was played and we were ushered to a hall on the first floor, where we were seated on wooden chairs.[13] Again, men and women sat separately with the men right from the altar and the women left. The altar was composed of a table covered with a white cloth with seven burning candles, a sword representing justice, a lily representing beauty, and a rose representing love. The windows were covered except for a skylight. The incoming sun illuminated the golden Grail cross above the altar.[14] The only sound was that of a recording of Beethoven. When the music stopped, the sacral leader delivered Lecture 7 from the first volume of *The Grail Message*, entitled 'Ascent'. Its message was that Grail members should 'free themselves by steadfast good volition', which would bring 'ascent to the light' and allow them to 'work off their karmic burden'.

[12] The Grail Movement uses the gender-neutral 'it' to refer to the Creator. To distinguish themselves from mainstream believers, Grail members hardly speak of 'God'.

[13] The Grail Circles, with their stylish worship halls and wooden instead of plastic chairs, stand in marked contrast with churches and mosques. For the aesthetic appeal of new spiritual movements in Congo, see Lambertz (2018: 165–6).

[14] The serene atmosphere in the Grail Circle begged for a photograph. However, I was not allowed to take photographs because, as I was told, my focus should be on the content of *The Grail Message* and not on the outward form of the Grail Movement.

After the reading, the sacral leader led the Lord's Prayer. The congregation stood up and prayed in silence. The sound coming from the Pentecostal church opposite the road broke the deafening silence.

After the silent prayer, the congregation sat down to listen to a piece of Mozart and a recording of organ music. When the tape with the ringing bells was played again, we went downstairs in silence where we sat down for another quiet moment of contemplation. I soon lost my concentration and I was glad when the children's worship service began at 9.30am and I could leave the hall. I was invited by Bob to join him and his friends at the restaurant next to the Grail Circle. Bottles of champagne and whisky were ordered to the table, which increased the cheerful mood. One of my table companions, who introduced himself as a former Muslim, explained to me that unlike Muslim and Christian sermons, the Grail worship service does not take long, 'Because the Lectures from *The Grail Message* are deep, members must concentrate on them very well. That's why our worship takes only 30 minutes.'

While several male Grail members socialized in the restaurant and some female members assembled under a canopy in the garden for a flower arrangement lesson, others joined a reading circle to discuss *The Grail Message*. The reading circle that I joined later was led by a cross-bearer (the designation for an initiated Grail member) who urged us to remove the bandage from our eyes so that we could see the truth, 'Genuine faith lies in conviction, and conviction comes solely through examination. You must search for yourself by reading. You will then find out that *The Grail Message* offers a path to the recognition of the Creator, the world, and the self.' The cross-bearer then addressed me, 'Don't read *The Grail Message* as a mere academic exercise; read it for your personal advantage. You can acquire knowledge only through experience.' Feeling confused, not by the alcohol that I had declined but by the overload of new impressions, I left. I did not have much time to reflect on my spiritual path because soon I was caught in another 'go-slow', which kept me busy for the next hours trying to find a backway to the guesthouse where I was staying.

Eckankar: The Doorway to Spiritual Freedom, Self-Mastery, Wisdom, and Love

Whereas silence marks worship in the Grail Movement, sound defines Eckankar's worship services, which are referred to as 'ECK Light and Sound Services' and are premised on the belief that through chanting the sound *HU* – the 'holy name of God' – Eckists can experience God's presence in their lives. Initially named 'The Ancient Science of Soul

Travel' and later 'The Religion of the Light and Sound of God',[15] Eckankar was founded by pulp fiction writer Paul Twitchell in Las Vegas in 1965. Before founding Eckankar, Twitchell had been a follower of the Sant Mat (literally, 'School of the Saints') movement established by Kirpal Singh in India, the controversial Indian guru Swami Premananda, and the Church of Scientology. After his death in 1971, Eckankar's leadership passed to Twitchell's appointed successor, Darwin Gross. During Gross's time as the Living ECK Master, there was adverse publicity about Eckankar's teachings having been plagiarized from the Indian Sant Mat movement.[16] Gross stepped down in 1981 and was succeeded by the current Living ECK Master Harold Klemp, who was born in 1942 and grew up on a Wisconsin farm, attended Divinity School, and served in the US Air Force. While stationed in Japan, he discovered Eckankar (Barrett 2004a: 178–9, 2004b: 643). Klemp popularized Eckankar by building the international ECK Temple in Chanhassan, Minnesota, from where the movement expanded to over 100 countries, including Nigeria.

Elucidating the history of Eckankar in Nigeria, the regional leader or RESA (Regional ECK Spiritual Aide),[17] Dr Ademola, told me over a cup of herbal tea in her office at the university where she lectures that the movement was introduced by Ben Anyaeji in Lagos in the mid-1970s. She described Anyaeji, a former physics teacher at Eko Boys High School in Lagos – a school that has produced some eminent alumni including former Lagos State Governor Babatunde Fashola – as a 'seeker' in search for 'higher levels of spiritual consciousness'. Dr Ademola, who herself came across Eckankar when studying different religious traditions during her undergraduate degree in Sociology and Anthropology at the University of Ife, apologized that this was all she could tell me about the beginnings of Eckankar in Nigeria because, 'unlike the orthodox religions, its history has not been recorded'. Although Lagos is still an

---

[15] Highlighting that Eckankar is a 'living religion' that transforms itself, Harold Klemp, the current leader of the movement, changed its name into 'Eckankar: The Path of Spiritual Freedom' in 2017.

[16] In 1978 David Lane published the book *The Making of a Spiritual Movement: The Untold Story of Paul Twitchell and Eckankar*, in which he claimed that Eckankar's teachings were not newly revealed but originated in the Sant Mat movement (an esoteric movement with Hindu and Sikh roots, which dates back to the nineteenth century), and that some of Twitchell's writings plagiarized the work of the Sant Mat teacher Julian Johnson. Initially, Eckankar ignored these accusations, but later Gross noted that fragments of Eckankar's writings could be found in all religions and that Twitchell had drawn these together (Barrett 2004a: 178–9).

[17] Nigeria is divided into three ECK regions; Dr Ademola is in charge of the western region.

Figure 6.2 ECK Centre.
Photographer: Akintunde Akinleye

important centre of ECK activities in Nigeria, Eckankar's headquarters have moved to Port Harcourt in the Niger Delta, hosting the largest ECK temple in the world.

On the internet I found a list with 14 ECK Centres in Lagos (altogether there are 120 Centres in Nigeria) and I selected the one in Isolo, a residential middle-class neighbourhood (Figure 6.2). At the ECK Centre in Isolo a signboard welcomed me with the following words, 'When you're ready for something more durable than philosophy, meta-physics, or orthodox religion, then you're ready for the knowledge that grants love, wisdom, and spiritual freedom. ... You are welcome to join this most grand journey to your Creator.' In the ECK Centre I received a warm welcome by an elderly Yoruba man named Mr Akindele, who introduced himself as the Centre's manager and showed me around.

The roof of the two-storey ECK Centre in Isolo resembled a pyramid composed of nine steps (*zikurat*) symbolizing the steps on the 'spiritual ladder' an Eckist takes. At the top of these steps s/he finds spiritual freedom, self-mastery, wisdom, and love. The ground floor of the ECK Centre was composed of a white-painted worship hall decorated with plants and blue ribbons. On the stage in front of the hall stood a table made from gold-painted wood on which the word HU was carved. Above the stage hung a painting of Paul Twitchell, a picture of Harold Klemp, and a no-smoking sign. The walls displayed portraits of the historical ECK Masters, who serve God by helping seekers find the *Mahanta*, the Living ECK Master, including Rebazar Tarzs (the Tibetan spiritual teacher of Paul Twitchell who is believed to be over 500 years old), Jesus's look-a-like Gopal Das, and the female Kata Daki who supports people during hardship. Mr Akindele explained: 'God is an abstract concept, which can't be grasped. It becomes personified in the ECK Masters.' Underlining God's abstract nature, Eckists – like Grail members – refer to God as 'it'. Next to the worship hall was a library with copies of the many ECK works. On the first floor the children's hall was located, where children learn about Eckankar through play.

Mr Akindele showed me a poster of the spiritual planes in Eckankar's conception of the universe. He explained that Eckists communicate directly with God. They do so through chanting HU and setting out on soul travel. Eckankar teaches that through these spiritual exercises the inner self or Soul can travel independently of the body on the higher spiritual planes. On these God planes – which can be recognized by their particular sounds and colours[18] – Eckists may meet and learn from the Living ECK Master, Harold Klemp, and the other ECK Masters. God or the *Sugmad* – 'the unpolluted name of God' – is the source of all the planes. From out of the *Sugmad* flows the ECK. It is the ECK or Divine Spirit that sustains life in all spiritual planes. Eckists' spiritual journey to the higher planes occurs during sleep and therefore Eckankar teaches its members to record their dreams in a dream diary. This dream diary

---

[18] For instance, the sound of the Physical Plane (the basic material level) is heard as thunder and the light is seen as green; the sound of the Causal Plane (where the memories of past lives are stored) is heard as the tinkling of bells and the light is seen as orange; and the sound of the Soul Plane (where self-realization is achieved) is the single note of a flute and the light is seen as yellow.

serves as a teaching tool in that dreams contain messages that enable Eckists to reach a higher spiritual consciousness.

After the tour, Mr Akindele narrated his life story,

I grew up in a Baptist church where I was a chorister, but after finishing secondary school I got tired of going to church. I looked for a place where I could worship the way I wanted and came across AMORC. AMORC didn't satisfy me and I left after three years. When I married my wife, a Pentecostal, she was unhappy that I wasn't going to church. So I attended a Pentecostal church for a while, but the pastor was unwilling to answer the questions I was struggling with. I read a book about Eckankar and that was an eye opener to me. The book answered all my questions, 'Who am I?' and 'Where do I go to after my life has ended?' Most Nigerians don't read and Eckankar is not a movement for you when you don't read. By reading more books about Eckankar, I fell in love with the teachings and discovered that it was not an orthodox religion but rather a spiritual one. Eckankar formed my doorway to a deeper level of existence.

Before seeing me off, Mr Akindele invited me to the ECK worship service the following Sunday. When I asked him whether there were certain rules, such as a dress code, that I needed to observe, he laughed, 'Churches prescribe a dress code but we don't believe in such trivialities; you are free here. But do come on time: we start at 9am and don't observe Nigerian time.'

The following Sunday at 9 am sharply, the choir, composed of seven young women, opened the service by singing 'Thank you *Mahanta*, thank you for everything'. Then the master of ceremony took the floor, instructing the congregation to switch off their phones and tablets so that they could better concentrate on the service. He introduced Edith, the local director of the ECK Centre in Isolo and the ECK cleric of that week. Edith, who works as the manager of a wellness business, entered the stage dressed in a fashionable dress with tiger print. She greeted the congregation with 'Good morning children of God', after which she explained the order of service. The first agenda item was reading a passage from Eckankar's scripture, the *Shariyat-Ki-Sugmad* ('Way of the Eternal'): a two-volume work written by Paul Twitchell based on his spiritual and visionary experiences in India and Tibet, which is believed to be the greatest of all sacred books. She then invited the congregants to join her in chanting 'the love song to God, HU' in a long, drawn-out breath while concentrating on their 'third eye',[19] followed by a few minutes of quiet contemplation. While the congregants sat with their eyes closed, I looked around me. I estimated that around 80 people

---

[19] In spiritual traditions from the East, the third eye – the point between the eyebrows – refers to the *chakra* that opens the gate to one's inner realm of higher consciousness.

(excluding the children who worshipped in the children's hall on the first floor), cutting across gender, age, and ethnicity attended the ECK service. Unlike in the Grail Movement, men and women sat next to each other. Whereas the services of the institutionalized religions in Lagos are attended by predominantly Yoruba – the largest ethnic group in the south-west – the ECK service was attended by quite some Igbo, including Edith and her husband. According to my research assistant, Igbos' entrepreneurial nature may explain why they were well represented in Eckankar, 'They are open to try new things in the hope that it could help their businesses to succeed.'

After chanting HU, Edith shared a personal experience relating to the topic of that week's service: overcoming fear. She told the congregation how she once travelled with her husband in a *danfo* (minibus) to an Igbo village in eastern Nigeria,

As soon as we entered the *danfo*, an old man started praying for protection. All the passengers prayed with him, except for my husband and me. Along the way, people started shouting. The driver of the *danfo* in front of us was flashing and our fellow passengers feared that this was a sign to warn our driver for armed robbers along the highway. The old man who had led the prayer earlier that morning was trembling. My husband and I were the only passengers who remained calm. When we reached our destination safely, the old man asked us why we had remained so calm although we had not participated in his prayer for protection. This example shows that although Nigerians spend much time praying, they do not always have faith in what they pray for. Eckankar teaches us the protective power of HU. Through chanting HU, we will be guided by love rather than fear.

After Edith's talk,[20] the choir sang two songs in English in which they thanked God for setting them free. They closed with Eckankar's anthem, 'I sing HU; I was lost, but now I'm found; now I can see.' During the singing, a chorister collected donations.

Edith then introduced three panelists, whom she invited to take a seat on the stage. During the panel discussion,[21] the panelists used the rhetoric of 'emerging from darkness' and 'personal transformation' to project an image of spiritual progress. A metaphor used by all the panelists was that of a 'path' on which the *chela* ('student' – Eckists' self-designation) sets out to achieve a higher level of 'self-realization' (the

---

[20] Edith referred to her speech as a 'talk' rather than as a 'sermon', the term used in mainstream religion.

[21] Whereas in Pentecostal churches the sharing of personal experiences is referred to as 'testimony', in Eckankar the term 'panel discussion' is used, which has an academic connotation. Highlighting Eckankar's intellectualism, Eckists refer to the monthly spiritual lessons that they receive by post from the US headquarters as 'discourses'.

realization of oneself as Soul) and 'God-realization' (the awareness of God in one's life). The first panelist – a young Igbo man dressed in a suit – testified that chanting HU had rescued him from a fire in his flat. For him, HU represents the origin of all religions, 'You find the word HU in all religions: HU is the root of "Hallelujah" and "*Allahu Akbar*".' When the 'timekeeper' held a sign that his five minutes of allotted speaking time had ended, a Yoruba university student dressed in a fashionable skirt and blouse took the floor. She narrated that she was born in Eckankar,

As a child, I had many Muslim and Christian friends at school. One day I followed my Muslim friend to her Qur'anic school but when I observed the teacher beating a student, I decided that Islam was not my piece of cake. I also followed my Christian cousin to church, but I found the service so boring that I fell asleep. After ECK worship services, I always feel energized. These experiences made me realize that Eckankar is the right path for me. I would like to thank my parents, who are long-established Eckists, for allowing me to experiment with different religions before making my own choice.

The final panelist was a middle-aged Igbo man dressed in native attire who confided to the congregation that he had wanted to leave Eckankar because he had grown tired of chanting HU. After taking the decision to withdraw, his car was confiscated by the police and he had to pay a huge sum to get it back. He called on the *Mahanta* for help. Help came in the form of a windfall, which made him decide to return to Eckankar. After the panel discussion, HU was chanted once more. Edith concluded the service at 10am by saying 'May the blessings be'. She encouraged new-comers to speak to the ECK clergy and those who had studied the ECK works and were convinced that they wanted to become Eckists, to fill in a membership form and pay their annual membership fees of 50 USD, or 75 USD for family membership.[22]

In addition to the weekly ECK Light and Sound Services, weekly reading classes and discussion groups or *satsang* take place in the ECK Centres. Every last Sunday of the month, Eckists from different Centres worship jointly in Lagos. Since Eckankar is still a relatively new movement, joint worship is considered important to build a social platform for Eckists. Other joint rituals are the life-cycle ceremonies: the ECK consecration ceremony for infants, the rite of passage into adulthood (around the age of 13), the ECK wedding, and the ECK memorial service. For young Eckists outdoor activities are organized. With the youths from the

---

[22] Since membership fees are transferred to the headquarters in the USA, they are paid in dollars rather than Naira. In return, the headquarters send monthly spiritual lessons or 'discourses' to the Nigerian members.

ECK Centre in Isolo, I attended the annual Youth Programme in a nature reserve on the outskirts of Lagos, where – surrounded by monkeys – we did sports, played games, took part in talent scouting to display our artistic skills, and participated in a quiz to test our knowledge of the Eck Masters. Every year an ECK Seminar with international guest speakers is organized in the ECK Temple at the headquarters in Port Harcourt. Many of my interlocutors also attend the annual Worldwide Seminar in the United States. That they have the financial means to fly to the United States shows their affluence.

At the end of the worship service that I attended in the ECK Centre in Isolo, I was hugged by several female Eckists who wished me strength on my spiritual path 'back to God'. One of them warned me, 'Don't give up; Eckankar is a spiritual adventure of a lifetime', before she stepped in her SUV with a customized number plate with the word HU and drove off.

Shifting Allegiances

Despite their differences in outlook and message, the Grail Movement and Eckankar have in common that they inspire religious practitioners to view religion differently. Although they share features with institutional-ized religion – in the sense that they have scriptures and a liturgy (their worship services are meticulously orchestrated like in a church or mosque) – and 'Yoruba religion' – in the sense that they believe that the physical world is affected by metaphysical forces – they see them-selves as beyond the realm of institutionalized religion. While the Grail Movement does not define itself in terms of a religion at all but rather a 'life science', Eckankar describes itself as a 'spiritual religion' that is freed from dogmatic strictures. In their mission to move 'beyond religion', the Grail Movement and Eckankar represent a novel trend of shifting alle-giances from normative religiosity to de-confessionalized spirituality on Lagos's religious marketplace.[23] In this section I go more deeply into this trend and discuss why and how it took root in Lagos.

The Grail sacral leaders and ECK clergy whom I interviewed por-trayed mainstream religion as being based on blind acceptance of dogmas dictated by authoritarian religious leaders, through which reli-gious practitioners are prevented from experiencing spirituality.

---

[23] The new trend of tailoring one's religious beliefs and practices to meet one's spiritual needs is in line with the New Age movement, which played a major role in the dissemination of new forms of spirituality in Europe and North America in the 1980s and 1990s (Hanegraaff 1996). However, New Age is, to a large extent, an etic and a Western category. The question whether what has been written about New Age in the Global North also applies to the Global South deserves further research.

Although the Grail Movement has sacral leaders, this leadership is not a hierarchical position attached to one person. Abd-Ru-Shin never wanted to be seen in person as central to the Grail teaching; the focal point of the Grail Movement was his Message and he told his followers to 'heed the Word and not the bringer'. In a similar vein, Eckankar turns away from charismatic leadership: each week another ECK cleric officiates. Women seem to have benefited most from the lack of institutionalized hierarchy in the Grail Movement and Eckankar: the loose organizational structure creates possibilities for women to take up (temporary) leadership roles. However, when I asked Dr Ademola about the gendered nature of her regional leadership, she responded, 'What matters is one's spiritual progress, not whether one is a woman or a man. Eckists do not believe in classifications according to gender. For us, even the Creator is neither male nor female.' Instead of in a religious leader or in the scriptures, the Grail Movement and Eckankar position authority in subjective spiritual experience.

In their shifting allegiance from normative religiosity to unconventional spirituality, the Grail Movement and Eckankar question many of the ingrained conceptions of religion, including the notion of a transcendent, omnipotent God and eschatological notions of the hereafter. While in mainstream religion the relationship between the worshipper and God is centred on God, the focus in the Grail Movement and Eckankar has shifted towards the individual seeker. God is no longer seen as a distant God but as a force living within oneself. For example, for Grail members God is not an abstract entity but stands for love, which one can experience not only during rituals but anytime when 'going inwardly'. Many Eckists told me that through chanting HU and soul travelling they had experienced the divine within themselves. Just as they do not believe in a God residing in heaven, Grail members and Eckists do not believe in a devil residing in hell. The concept of the devil does not only conflict with their belief in the goodness of the universe but also with their idea of self-responsibility: rather than an external agent, such as Satan, one is responsible for one's own actions. This does not mean that Grail members and Eckists do not believe in evil: they do, but for them suffering exists for the purpose of spiritual progress and anything evil can therefore be transformed into something good from which one could learn.

Underscoring the idea of individual responsibility, Bob elucidated the Grail Movement's eschatological notions of the hereafter as follows, 'Heaven and hell do not exist as specific sites created by the Creator. Instead, heaven and hell are created by ourselves. If one engages in good deeds, one's soul rises to a higher level. If one does evil, one creates one's own hell.' Contrary to mainline Christianity, in which human beings are regarded as sinful and in need of redemption, Grail members believe they have the capacity to perfect themselves spiritually. This idea of spiritual perfection is premised on the principle of reincarnation. According to the ECK cleric Edith: 'Life does not end when you die. You only leave your body behind. The body is just flesh. We believe that Soul has no beginning and end, which is the principle of reincarnation.' Reincarnation teaches that one is born again and again until one has learned the spiritual lessons of life: one reaps in life what one has sown in an earlier life. Hence, Judeo-Christian conceptions such as predestination and salvation do not have much significance in the Grail Movement and Eckankar. Rather than resigning oneself to one's fate, the Grail Movement and Eckankar teach their adherents to take an active role in life. An Eckist explained to me, 'Eckankar is not a passive path to God. Spiritual maturity comes when we realize we are the creator of our own life.' Remarkably, although their beliefs and practices are radically different from those in institutionalized religion, the Grail Movement and Eckankar have gained a strong foothold on Lagos's religious marketplace since the 1970s. This raises the question how exogenous movements have become indigenized in Lagos; a question that I will try to answer here.

In a country that is, according to the 2017 Gallup International poll, the world's second most religious, turning away from religion is seen as socially unacceptable. Still, an increasing number of the newly emerging middle class of Lagosians – university-educated professionals employed in the private business sector or having well-paid jobs in the public sector – experience rising sentiments of uneasiness with the excesses of Pentecostal Christianity and reformist Islam – the two largest religious movements of contemporary times – in the sense of their perceived noisiness, flashiness, rigidity, and fanaticism. An example is Bob, for whom reformist religion has lost its significance, 'I don't believe in religion; religion has become reduced to power and politics. Where religion falls short, the Grail Movement provides spiritual guidance.' Because it is not a religion, Bob did not consider it contradictory to simultaneously worship in the Grail Movement and occasionally in the Anglican Church, where his roots lie. Unlike Bob, Mr Akindele did not deny that Eckankar is a religion, but he defined it in terms of a 'spiritual religion' that is 'higher and richer' than what he called 'orthodox religion'. Disillusioned with what they termed 'old-fashioned' forms of mainstream religion and 'radical' types of reformist religion, professionals such as Bob and Mr Akindele started experimenting with new forms of spirituality.

Although somewhat difficult to pin down, I use spirituality here as a concept to denote new forms of religiosity that exist outside conventional religious structures (van der Veer 2008: 790). A Muslim friend who considered himself both religious and spiritual explained the difference between the two as follows, 'If I sit at Lagos Lagoon and meditate, I may have a spiritual experience. Religion tells me how to meditate, the rules and regulations of meditation. Whereas spirituality is experiential, religion has to do with doctrines.' Because they fall outside conventional religious models, religio-spiritual movements such as the Grail Movement and Eckankar are in New Religious Studies (NRS) – an interdisciplinary field that was established in the 1970s – sometimes called 'secular religions' (Hanegraaff 1996). Since this term reinforces the problematic religion–secularism binary (see Chapter 3), I think Riesebrodt's (2010: 178) notion of 'do-it-yourself religions' is more accurate. Indeed, there is a strong orientation towards goal-attainment and problem-solving in the Grail Movement and Eckankar. Through teaching their members spiritual exercises, they allow personal development and spiritual self-fulfillment. Although these exercises depart from the core doctrines and practices of Christianity and Islam, they are consonant with the pragmatic orientation of 'Yoruba religion'.

Their pragmatism may explain the popularity of the Grail Movement and Eckankar in Lagos. To overcome the obstacles of everyday living in the megacity and advance spiritually, *The Grail Message* promises its readership a 'shining light' that will offer a way out of 'the chaos of the present-day confusion', and eventually lead to the Holy Grail, 'the sacred vessel of the pure love of the Almighty'. In a similar vein, Eckankar offers its members tools to free themselves from physical and psychological impediments so that they can liberate themselves spiritually. The Grail Movement and Eckankar's do-it-yourself spirituality aligns with the do-it-yourself attitude that prevails in Lagos. In a cityscape where jobs in the formal sector are scarce, and where many migrants cannot fall back on extensive kinship networks, one needs to be ingenious to make a living. During my field research, I met numerous Lagosians who earned a living in inventive ways. For instance, the young entrepreneur in the photograph in Figure 6.3, visualizing Lagosians' creativity in coping with frequent blackouts, set up a mobile battery charging service from his car boot. The career paths of urbanites like this do-it-yourself man[24]

---

[24] Note that the Lagosian 'do-it-yourself man' is more in line with what Lévi-Strauss (1966) calls a *bricoleur* in French than the English working-class 'handyman'. The *bricoleur* is involved in 'make do and mend', based on the recycling of existing materials to make new forms (Johnson 2012: 367).

Figure 6.3 Mobile battery charger.
Photographer: Akintunde Akinleye

often merge with their spiritual journeys, which show a similar level of entrepreneurialism in the sense of trying out different religious traditions and mixing and matching elements from divergent religious and spiritual traditions. For instance, Mr Akindele's spiritual journey started in the Baptist church and moved via AMORC and Pentecostalism to Eckankar. Religious shoppers, or 'seekers' to use Eckankar's terminology, like Mr Akindele are open to religio-spiritual movements that allow for the assemblage of multiple traditions in meeting their needs. Here it is important to note that unlike Chrislamists and the adherents of *Ijo Orunmila*, the religious shopping of Grail members and Eckists – many of whom are from an upper middle-class background – is not so much induced by the need to survive in Lagos's cityscape, but rather by their aspiration to develop themselves spiritually and distinguish themselves from mainstream believers who submit to religious authorities and their doctrines. In short, in the context of religio-spiritual movements religious shopping can be regarded as a sign of a progressive attitude and a sophisticated lifestyle.[25]

---

[25] Historians have noted that in early modern times both the Protestant and Catholic Reformations produced a rhetoric of religiosity that similarly distinguished the emerging elites from non-elites. Popular religion was denigrated as 'magic',

Bob told me that unlike the Anglican Church in which he grew up, the Grail Movement encourages him to map out his personal spiritual journey by promoting critical consideration and self-reflection. Such an intellectualist-oriented model is particularly appealing to the expanding middle classes among the urban sections of Africa's population. The majority of the Grail members and Eckists are indeed highly educated urbanites. During worship services in Grail Circles and Eck Centres, I met not only university lecturers, lawyers, engineers, IT consultants, and businesspeople but also artists and others involved in the creative industries. A painter who acted as an ECK cleric told me that Eckankar stimulates him to tap his creativity in developing his spirituality. According to a fashion designer who designs costumes for the Nollywood film industry, people like him who 'dare to be different' are welcomed in Eckankar, while he felt excluded in his church. Besides the intellect to read the voluminous *The Grail Message* or the many ECK works, and the creativity and imagination to engage in spiritual exercises and keep dream diaries, one also needs the financial means to buy books.[26] Dr Ademola told me, 'Most Nigerians adhere to a one-book religion: they buy either the Qur'an or Bible. I have over 100 ECK works at home. They are expensive, but if you want to study them, you will find a way to buy them.' With annual membership fees of 50 USD, Eckankar is too expensive for the average Lagosian. Like Eckists, many of the Grail members are well-off. When I asked Chief Lawson's son whether the Grail Circles receive funding from Austria, he responded indignantly that rather than receiving money, he and his fellow Nigerian Grail members support the Grail Movement in Austria financially. To sum up, only the middle class can afford – literally as well as metaphorically – membership of the Grail Movement and Eckankar.

Although the popularity of the Grail Movement and Eckankar is on the rise in Lagos, their perceived alterity means that they still have a relatively small membership compared with the Pentecostal megachurches and Muslim mass organizations such as NASFAT. While these organizations measure their success in numbers of worshippers, Dr Ademola prided herself on having a small membership, 'Being an Eckist requires perseverance and self-discipline; it is not granted to everyone.' This exclusivity is yet another factor explaining the popularity of religio-spiritual

'superstition', and 'impure', whereas middle- and upper-class religiosity was valorized as 'spiritual', 'sober', and 'proper' (McGuire 2008b: 219).

[26] The ECK works cost between 3,000 and 4,000 Naira (on average around 8 GBP) per volume, while a paperback edition of the *Shariyat-Ki-Sugmad* costs 25,000 Naira (around 55 GBP). *The Grail Message* is subsidized by the Grail Foundation in Stuttgart and costs 750 Naira.

movements among the rising middle class eager to distinguish themselves through their lifestyle. But because also exclusive movements need members, the Grail Movement organizes public lectures and has its own radio programme, while Eckankar organizes seminars and advertises these events in newspapers. Yet, they are not missionary movements. According to a Grail sacral leader, 'We want to spread the joy of spiritual progress to others but we don't want to force them to join us. Conviction is something personal. You must find out for yourself whether *The Grail Message* is true.' Like seekers are free to join, they are also free to resign without the risk of being regarded as apostates. For instance, Eckists are encouraged to review their spiritual path on an annual basis. If they are happy with the path they have chosen, they renew their membership fees. If not, they simply stop paying.

Although the Grail Movement keeps a record of sealed cross-bearers and Eckankar gives out membership cards, it turned out difficult to obtain membership figures. After much probing, a Grail sacral leader estimated that the Grail Movement has about 4,000 members in Nigeria, and an ECK cleric estimated Eckankar's Nigerian membership at 10,000. The difficulty in obtaining membership figures can be explained by the fact that religio-spiritual movements do not require exclusivist membership or conversion; a disjunction that Davie (1994) in her study of religion in post-war Britain referred to as 'believing without belonging'. Although the Grail Movement and Eckankar organize weekly worship services and other group activities, their orientation focuses less on community building and tends to be more individualistic, encouraging home study, private meditation, and self-development. Nor do the Grail Movement and Eckankar require their members to convert. Since being involved in the Grail Movement is for seekers such as Bob a source of supplementary spirituality, it is common to find them experimenting with different movements and methods. As a result, religio-spiritual movements such as the Grail Movement and Eckankar have high rates of membership turnover. This has moved theorizing on new modes of spirituality away from traditional interpretations of conversion toward a process of shifting allegiances (Bromley 2009: 731–4).

From the aforementioned, it can be concluded that many of the conventional assumptions about religion, according to which it ought to be dogmatic, structured around a commonly shared source of authority, congregational, based on conversion, exclusive and bounded, are missing in the Grail Movement and Eckankar. Instead, they allow for a broader conception of spirituality in which institution, doctrine, and creed have given way to personal conviction, experience, and an awareness of innermost realities, thereby catering for the needs of the emerging middle class in Lagos. Taking this course, religio-spiritual movements such as the Grail Movement and Eckankar open an avenue for a consumer-based approach to religion, which might eventually swamp Lagos's religious marketplace.

The Dialectic between Boundary Crossing and Boundary Making

While all the religious movements described in this monograph show modalities of assemblage in that they mix elements from Islam, Christianity, and/or 'Yoruba religion', the Grail Movement and Eckankar display a multiplication of assemblages in that they mix elements from Islam, Christianity, ATR, the 'Eastern' religions, as well as non-religious sources. In line with Vertovec's (2007) notion of 'super-diversity' that characterizes the pluralization of immigrants in European cities, the Grail Movement and Eckankar display a 'super-plurality'. This super-plurality exists both in the quantity of religious and spiritual traditions available on Lagos's religious marketplace and in the boundary crossing between religious traditions and non-religious sources. Yet, stressing the fluidity and flexibility of religious boundaries should, as I already mentioned, not lead us to declare that religious boundaries are irrelevant. Rather, the crossing of boundaries coincides with a strong movement towards boundary making. This section illustrates that boundary crossing and boundary making are two aspects of the same movement taking place in present-day Lagos.

Although the Grail Movement is premised on Christianity, its conceptualization of Jesus seems more in line with Islam. While Grail members consider Jesus the son of God, like Muslims they believe that he has not been crucified but raised into heaven by God. Compared with the Grail Movement, Eckankar is more of an esoteric movement but, according to its founder Paul Twitchell, it bears resemblance with Islam. In his introduction to the *Shariyat-ki-Sugmad*, Twitchell writes that the thirteenth-century Persian Sufi mystic Jalal ad-Din Muhammad Rumi first hinted at Eckankar. Although Eckists' esoteric practices such as soul travelling are foreign to Nigeria, the ECK clergy stressed that there are similarities with ATR. For example, several ECK clerics saw in traditional Yoruba names such as Babatunde, meaning 'Father returns', and Yetunde, meaning 'Mother returns', the proof that practitioners of 'Yoruba religion' believe in reincarnation – one of the core principles in Eckankar. Also, the belief in the Eck Masters who reside on different spiritual planes resembles the Yoruba belief in spirits. An Eckist of long standing explained to me that Eckankar's teachings about nature as bearer of spiritual virtue are consonant with beliefs about nature in 'Yoruba religion': the earth, water, and rocks are regarded as the abodes of the *orisas*.

In addition to Islam, Christianity, and 'Yoruba religion', the Grail Movement and Eckankar have appropriated elements from the 'Eastern' religions, including Hinduism and Buddhism. Here it should be noted that Hinduism is no longer an exogenous movement that was brought by the Gujarati traders who came to dominate the trade in electronics in Lagos; it has become an indigenous movement under the influence of the establishment of the International Society for Krishna Consciousness (ISKCON), better known as 'Hare Krishna', in Lagos in 1981.[27] But compared with the Grail Movement and Eckankar, ISKCON is still very small in Lagos. An example of an Eastern belief appropriated by both the Grail Movement and Eckankar is *karma*: the spiritual principle of cause and effect whereby good deeds contribute to good karma and future happiness, while bad deeds contribute to bad karma and future suffering. Because Grail members and Eckists believe in reincarnation, bad deeds can be turned into good deeds in future lives. Reincarnation is not only close to Yoruba beliefs; it is also influenced by Hinduism and Buddhism.

Furthermore, the methods for spiritual evolution in which Grail members and Eckists engage are inspired by methods prevailing in Hinduism and Buddhism, including chanting, meditating, dreaming, and out-of-body experiences. These methods often go together with fasting. While Grail members fast by abstaining from eating and drinking, Eckists practise 'mental fasting' by concentrating on the *Mahanta* all day long on Friday and visualizing their negative thoughts as snowballs melting in radiant light. Like ISKCON devotees, several Grail members and Eckists keep a vegetarian diet. According to a Grail member, the body is the Creator's temple, which explains why one must look after it well. The no-smoking sign that one finds in every ECK Centre is meant to discourage Eckists from indulging in 'bodily passions' and endure self-discipline. Nevertheless, Eckankar does not forbid its members to smoke. According to Edith, 'We encourage smokers to quit when they join us, but we don't forbid smoking; this is Eckists' own responsibility.'

The focus on the union of the spirit and body in the Grail Movement and Eckankar aligns with the holistic approach of several 'Eastern' religions. Grail members and Eckists believe that what happens to the

---

[27] Given the prominence of Indian traders in Lagos, everything coming from the East is defined as 'Indian'. As such, 'Eastern' religions like ISKCON are often assimilated under the label of 'Indian religion' (Wuaku 2013).

external world happens to the self. This belief corresponds with the notion of *dharma* in Hinduism and Buddhism, which can be translated as 'cosmic laws'. Indeed, the Grail Movement and Eckankar conceive of the universe as a cycle in which 'everything is connected with everything'. Underlining the idea of interconnectedness, the circle is an important symbol as reflected in the Grail isosceles cross and the ECK logo: a blue circle formed of the letters E and K. The belief that what happens to the external world happens to the self explains why Grail members and Eckists are actively involved in nature conservation. Nature, as symbolized by the flowers and plants in the Grail Circles and Eck Centres, is a life-giving force in which the divine is believed to be immanent.

Not only are the boundaries between 'Western' and 'Eastern' religious traditions stretched in the Grail Movement and Eckankar but also between religious traditions and non-religious sources, including science. Unlike in mainstream religion, religion and science are seen not as opposing but rather as compatible meaning systems. The Grail Movement derives several of its teachings from physics. Its first teaching is the Law of the Attraction of Homogeneous Species, which is known in physics as resonance. Grail members experience this law when 'like-minded people affiliate'. Similar to the Law of Gravitation, *The Grail Message* teaches that 'if one's heart is burdened with worries one sinks, while a relieved soul rises'. In line with biomedical science, *The Grail Message* describes seekers' spiritual path in terms of a 'circular movement', similar to the 'blood circulation' or the 'current circuit', which allows 'all that originated from you to return to you', that is, the Law of Reciprocal Action. Underlining that spirituality is a mix of religious and scientific worldviews, Eckankar was initially known as 'The Ancient Science of Soul Travel'. Given the close link between religion and science in Eckankar, it is not coincidental that a former physics teacher introduced Eckankar in Lagos. By assembling religion and science, the Grail Movement and Eckankar serve as 'life sciences' that help the modern religious practitioner to find pragmatic solutions to the problems of our time.

The Grail Movement and Eckankar's assemblage of elements from diverse religious and spiritual traditions, and religious elements with science, suggests that Lagos has turned into a religious marketplace with almost unlimited consumer choice. Drawing on Beyer's (1997) model of the religious market we could say that,

most religious consumers, with a relatively modest demand for purely religious product, will consume eclectically, with perhaps a fair degree of 'brand' loyalty, but more often than not without membership and the sort of commitment that produced regular participation and communal incorporation in an organized body (286).

In a similar vein, Grail members and Eckists consume religious beliefs and spiritual practices eclectically. Unconstrained by formal membership of institutionalized religion, they are free to pick and choose different religious and spiritual traditions available on Lagos's religious market-place and in the process (re)assemble, combine, and adapt existing religious beliefs and spiritual practices.

As Hanegraaff (1996) points out, spirituality has become increasingly subservient to the laws of the marketplace. Indeed, the Grail Movement and Eckankar responded to their members' spiritual needs by marketing, often at exorbitant prices, religio-spiritual merchandise ranging from books, calendars, Grail crosses, necklaces with the word HU, to T-Shirts and other spiritual paraphernalia. During the ECK worship services that I attended, the posters with the picture of Harold Klemp, grinning as in a toothpaste advertisement, sold like hot cakes despite its considerable cost of 2,000 Naira. Ironically, spiritual consumerism is sold in the Grail Movement and Eckankar alongside a second trend that rejects a material-istic lifestyle and perceives the spiritual as an alternative and higher way of being. It is not uncommon for an Eckist to drive her/his posh car to the ECK Centre where s/he listens for an hour to a talk that motivates Eckists to detach themselves from material belongings and lead a spiritual life. A similar tension between spirituality and materiality I noticed in the Grail Circle when, after listening to a reading from *The Grail Message* that propagated soberness, Bob and his friends went to a restaurant where they ordered expensive bottles of champagne and spirits. For them, spirituality and materiality are not necessarily contradictory; both are seen as markers of their middle-class lifestyle. It seems that by simultaneously participating in religio-spiritual movements and indulging in a luxurious life, the newly emerging middle class in Lagos distinguishes itself from mainstream believers. Thus, although the Grail Movement and Eckankar present themselves as non-denominational and open to everyone regardless of creed, they are actually fed by class dispositions.

Despite their exclusive aura, in their crossing of the boundaries between religion and non-religion, the Grail Movement and Eckankar market plurality. Still, there is growing evidence of religious hardening and intolerance, also in a highly pluriform setting such as Lagos. The challen-ging and sometimes outward rejection of established core theological tenets by the Grail Movement and Eckankar leads to their condemnation as 'cults' or 'false religions' and their demonization as '419' by many mainstream believers.[28] '419' is what Nigerians call fraud, apparently after

---

[28] In this, religio-spiritual movements resemble ATRs. As I have discussed in Chapter 5, 'Yoruba religion' is perceived as devil worship and the epitome of evil by Pentecostals

a section in the Nigerian criminal code that describes these crimes. But 419 does not refer only to fraud in Nigerian slang; it has become a descriptor for all things morally corrupt, which attests to the pervasiveness of corruption and its centrality as a metaphor for modern life in Nigeria (Smith 2007). Because religio-spiritual movements such as the Grail Movement and Eckankar are neither institutionally nor doctrinally framed and engage in practices that are deemed strange, they are considered suspect by many mainstream believers. During my field research I heard several stories of families that had fallen apart after children decided to join the Grail Movement or Eckankar. Thus, to pursue the market analogy further, religious pluralism has its price.

Dr Ademola recalled how in the beginning of the history of Eckankar in Lagos, the monthly spiritual study lessons or 'discourses' that arrived by post from the United States were torn up by the local postal workers who feared that the envelopes contained 'occult' messages. Although Eckankar has become more widely accepted over the years, prejudices have not disappeared. For example, an Eckist told me that his wife, who is a member of the RCCG, was prevented by RCCG's security from parking their car in front of the church. The security had spotted an Eckankar sticker on the car window and they took the woman for a cult member. An Eckist of long standing told me that through engaging in spiritual exercises he had learnt how to heal himself and others but he does not advertise his skills because otherwise he will be accused of 'practising *juju*' and perceived as a 'sorcerer'.

Whereas their 'foreignness' explains the popularity of the Grail Movement and Eckankar among the rising middle class, who embrace it as a source of pride that makes them stand out, their alterity also evokes antagonism, fear, and suspicion (see also Louveau 2012; Lambertz 2018). For example, when we were offered red juice made from hibiscus flowers by a Grail member to celebrate her birthday, my research assistant refused to drink it because he thought it contained human blood. Whereas in the Grail Movement flowers connote beauty, purity, and divinity, for some Pentecostals they represent occult power. A Grail member told me that she had wanted to give her cousin, who is a dedicated Pentecostal, lilies for her birthday. The cousin declined the gift since she was told by her pastor that flowers are 'satanic'. The Grail Movement's silent worship exacerbates the image of alterity: it is interpreted as the proof that Grail members are hiding something.

and reformist Muslims. This diabolization nurtures a widespread animosity towards practitioners of 'Yoruba religion'.

What we see here is a double-sided process in which, on the one hand, religious boundaries are becoming more fluid in Lagos, whereas, on the other hand, they are hardening, especially under the influence of the rise of more strenuous forms of devotion within the established religions: Pentecostalism on the Christian side and more rigorous versions of Islamic reformism on the Muslim side, which have conquered urban space over the past decades. As underlined by the reformist ideology of 'spiritual warfare', Pentecostals and reformist-oriented Muslims wield a 'moral sword' with which they split society into 'good' and 'bad' ones (Englund 2011). Whereas in this ideology reformist Christians and Muslims are the 'good ones',[29] the 'bad ones' are represented by the deviant, that is, 'traditionalists' such as the adherents of *Ijo Orunmila* and alleged 'cultists' such as the Grail members and Eckists. This affirms Berger's (2014: 9) conclusion that pluralism and fundamentalism are seemingly opposite, but actually profoundly similar, attempts to cope with diversity in multifaith settings.

Conclusion

The case studies in this chapter illustrate that the decline in established, institutionalized religion among the newly emerging, highly educated, middle class in Lagos is accompanied by a rise in de-confessionalized spirituality. These unconventional forms of spirituality emerged at a time when an increasing number of religious practitioners felt that modern developments engendered life questions that the religious traditions in which they were born and raised could no longer answer. Moreover, they regarded the newer forms of religion, as represented by Pentecostalism and reformist Islam, as 'too loud' and 'too radical'. Their spiritual seeking led them to religio-spiritual movements such as the Grail Movement and Eckankar, which offer an alternative to institutionalized religion. Their exogeneity and exclusivity explains their appeal among the middle class in Lagos, whereas their pragmatic approach resonates with that of ATR. By navigating between 'old' traditions and 'modern' developments, the Grail Movement and Eckankar could secure a foothold in Lagos since the 1970s.

In their search for spiritual self-development, Grail members and Eckists have moved away from institutionalized religion to a 'do-it-yourself' spirituality outside of formal structures, which is based on individual experience and makes no claim to theological coherence. In line with the

---

[29] Although reformist Christians and Muslims have much in common, they also demonize each other (see Chapter 2).

Grail members and Eckists' consumerist approach to religion, it could be argued that they have turned Lagos's religious marketplace into a fast food restaurant with '*à la carte* spirituality' (Bibby 1987: 80–83), in which consumers taste from different religious 'dishes' in an attempt to satisfy their spiritual hunger. In this fast food restaurant God is still on the menu, but Grail members and Eckists no longer consider Him a distant Supreme Being. Instead, they are seeking what theologian Henry Maier calls an 'easier, faster, no-fuss, microwavable God' (in Nolen 1999: A1, A6).[30] This shift from normative religion towards a custom-made approach to spirituality is an important dimension of religion as assemblage in contemporary Lagos.

While the Grail Movement and Eckankar cross religious boundaries in that they mix 'Western' with 'Eastern' and ATR, and religious elements with science, in an eclectic assemblage, more rigorous types of Pentecostalism and Islamic reform that have emerged in Lagos over recent decades strengthen religious boundaries and demonize those who cannot be religiously pigeonholed as 'occultists' and '419'. Thus, whereas for the newly emerging middle class shifting allegiances from institutionalized religion to new religio-spiritual movements is a means to differentiate themselves, for others boundary making is a way to manage religious pluralism and maintain the religious status quo in Lagos.

The Grail Movement and Eckankar's crossing of religious boundaries and of the boundaries between religion and non-religious sources raises the larger question as to what 'religion' is. While the focus in this chapter was on rethinking established ways of studying religion in order to offer a fresh perspective on un-institutionalized forms of religion in which religiosity is less a matter of doctrine and more of practice and experience, the final chapter asks what place 'religion' has in the future anthropology of religion.

---

[30] Analogous with fast food restaurants, Robbins (2001: 176) refers to new religious movements as 'fast religions'.

7 Conclusion
Towards a New Framework for the Study of Religious Pluralism

'Religion' may – or may not – be here to stay. As a 'concept' (but which or whose, exactly?), from one perspective it might seem to be losing its received reference (the transcendent, the world beyond, and the life hereafter) and its shared relevance (a unified view of the cosmos and all beings in it; a doctrine of the origin, purpose, and end of all things; an alert, enlightened, or redeemed sense of self; a practice and way of life), if it has not done so already. Yet from another perspective, it continues to claim a prominent role in attempts to understand the past, to grapple with the present, and to anticipate, if not to prophesy, the future
(de Vries 2008: 1).

Religion in Nigeria is as diverse as its people, with millions of Yoruba subscribing to varieties of Islam, Christianity, and 'Yoruba religion', which sometimes contest and at other times entangle and borrow from each other. Religious pluralism, as we encounter in a multifaith setting such as Yorubaland in south-west Nigeria, challenges most of what we have long taken for granted about religion, including ready-made binaries such as Christianity versus Islam, religion versus secularism, spirit versus matter, religious monism versus polytheism, tradition versus modernity, and ultimately the one-sided equation of religion with belief. This prompts us to develop a broader conception of religion in which doctrine and creed give way to individual experience and practice.

In Yorubaland's teeming centre, Lagos, where 65 per cent are urban poor living in slums and informal settlements without access to clean water, electricity, and jobs in the formal economy, religion is for many less a matter of belief and more one of practice. By mixing Christian and Muslim elements, or the 'world religions' and 'Yoruba religion', Lagosians hope to overcome the contingencies of everyday living in the megacity. This is reflected in the spiritual journeys of Prince Charles and Peter, which I recorded in Chapter 3. Both turned to Chrislam at a crisis in their lives: they had lost their jobs and had difficulties making ends meet. By joining Chrislam, they were expecting a 'breakthrough' in their lives. During a service in the oldest Chrislam movement, *Ifeoluwa*, I met a young woman who had exchanged her *Aladura* church for Chrislam. She believed that by combining Christian and Muslim rituals, her chances of getting a visa to travel to Europe would increase. Others, such as the adherents of *Ijo Orunmila*, engage in religious pluralism in the hope it will cure physical illnesses or metaphysical afflictions. In short, by engaging in practices of religious pluralism – or what my interlocutors described as 'religious shopping', whereby they move in and out of religious movements and engage simultaneously with different religious traditions – Lagosians strive to achieve *alafia*, that is, a condition of well-being with health and prosperity as its main components.

This is not to say, however, that only marginalized Lagosians engage in religious shopping. For the emerging middle class, as represented by Bob and Mr Akindele, who were introduced in Chapter 6, practices of religious pluralism are a way to distinguish themselves from mainstream believers and free themselves from the dogmatic strictures associated with institutionalized religion. It is therefore important to study lived religion in relation to class dispositions within Lagos's political economy. Not only does religious affiliation, or rather lack of affiliation since religious shoppers cross religious boundaries, intersect with class; it also intersects with gender and age. It appears that women and youth are overrepresented in the religious movements that have emerged in Lagos since the religious revival of the 1970s. The organizational structure of Chrislam, NASFAT, and Eckankar creates possibilities for women to take up (temporary) leadership roles. These movements offer special programmes for youth, with NASFAT targeting youth most directly. Since the last two decades, NASFAT has grown into the largest contemporary Muslim organization in Nigeria, which attracts a mainly youthful upwardly mobile middle class. They feel attracted to NASFAT's innovative approach to religion that offers new prospects to cultivate a modernist form of Islam. Whereas the link between religion, gender, and age is obvious, the link between religion and ethnicity is more complex. While Chrislam, NASFAT, and the Grail Movement are composed predominantly of Yoruba – the largest ethnic group in the south-west – and NASFAT and *Ijo Orunmila* can be described in terms of Yoruba emancipation movements, I also met some Igbo in *Ijo Orunmila* and Eckankar. Igbo are known for their entrepreneurial spirit and religious shopping may be considered a reflection of that.

The issue at stake in the previous chapters has been to critically engage with religious pluralism in Lagos in order to move beyond normative and idealized notions of religion as a singular, self-contained entity with well-defined borders. From this perspective, the way religion is practised in everyday living in Lagos is anomalous and Lagosians who cross religious boundaries are aberrations. But, as the extended case studies in this book illustrate, rather than an exception, the crossing of religious boundaries is the norm in Lagos and an integral part of daily experience. Thus, rather than reconciling the ambivalence and contradictions in lived religion as in syncretism – a commonplace in the study of religion that reinforces essentialist conceptions of religion and passes over the ways in which religious practitioners actually live and do religion – we must get to grips with them. A focus on lived religiosity allows us to develop a more inclusive anthropology of religious pluralism that shifts attention from a narrow analysis of religious traditions as mutually exclusive towards a perspective that focuses on the complex dynamics of their actual entanglements.

Assemblage as Concept

In order to come to terms with the idiosyncratic ways in which religion is practised in everyday living in Lagos, I used assemblage as a trope and technique. The benefit of assemblage over syncretism is that it overcomes conceptions of religion that are built on dichotomies. In assemblage thinking there are no separate compartments and therefore it is not considered contradictory to simultaneously be a Christian and a Muslim, a religious monist and a polytheist, or a religious practitioner engaging with 'Western' and 'Eastern' traditions. In this spirit, an approach in terms of assemblage overcomes not only the compartmentalized study of religion along theological boundaries but also goes a step further by dissolving religion as a bounded and distinct category. By taking assemblage as my analytical tool, I have shifted the focus from idealized conceptions of religion as a coherent, internally consistent belief system to the ambivalences and incompatibilities that emerge when religious shoppers combine multiple religious traditions, for these are what lived religion in Lagos is about.

The pluriform religious movements that form the core of this monograph all exemplify different modes of assemblage. My point of departure was that assemblage foregrounds the ongoing and open-ended processes through which new religious formations, fusing diverse religious elements without unifying them, emerge and transform. A case in point is Chrislam, a series of religious movements that combine Christianity and Islam, which found fertile soil in Lagos's pluriform setting where, according to Section 10 of the Nigerian constitution, 'the Government of the Federation or of a State shall not adopt any religion as State Religion'. Chrislamists assemble Christian and Muslim beliefs and practices in an effort to hedge their bets by combining the powers in

Christianity and Islam, thereby doubling their chances of achieving a good life. However, as we saw in Chapter 3, there are limits to religious assemblage. In 2011, the Lagos State Government determined Jamiu Yusuf's Chrislam movement to be illegal; not only was it banned but Yusuf and his disciples were detained for over a year. This suggests that the Nigerian state's management of religious pluralism tends to reify a normative, monotheistic model of religion. The case of Chrislam thus shows that if we want to gain a better understanding of religion as part of Lagosians' lifeworld, we should move beyond politically entrenched notions of religions as mutually exclusive entities and the conventional religious–secular divide. Rather than separating religious traditions from each other, and the religious sphere from the secular domain, we should study them in tandem.

Nigeria's secular state has given rise to a whole range of pluriform movements, of which Chrislam is just one. Similar to Chrislam, NASFAT appropriates Pentecostal prayer styles and techniques, as a result of which the movement is popularly known as 'Pentecostal Islam'. Although appealing, such an appellation has, as I argued in Chapter 4, limited utility in shedding light on NASFAT's particular mode of religious assemblage. Whereas Chrislamists assemble Christian and Muslim beliefs and practices to multiply their chances of achieving a good life, NASFAT's leadership appropriates Pentecostal prayer forms in order to emphasize its Muslim doctrine, thereby enhancing its competitiveness in the religious marketplace that is Lagos. Rather than suggesting that religious boundaries no longer matter, the case of NASFAT thus powerfully exemplifies how religious assemblage can in fact be dedicated to the preservation of religious differences.

Like NASFAT, *Ijo Orunmila* – a movement aiming to revive 'Yoruba religion' – has also appropriated a Christian form in order to compete with the rival Christian faith. While *Ijo Orunmila*'s doctrines are based on *Ifa* – a Yoruba divination cult – the movement's worship is composed of hymns, prayers, sermons, and scriptures modelled closely on those of the mission church, and, more recently, the Pentecostal church. But instead of synthesizing 'Yoruba religion' and Christianity, *Ijo Orunmila*'s founding father, Olorunfumi Oshiga, maintained the religious boundaries between the two traditions, which he viewed as equal. His approach reflected the ideology of cultural nationalism that was current at the time of *Ijo Orunmila*'s foundation in 1920, which considered 'Yoruba religion' and Christianity to be coterminous. From such a perspective, *Ijo Orunmila*'s revival of 'Yoruba religion' does not imply a relapse into a temporalizing device that locates tradition in the past but needs to be seen as a mode for responding to developments in the present, such as (Pentecostal) Christianity's inroads in south-western Nigeria. In order to gain a better understanding of neo-traditionalist groups such as *Ijo Orunmila*, we must therefore abandon the discursive framework that conceptualizes so-called African Traditional Religion (ATR) in opposition to the world religions. As I showed in Chapter 5, 'Yoruba religion' is not an ossified tradition but rather part and parcel of Christianity and Islam. This explains why I opted for using the term 'Yoruba religion' in inverted commas.

A wave of Pentecostal churches, mushrooming in the 1970s, transformed the urban landscape in Lagos. Whereas Chrislam, NASFAT, and *Ijo Orunmila* borrowed heavily from Pentecostalism, other religious assemblages, such as the Grail Movement and Eckankar, expanded because they turned away from Pentecostalism and offered an alternative that promised individual spiritual liberation in the here and now. Today their 'otherness' attracts especially the newly emerging middle class, who are looking for ways to distinguish themselves from 'dogmatic' mainstream believers. Chapter 6 illustrated that spirituality is one way of distinguishing oneself in the anonymous megacity that is Lagos. Even more than Chrislam, NASFAT, and *Ijo Orunmila*, the Grail Movement and Eckankar are eclectic in nature because they assemble Islam, Christianity, indigenous traditions, 'Eastern' religions, spirituality, and science. The resulting 'super plurality' is more than simply an aggregate of its component parts, which explains their appeal among a growing membership who feel that the religious traditions in which they were born and raised can no longer answer the life questions they are struggling with. Yet, while Grail members and Eckists believe that the assemblage of various religious and spiritual traditions will bring about spiritual liberation, it may equally result in the hardening of religious boundaries. The rejection of established core theological tenets by the Grail Movement and Eckankar led to their condemnation as 'cults' and their demonization as '419' – a popular appellation for what Nigerians call fraud, apparently after a section in the Nigerian criminal code that describes these crimes – by many mainstream believers. What we see here is a double-sided process in which, on the one hand, religious boundaries are becoming more fluid in Lagos, while on the other hand, they are hardening, especially under the influence of the more strenuous forms of Pentecostalism and Islamic reformism that have cropped up over recent decades.

Despite their differences, what these various modes of religious pluralism have in common is that they are premised on the idea that different religious traditions solve different problems and may therefore coexist without conflict. From such a perspective, 'religious otherness' is not framed as a 'lack' but rather as 'plenitude' (Das 2013: 82). Indeed, by combining elements from different religious traditions, the religious shoppers who are the protagonists of this monograph believe their chances of having success in this world and the hereafter can be multiplied. This study points to the need for a broader comparative orientation that does not essentialize religious traditions but leaves room for double standards, ambiguity, and contradiction. The challenge for us is to develop a new conceptual frame to explore mutual influences between divergent, and often contradicting, religious traditions. Indeed, the heterogeneity of everyday living and the pluriform religious cityscape in Lagos force us to think about networks of entanglement instead of distinct religious traditions. To avoid clichés about religion in terms of theological partition, doctrinal rigidity, and boundedness, assemblage provides us with a heuristic device for shedding a fresh light on the porosity of religious boundaries and the fluidity of religious subjectivities in Lagos. By exploring the complex assemblages between religious traditions in a comparative frame and by tracing their interactions over time, we may eventually reform the study of religion beyond the compartmentalization of an anthropology of Islam and an anthropology of Christianity, and beyond ontological boundaries between Islam, Christianity, and ATR.[1]

Assemblage as Method

Our terms for conceptualizing religious pluralism frame how we study it. Assemblage is not just an analytical tool for studying modes of religious pluralism but it can also serve as a method to bring about a decompartmentalized study of religion that illuminates the internal dynamics of multifaith settings. During my field research I employed assemblage as a method that, in line with my interlocutors' assumption that religious truth does not reside permanently in one religious tradition, allowed me to shift from one religious perspective to another without seeing them as conflicting.

As Soares (2016: 674) points out, particularly in the study of religious pluralism there are methodological challenges. Relating to the very

---

[1] The recent 'ontological turn' in anthropology (Holbraad and Pedersen 2017) has seen a comeback of binary oppositions and essentialist categorizations. I strongly believe that the challenge to develop concepts for the study of religious pluralism cannot be met by approaching religions as separate ontological belief systems.

nature of our PhD training, most scholars tend to study either Islam or Christianity, and sometimes their interaction with ATR, but not all three religious traditions within a single analytical frame. Moreover, there are additional practical problems, such as language learning and funding, which prevent scholars from acquiring the expertise to deal sufficiently with multiple religious traditions. This raises the question as to how we should 'measure' and map religion.

The multiplicity and indeterminacy that are part of lived religion in a pluriform setting such as Lagos require a different approach from the theories and methods that anthropologists of religion have long employed. For example, how do we analyse religious belonging in a context where Chrislamists believe without necessarily belonging? The opposite applies to Grail members and Eckists, who belong without necessarily believing. In such contexts, conversion is not automatically considered a marker of religious belonging. For instance, Chrislam does not have a conversion ritual: one simply buys a Bible and Qur'an and starts participating in Chrislam rituals. The case of *Ijo Orunmila* shows the limitations of ingrained conversion theories: rather than converting from 'Yoruba religion' to Christianity, *Ijo Orunmila*'s founding father Oshiga put the two into conversation and within the dialogue a particular religious assemblage occurred. In Chapter 6 I brought up the notion of shifting allegiances to go beyond the teleological inclinations of conventional conversion theory. The idea of shifting allegiances sheds light on the evolving memberships in the Grail Movement and Eckankar, whose members act as consumers in a religious marketplace, picking and choosing from the religious traditions that are available. Because religious shoppers understand processes of religious affiliation in terms other than conversion, we must look beyond institutional membership and belief as indications of religious belonging and focus instead on religious practice and lived experience.

Studying religion through the vector of religious practice and lived experience requires a pluralistic approach, that is, an open, hermeneutical way of understanding differences between religious practitioners, as well as between scholars of religion (Spies 2013: 118). Even if it is now acknowledged by some scholars that it is no longer sufficient to study different religions as separate units, scholars with expertise regarding either Islam or Christianity still barely engage in conversations with each other. And yet, the old division of labour between anthropologists of Islam and anthropologists of Christianity has become obsolete against the backdrop of religious pluralism (Janson and Meyer 2016). Therefore, rather than focusing on single, self-contained religious traditions, it makes more sense to work with the broader notion of a pluriform field[2] in which different religious traditions coexist and copy from each other, and in which scholars of religion collaborate transdisciplinarily.

Clearly, a pluralistic approach leaves room for new synergies to evolve from a polylogue among scholars across the globe and across disciplines, which so far have remained more or less unrelated. By employing assemblage theory, a theory that originated in philosophy, and applying it to the study of religious pluralism in Lagos, I have tried to bring anthropology, philosophy, religious studies, African studies, and urban studies into conversation. In this way, we can cut across not only disciplinary boundaries but also religious boundaries, whereby one scholar studies Islam, another Christianity, and the third ATR. As exemplified by my collaboration with the Nigerian photographer Akintunde Akinleye, it could also be productive to collaborate with non-academic research partners. Such collaboration in the interface of the arts, but also with NGO workers and interfaith activists, promises to give a new impetus to the study of religious pluralism. By bringing about novel connections among scholars and among scholars and practitioners, a pluralistic approach renders possible a truly comparative study of religion, one that avoids typologies and transcends boundaries.

Although transdisciplinarity has become the charm in getting research grants awarded, in practice it is often an attempt to convince the disciplinary 'other' of the strength of one's own concepts and methods. A pluralistic approach, however, requires that we seriously attempt to learn from one another: by overcoming our 'intellectual sectarianism' (Ilesanmi 1997: 253), we can meet common theoretical and methodological challenges. Opting for a transdisciplinary and cross-cultural approach is to attach more importance to listening to and engaging with 'the Otherness of the other' (Bernstein 1991: 91). This is not only an important methodological issue but also a major epistemological challenge for the production of knowledge beyond Eurocentric claims.

The study of religion in Africa has long been pursued from a hegemonic Western perspective, reinforcing a Christian concept of religion

---

[2] Inspired by Bourdieu's concept of the 'field', Janson and Meyer (2016) coined the term 'religious field'. According to Bourdieu (1991), the visions and stances of actors in a field have a relational status, they make sense only in relation to those of others, 'the field as a whole is defined as a system of deviations on different levels and nothing, either in the institutions or in the agents, the acts or the discourses they produce, has meaning except relationally, by virtue of the interplay of oppositions and distinctions' (185). Drawing on Bourdieu, a relational approach to religion may provide a better grasp of religious pluralism and encourage transdisciplinarity.

that emphasizes belief, knowledge, and cosmology at the expense of the practical dimension of Africans' lived religiosity. Therefore, there is a pressing need for a reorientation of the study of religion, taking into account the transregional connections between the European centres of knowledge production and the former areas of imperial European outreach and acknowledging the validity of different ways of seeing the world (Tayob 2018; Meyer 2018). Taking this course, a pluralistic approach may create a less inward-looking and parochial attitude and a more open 'pluriversity', defined by Mbembe (2016) as,

a process of knowledge production that is open to epistemic diversity. It is a process that does not necessarily abandon the notion of universal knowledge for humanity, but which embraces it via *a horizontal strategy of openness to dialogue among different epistemic traditions* (37; emphasis in the original).

In short, studying religion in the pluriversity enables us to transcend the disciplinary, methodological, and epistemological rigidity that dominates much scholarship on religion (van Klinken 2020).

The merit of a pluralistic approach is that it prompts us to study religious pluralism without reducing religious diversity to unity. We do not all need to study religion in the same way; the intellectual purchase of a pluralistic approach lies in the dissonance between the different voices in the debate (Adogame, Echtler, and Freiberger 2013). In a similar vein, a pluralistic approach underlines that religious phenomena need not be commensurable or made mutually consistent in order to coexist. Hence, Spies (2013) proposes to take incommensurability as the starting point in the study of religious pluralism. By acknowledging incommensurability, we can come to terms with situations that at first sight seem ambivalent or contradictory, where Chrislamists, Grail members, and Eckists do not feel the need for one practice or belief to exclude another, where Muslim reformers founded NASFAT on a Pentecostal blueprint, and where different ways of doing and seeing things do not stand against each other but exist side by side as in *Ijo Orunmila*. From this perspective, religious pluralism is no longer a problem opposing the tradition of monism but an opportunity to offer a fresh perspective on religious entanglements in multifaith settings.

Just as scholars of religion might disagree among themselves about how to study religion, a pluralistic approach does not imply that religious boundaries do not matter. Though the Yoruba continue to be a beacon of religious amity, with the rise of stricter forms of devotion as represented by Islamic reform movements on the one side, and neo-Pentecostalism on the other, Muslim–Christian relations have become more tense than they used to be before the 1980s (Peel 2016a: 221).[3] Still, even Islamic reformism and Pentecostalism, which emphasize religious boundaries, are themselves the product of engagement with religious others. A case in point is NASFAT. Although it calls for a reform of the way Islam has long been practised locally, in its mission to reform Islam it borrows openly and heavily from Pentecostalism. What we find here is an intriguing case of 'agonistic belonging' (Das 2010: 399), where entanglement happens through opposition.

Ultimately, adopting a pluralistic approach may break the deadlock of essentializing religious and disciplinary boundaries and enable us to better understand how our research participants experience religious differences and how our research collaborators frame disciplinary differences. 'Otherness' is then no longer understood as a threat but as a potential resource to gain from. As a result, religious pluralism may become a political asset: the Yoruba teach us an important lesson about how different religious traditions can live together in peace.

The City as Assemblage

Religious pluralism is often associated with cities (Albera 2012). Cities are places where people from different socio-religious backgrounds, ethnicities, and nationalities interact and assemblage begins its creative job. In this spirit, Lagos is a good place to think about assemblage. The insecurity and unpredictability of everyday living in the megacity has produced a tremendous explosion of religious improvisation and experimentation. Lagosians pick and choose elements from various religious traditions and recycle infrastructural fragments to reorder urban space and secure a livelihood through the makeshift combinations of spaces, objects, beliefs, and practices. The city in itself can therefore be regarded as an 'assemblage of assemblages', 'cities are assemblages of people, networks, organizations, as well as a variety of infrastructural components, from buildings and streets to conduits for matter and energy flows' (DeLanda 2006: 5–6). As in Bender's (2002) book title *The Unfinished City*, the basic idea behind the city as an assemblage is that there is no city as a bounded space; the city is an ongoing construction. With the soaring luxury apartments being built on Lagos Island and bought by NASFAT leaders, Grail members, and Eckists, and the ever-expanding slum

---

[3] For instance, riots between Yoruba and Hausa gangs in the Mushin district of Lagos left at least a hundred people dead and many more injured in February 2002. The riots started after Hausas claimed a young Yoruba man had desecrated a mosque (www.news.bbc.co.uk/1/hi/world/africa/1802175.stm).

Figure 7.1 'Face Me I Face You'.
Photographer: Akintunde Akinleye

settlements on the mainland inhabited by the members of *Ijo Orunmila*, Lagos indeed resembles a permanent construction site.

A notable example of urban dwelling as an assemblage is the socio-material composite of the 'Face Me I Face You' housing in Lagos (Figure 7.1). Many lower- and lower-middle class Lagosians live in this type of communal housing referred to as 'Face Me I Face You' because it squeezes occupants into rooms laid out facing each other along a narrow corridor. Public space is used here as an extension of private space. Because the occupants share facilities, it is common to see people queuing up for the outside bathroom in the early morning. While there is a shared bathroom for toileting and bathing, less private acts of personal hygiene are moved to the public domain. At morning rush hour one can spot men with towels tied to their waist brushing their teeth and shaving above the open sewers in front of their 'Face Me I Face You', and women plaiting each other's hair or straightening it before their workday starts. Not only in the occupants' use of space but also in its physical structure the 'Face Me I Face You' is an assemblage: electricity lines are reassembled, dissembled, or tapped from one's neighbours, making the walls 'palimpsests of wire-on-concrete' (Trovalla and Trovalla 2015: 335). In addition to the heterogeneous connections of material space, the 'Face Me I Face You' facilitates particular forms of sociality, commonality, and conflict. For instance, in the densely populated neighbourhood of Ebute-Metta, where *Ijo Orunmila* is located, Muslim Hausa immigrants from the north live together with Christian Yoruba from the south. This cohabitation results in the (re)drawing of religious boundaries and the (re)negotiation of religious coexistence on a routine basis. Thus, the infrastructure of the 'Face Me I Face You' aligns with religious assemblage.

This snapshot of lived space in Lagos spells out a conception of the megacity as a socio-material assemblage that does not fit in any pre-given, fixed design as developed by urban planners. By mapping Lagos as an assemblage that has become a driving force of urban transformation and reconfiguration, dystopian projections of the megalopolis as a ticking 'population bomb' on the brink of collapse (Liotta and Miskel 2012), or a 'mega-slum of despair' (Ilesanmi 2010), are redressed by conceptions of the megalopolis as a site of 'generative capacity' (Pieterse 2011) and 'creativity of practice' (Diouf and Fredericks 2014). In the latter view, the urban-religious assemblages discussed in this book can be interpreted as experiments in Lagosians' resourcefulness and aspiration, and the religious shoppers who inhabit them as experts at assemblage. In a cityscape where jobs in the formal sector are scarce and where many migrants cannot fall back on extensive kinship networks, one needs to be inventive to make a living. Urbanites' improvisation in creating homes by assembling materials and their ingenuity in mixing and matching religious elements need to be studied as part of the same trend: a do-it-yourself attitude that ties in with the do-it-yourself religiosity displayed by religious shoppers.

While religious shoppers show a high level of entrepreneurialism in the sense of trying out different options in their attempt to navigate the chaotic flux of life in Lagos, the religious leaders who founded Chrislam, NASFAT, *Ijo Orunmila*, the Grail Movement, and Eckankar show a similar level of entrepreneurialism in their attempts to win souls and secure urban space. Following the example of the Pentecostal movement, most of them have invested in urban renewal and religiously owned real estate, thereby reconfiguring Lagos into what is dubbed a 'Prayer City' (Ukah 2013). For instance, Samsindeen Saka – the leader of the most popular Chrislam movement – has recently started developing '*Oke Tude* Village' close to RCCG Redemption City, the largest Pentecostal prayer camp along the Lagos–Ibadan Expressway. In a similar vein, in an effort to inscribe itself in the Pentecostal-dominated public space, NASFAT has opened a prayer camp along the Lagos–Ibadan Expressway where it plans to build a mega-mosque. To escape from

Lagos's overcrowded and polluted cityscape, the founder of the Grail Movement in Nigeria has invested in Grailland, a green oasis on the outskirts of Lagos that, similar to the prayer camps along the Lagos–Ibadan Expressway, serves as a model city for those seeking spiritual awakening. To establish its public presence in Lagos's cityscape, *Ijo Orunmila*, despite its small size, makes use of a public address system. This had some effect: services now attract a small number of non-Yoruba neighbours who came to the temple out of curiosity on hearing the amplified services. By claiming urban space, the religious entrepreneurs who created the religious-urban assemblages that are central here have converted themselves from victims of a crumbling urban infrastructure into agents who actively engage the religious worlds they help to create. At stake in this urban-religious place-making is a particular attitude towards Lagos as a site to realize one's dreams and to achieve a successful life; an attitude that is encapsulated well in Garbin's (2012) characterization of urban religiosity as 'believing in the city'.

This monograph has underlined Lagosians' tactics of religious shopping in asserting composite urban identities for themselves while assembling multiple religious traditions. Against the ubiquitous rhetoric of Nigeria as a nation torn by religious conflict that is doomed to an apocalypse, my urban ethnography has given expression to the novel and regenerated capacities and potentials that characterize lived religion in Lagos. By charting the idiosyncratic ways in which religion is lived in the megacity – often marked by ambiguity, inconsistency, and contradiction – we may develop new ground in the field of religion from which something fresh can sprout.

Bibliography

Abimbola, W. 1976. *Ifá: An Exposition of Ifá Literary Corpus*. Ibadan: Oxford University Press.

Abou-El-Haj, B. 1991. Languages and Models for Cultural Exchange. In *Culture, Globalization and the World-System: Contemporary Conditions for the Representation of Identity*, ed. A. D. King, 139–44. Basingstoke and New York: Palgrave.

Abu-Lughod, L. 1993. *Writing Women's Worlds: Bedouin Stories*. Berkeley: University of California Press.

Adebanwi, W. 2017. Approaching the Political Economy of Everyday Life. In *The Political Economy of Everyday Life in Africa: Beyond the Margins*, ed. W. Adebanwi, 1–31. Woodbridge: James Currey.

Adeniyi, M. O. 2013. Dynamics of Islamic Religious Movements in Nigeria: A Case Study of Nasru-Lahil-Fatih Society of Nigeria. In *Religion on the Move! New Dynamics of Religious Expansion in a Globalizing World*, eds. A. Adogame and S. Shankar, 323–38. Leiden: Brill.

Adetona, L. M. 2012. NASFAT: A Modern Prayer Group and Its Contributions to the Propagation of Islam in Lagos. *World Journal of Islamic History and Civilization* 2 (2): 102–7.

Adogame, A. 2010. How God Became a Nigerian: Religious Impulse and the Unfolding of a Nation. *Journal of Contemporary African Studies* 28 (4): 479–98.

Adogame, A., M. Echtler, and O. Freiberger. 2013. Introduction. In *Alternative Voices: A Plurality Approach for Religious Studies. Essays in Honor of Ulrich Berner*, eds. A. Adogame, M. Echtler, and O. Freiberger, 9–17. Göttingen: Vandenhoeck & Ruprecht.

Ajayi, J. F. A. 1965. *Christian Missions in Nigeria 1841–1891: The Making of a New Elite*. London: Longmans.

Akinleye, A. and M. Janson. 2014. *The Spiritual Highway: Religious World Making in Megacity Lagos*. Exhibition catalogue with photographs by A. Akinleye, curated by M. Janson. London: SOAS University of London.

Albera, D. 2012. Conclusion: Crossing the Frontiers between the Monotheistic Religions, an Anthropological Approach. In *Sharing Sacred Spaces in the Mediterranean. Christians, Muslims, and Jews at Shrines and Sanctuaries*, eds. D. Albera and M. Couroucli, 219–44. Bloomington: Indiana University Press.

Anderson, A. 2004. *An Introduction to Pentecostalism: Global Charismatic Christianity*. Cambridge: Cambridge University Press.

Anonymous. 2012. The Popular Discourses of Salafi Radicalism and Salafi Counter-Radicalism in Nigeria: A Case Study of Boko Haram. *Journal of Religion in Africa* 42: 118–44.

Apostolov, M. 2004. *The Christian–Muslim Frontier: A Zone of Contact, Conflict or Cooperation*. London: Routledge.

Apter, A. H. 2005. *The Pan-African Nation: Oil and the Spectacle of Culture in Nigeria*. Chicago, IL: University of Chicago Press.

Asad, T. 1983. Anthropological Conceptions of Religion: Reflections on Geertz. *Man* 18 (2): 237–59.

   1993. *Genealogies of Religion: Discipline and Reasons of Power in Christianity and Islam*. Baltimore, MD: Johns Hopkins University Press.

   2003. *Formations of the Secular: Christianity, Islam, Modernity*. Stanford, CA: Stanford University Press.

Asamoah-Gyadu, K. 2016. 'Meccanizing' Jerusalem: Christianization of Islamic Traditions in Contemporary African Christianity. Unpublished paper presented at the Summer School Christians and Muslims in Africa: Towards a Framework for the Study of Multi-Religious Settings, convened by B. Meyer, A. Sounaye, M. Janson, and K. Kresse, ZMO, Berlin, 14–20 July.

Atiemo, A. 2003. Zetaheal Mission in Ghana: Christians and Muslims Worshipping Together? *Exchange* 32 (1): 15–36.

Ayandele, E. A. 1966. *The Missionary Impact on Modern Nigeria 1842–1914: A Political and Social Analysis*. London: Longmans, Green and Co.

Bach, D. C. 2006. Inching Towards a Country without a State: Prebendalism, Violence and State Betrayal in Nigeria. In *Big African States: Angola, Sudan, DRC, Ethiopia, Nigeria, South Africa*, eds. C. Clapham, J. Herbst, and G. Mills, 62–96. Johannesburg: Wits University Press.

Barber, K. 1981. How Man Makes God in West Africa: Yoruba Attitudes towards the 'Orisa'. *Africa: Journal of the International African Institute* 51 (3): 724–45.

   1989. Interpreting Oríkì as History and Literature. In *Discourse and Its Disguises: The Interpretation of African Oral Texts*, eds. K. Barber and P. F. de Moraes Farias, 13–23. Birmingham: Birmingham University.

   1990. Discursive Strategies in the Texts of Ifa and in the 'Holy Book of Odu' of the African Church of Orunmila. In *Self-Assertion and Brokerage: Early Cultural Nationalism in West Africa*, eds. P. F. de Moraes Farias and K. Barber, 196–224. Birmingham: Centre of West African Studies, University of Birmingham.

Barnes, S. T. 1986. *Patrons and Power: Creating a Political Community in Metropolitan Lagos*. Manchester: Manchester University Press for the International African Institute, London.

   1997. The Many Faces of Ogun: Introduction to the First Edition. In *Africa's Ogun: Old World and New*. Second Edition Expanded, ed. S. T. Barnes, 1–26. Bloomington: Indiana University Press.

Barrett, D. V. 2004a. Eckankar. In *Encyclopedia of New Religious Movements*, ed. P. B. Clarke, 178–9. London and New York: Routledge.

2004b. Twitchell, Paul. In *Encyclopedia of New Religious Movements*, ed. P. B. Clarke, 643. London and New York: Routledge.

Bascom, W. 1969. *Ifa Divination: Communication between Gods and Men in West Africa*. Bloomington: Indiana University Press.

Bastian, M. L. 1993. 'Bloodhounds Who Have No Friends': Witchcraft and Locality in the Nigerian Popular Press. In *Modernity and Its Malcontents: Ritual and Power in Postcolonial Africa*, eds. J. Comaroff and J. L. Comaroff, 129–66. Chicago, IL: University of Chicago Press.

1998. Mami Wata, Mr. White, and the Sirens off Bar Beach: Spirits and Dangerous Consumption in the Nigerian Popular Press. In *Afrika und das Andere: Alterität und Innovation*, eds. H. Schmidt and A. Wirz, 21–31. Hamburg: Lit Verlag.

Bayart, J.-F. 1993. *The State in Africa: The Politics of the Belly*. New York: Longman.

Bayat, A. 2007. Radical Religion and the Habitus of the Dispossessed: Does Islamic Militancy Have an Urban Ecology? *International Journal of Urban and Regional Research* 31 (3): 579–90.

Bender, T. 2002. *The Unfinished City: New York and the Metropolitan Idea*. New York: New Press.

Berger, P. L. 2014. *The Many Altars of Modernity: Toward a Paradigm for Religion in a Pluralist Age*. Boston, MA and Berlin: De Gruyter.

Bernstein, R. J. 1991. Incommensurability and Otherness Revisited. In *Culture and Modernity: East-West Philosophic Perspectives*, ed. E. Deutsch, 85–103. Honolulu: University of Hawaii Press.

Beyer, P. 1997. Religious Vitality in Canada: The Complementarity of Religious Market and Secularization Perspectives. *Journal for the Scientific Study of Religion* 36 (2): 272–88.

Bhabha, H. 1994. *The Location of Culture*. London: Routledge.

Bibby, R. 1987. *Fragmented Gods: The Poverty and Potential of Religion in Canada*. Toronto: Stoddart.

Blier, S. P. 2018. Design. In *Critical Terms for the Study of Africa*, eds. G. Desai and A. Masquelier, 86–101. Chicago, IL and London: University of Chicago Press.

Bochinger, C. 2013. Ist religiöse Vielfalt etwas Gutes? Pluralismus und Pluralität in der Religionswissenschaft [Is Religious Diversity a Good Thing? Pluralism and Plurality in Religious Studies]. In *Alternative Voices: A Plurality Approach for Religious Studies. Essays in Honor of Ulrich Berner*, eds. A. Adogame, M. Echtler, and O. Freiberger, 285–307. Göttingen: Vandenhoeck & Ruprecht.

Bourdieu, P. 1991. *Language and Symbolic Power*, edited and introduced by J. B. Thompson, translated by G. Raymond and M. Adamson. Cambridge: Polity Press.

Brenner, L. 1989. 'Religious' Discourses in and about Africa. In *Discourse and Its Disguises. The Interpretation of African Oral Texts*, eds. K. Barber and P. F. de Moraes Farias, 87–105. Birmingham: Centre of West African Studies, University of Birmingham.

2000. Histories of Religion in Africa. *Journal of Religion in Africa* 30 (2): 143–67.

Bromley, D. G. 2009. New Religions as a Specialist Field. In *The Oxford Handbook of the Sociology of Religion*, ed. P. B. Clarke, 723–41. Oxford: Oxford University Press.

Bruder, E. 2008. *The Black Jews of Africa: History, Religion, Identity*. Oxford: Oxford University Press.

Butticci, A. 2013. Crazy World, Crazy Faith! Prayer, Power and Transformation in a Nigerian Prayer City. In *Prayer in Religion and Spirituality*, eds. G. Giordan and L. Woodhead, 243–62. Leiden: Brill.

Capps, W. H. 1979. Commentary. In *Science of Religion: Studies in Methodology*, ed. L. Honko, 177–85. The Hague: Mouton.

Casanova, J. 1994. *Public Religions in the Modern World*. Chicago, IL: University of Chicago Press.

2008. Public Religions Revisited. In *Religion: Beyond a Concept*, ed. H. de Vries, 101–19. New York: Fordham University Press.

Chidester, D. 1996. *Savage Systems: Colonialism and Comparative Religion in Southern Africa*. Charlottesville and London: University Press of Virginia.

2018. *Religion: Material Dynamics*. Oakland: University of California Press.

Clifford, J. 1988. *The Predicament of Culture: Twentieth-Century Ethnography, Literature, and Art*. Cambridge, MA: Harvard University Press.

Coleman, S. 2009. The Protestant Ethic and the Spirit of Urbanism. In *When God Comes to Town: Religious Traditions in Urban Contexts*, eds. R. Pinxten and L. Dikomits, 33–44. New York: Berghahn Books.

Collier, S. J. and A. Ong. 2005. Global Assemblages, Anthropological Problems. In *Global Assemblages. Technology, Politics, and Ethics as Anthropological Problems*, eds. A. Ong and S. J. Collier, 3–21. Malden, MA: Blackwell Publishing.

Comaroff, J. and J. Comaroff. 1991. *Of Revolution and Revelation: Christianity, Colonization and Consciousness in South Africa*. Chicago, IL: University of Chicago Press.

Connolly, W. E. 2005. *Pluralism*. Durham, NC: Duke University Press.

Cooper, B. M. 2006. *Evangelical Christians in the Muslim Sahel*. Bloomington: Indiana University Press.

Danmole, H. O. 2008. Religious Encounter in Southwestern Nigeria: The Domestication of Islam among the Yoruba. In *Orisa Devotion as World Religion: The Globalization of Yoruba Religious Culture*, eds. J. K. Olupona and T. Rey, 202–21. Madison: University of Wisconsin Press.

Das, V. 2010. Engaging the Life of the Other: Love and Everyday Life. In *Ordinary Ethics: Anthropology, Language, and Action*, ed. M. Lambek, 376–99. New York: Fordham University Press.

2013. Cohabiting an Interreligious Milieu: Reflections on Religious Diversity. In *A Companion to the Anthropology of Religion*, eds. J. Boddy and M. Lambek, 69–84. Chichester: Wiley-Blackwell.

Davie, G. 1994. *Religion in Britain since 1945: Believing without Belonging*. Oxford: Blackwell Publishing.

De Boeck, F. 2013. Global Prayers: How the Academy and the Arts Circumambulate the City. In *Global Prayers: Contemporary Manifestations of the Religious in the City*, eds. J. Becker, K. Klingan, S. Lanz, and K. Wildner, 559–65. Berlin: Lars Müller Publishers.

De Boeck, F. and M.-F. Plissart. 2014. *Kinshasa: Tales of the Invisible City*. Leuven: Leuven University Press.

De Boeck, F. and S. Baloji. 2016. *Suturing the City: Living Together in Congo's Urban Worlds*. London: Autograph ABP.

De Certeau, M. 1984. Walking in the City. In *The Practice of Everyday Life*, 91–110. Berkeley: University of California Press.

De Vries, H. 2008. Introduction: Why Still 'Religion'? In *Religion: Beyond a Concept*, ed. H. de Vries, 1–98. New York: Fordham University Press.

De Witte, M. 2012. Neo-Traditional Religions. In *The Wiley-Blackwell Companion to African Religions*, ed. E. K. Bongmba, 171–83. Chichester: Blackwell Publishing.

Deeb, L. 2006. *An Enchanted Modern: Gender and Public Piety in Shi'i Lebanon*. Princeton, NJ: Princeton University Press.

DeLanda, M. 2006. *A New Philosophy of Society: Assemblage Theory and Social Complexity*. London and New York: Continuum.

Deleuze, G. and F. Guattari. 1987. *A Thousand Plateaus: Capitalism and Schizophrenia*. Minneapolis, MN: University of Minneapolis Press.

Derrida, J. 1982. *Margins of Philosophy*, translated by A. Bates. Chicago, IL: University of Chicago Press.

Dilger, H and M. Janson. Forthcoming. Religiously-Motivated Education as 'Moral Enclaves': Reforming Urban Youths in Tanzania and Nigeria.

Diouf, M. and R. Fredericks, eds. 2014. *The Arts of Citizenship in African Cities: Infrastructures and Spaces of Belonging*. New York: Palgrave Macmillan.

Droogers, A. 1989. Syncretism: The Problem of Definition, the Definition of the Problem. In *Dialogue and Syncretism: An Interdisciplinary Approach*, eds. J. G. Gort, H. Vroom, R. Fernhout, and A. Wessels, 7–25. Amsterdam: Wm. B. Eerdmans Publishing.

2014. Playing with Perspectives. In *Methods for the Study of Religious Change: From Religious Studies to Worldview Studies*, eds. A. Droogers and A. van Harskamp, 61–79. Sheffield: Equinox.

Eck, D. L. 2007. Prospects for Pluralism: Voice and Vision in the Study of Religion. *Journal of the American Academy of Religion* 75 (4): 743–76.

Ekelund, R. B., R. F. Hébert, and R. D. Tollison. 2006. *The Marketplace of Christianity*. Cambridge, MA: MIT Press.

Engelke, M. 2004. Text and Performance in an African Church: The Book, 'Live and Direct'. *American Ethnologist* 31 (1): 76–91.

Englund, H. 2011. From Spiritual Warfare to Spiritual Kinship: Islamophobia and Evangelical Radio in Malawi. In *Christianity and Public Culture in Africa*, ed. H. Englund, 167–88. Athens: Ohio University Press.

Enwerem, I. M. 1995. *A Dangerous Awakening: The Politicization of Religion in Nigeria*. Ibadan: IFRA.

Enwezor, O., C. Basualdo, U.M. Bauer, S. Ghez, S. Maharaj, M. Nash, and O. Zaya, eds. 2002. *Under Siege: Four African Cities: Freetown, Johannesburg, Kinshasa, Lagos. Documenta 11_Platform 4*. Ostfilderns-Ruit: Hatje Cantz Publishers.

Evans-Pritchard, E. E. 1937. *Witchcraft, Oracles and Magic among the Azande*. Oxford: Clarendon Press.

1956. *Nuer Religion*. Oxford: Clarendon Press.

Ewing, C. 1990. The Illusion of Wholeness: Culture, Self, and the Experience of Inconsistency. *Ethos* 18: 251–78.

Fabian, J. 1985. Religious Pluralism: An Ethnographic Approach. In *Theoretical Explorations in African Religion*, eds. Wim van Binsbergen and Matthew Schoffeleers, 138–63. London: KPI Limited.

Falola, T. 1998. *Violence in Nigeria: The Crisis of Religious Politics and Secular Ideologies*. Rochester, NY: University of Rochester Press.

Fardon, R. 2015. 'Do You Hear Me? It Is Me, Akiga': Akiga's Story and Akiga Sai's History. *Africa: Journal of the International African Institute* 85 (4): 572–98.

Ferguson, J. 2006. *Global Shadows: Africa in the Neoliberal World Order*. Durham, NC and London: Duke University Press.

Finnegan, R. 2012 [1970]. *Oral Literature in Africa*. Cambridge: Open Book Publishers.

Fisher H. J. 1963. *Ahmadiyyah: A Study in Contemporary Islam on the West African Coast*. London: Oxford University Press.

1985. The Juggernaut's Apologia: Conversion to Islam in Black Africa. *Africa: Journal of the International African Institute* 55 (2): 153–73.

Fourchard, L. 2011. Lagos, Koolhaas and Partisan Politics in Nigeria. *International Journal of Urban and Regional Research* 35 (1): 40–56.

Frederiks, M. 2009. Methodists and Muslims in the Gambia. *Islam and Christian–Muslim Relations* 20 (1): 61–72.

Gandy, M. 2005. Learning from Lagos. *New Left Review* 33: 36–52.

2006. Planning, Anti-Planning and the Infrastructure Crisis Facing Metropolitan Lagos. *Urban Studies* 43 (2): 371–96.

Garbin, D. 2012. Introduction: Believing in the City. *Culture and Religion* 13 (4): 401–4.

Gbadegesin, S. 1991. *African Philosophy: Traditional Yoruba Philosophy and Contemporary African Realities*. New York: Peter Lang.

Geertz, C. 1973. Religion as a Cultural System. In *The Interpretation of Cultures*, ed. C. Geertz, 87–125. New York: Basic Books.

Gellner, D. N. 1997. For Syncretism: The Position of Buddhism in Nepal and Japan Compared. *Social Anthropology* 5 (3): 277–91.

Geschiere, P. 1997. *The Modernity of Witchcraft. Politics and the Occult in Postcolonial Africa*. Charlottesville and London: University of Virginia Press.

Gez, Y. N., Y. Droz, E. Soares, and J. Rey. 2017. From Converts to Itinerants: Religious *Butinage* as Dynamic Identity. *Current Anthropology* 2: 141–59.

Gifford, P. 1998. *African Christianity: Its Public Role*. London: Hurst.

Goody, J. 1987. *The Interface between the Written and the Oral*. Cambridge: Cambridge University Press.

Gooren, H. 2006. The Religious Market Model and Conversion: Towards a New Approach. *Exchange* 35 (1): 39–60.

Gore, C. and D. Pratten. 2003. The Politics of Plunder: The Rhetorics of Order and Disorder in Southern Nigeria. *African Affairs* 102 (407): 211–40.

Griffith, R. M. 2004. *Born Again Bodies: Flesh and Spirit in American Christianity*. Berkeley: University of California Press.

Guyer, J. I. 1996. Traditions of Invention in Equatorial Africa. *African Studies Review* 39 (3): 1–28.

Hackett, R. I. J. 1989. *Religion in Calabar: The Religious Life and History of a Nigerian Town*. Berlin and New York: Mouton de Gruyter.

2001. Prophets, 'False Prophets,' and the African State: Emergent Issues of Religious Freedom and Conflict. *Nova Religio: The Journal of Alternative and Emergent Religions* 4 (2): 187–212.

2011. Is Satan Local or Global? Reflections on a Nigerian Deliverance Movement. In *Who is Afraid of the Holy Ghost? Pentecostalism and Globalization in Africa and beyond*, ed. A. Adogame, 111–31. Trenton, NJ: Africa World Press.

Hanegraaff, W. J. 1996. *New Age Religion and Western Culture: Esotericism in the Mirror of Western Thought*. Leiden: Brill.

Hannerz, U. 1987. The World in Creolisation. *Africa: Journal of the International African Institute* 57 (4): 546–59.

Harvey, D. 2012. *Rebel Cities: From the Right to the City to the Urban Revolution*. London: Verso Books.

Haynes, J. 2007. Nollywood in Lagos, Lagos in Nollywood Films. *Africa Today* 54 (2): 131–50.

Heelas, P. and L. Woodhead. 2005. *The Spiritual Revolution: Why Religion Is Giving Way to Spirituality*. Oxford: Blackwell Publishing.

Higazi, A. 2008. Social Mobilization and Collective Violence: Vigilantes and Militias in the Lowlands of Plateau State, Central Nigeria. *Africa: Journal of the International African Institute* 78 (1): 107–35.

2013. Les origins et la transformation de l'insurrection de Boko Haram dans le nord du Nigeria [The Origins and Transformation of the Boko Haram Insurgency in Northern Nigeria]. *Politique africaine* 130: 137–64.

Hirschkind, C. 2006. *The Ethical Soundscape: Cassette Sermons and Islamic Counterpublics*. New York: Columbia University Press.

Hobsbawm, E. and T. Ranger, eds. 1983. *The Invention of Tradition*. Cambridge: Cambridge University Press.

Hock, K. 2004. *The Interface between Research and Dialogue: Christian–Muslim Relations in Africa*. Münster: Lit Verlag

Holbraad, M. and M. A. Pedersen. 2017. *The Ontological Turn: An Anthropological Exposition*. Cambridge: Cambridge University Press.

Honwana, A. 2012. *The Time of Youth: Work, Social Change, and Politics in Africa*. Sterling, VA: Kumarian Press.

Horton, R. 1975a. On the Rationality of Conversion, Part I. *Africa: Journal of the International African Institute* 45 (3): 219–35.

1975b. On the Rationality of Conversion, Part II. *Africa: Journal of the International African Institute* 45 (3): 373–99.

Hunwick, J. 1992. An African Case Study of Political Islam: Nigeria. *The Annals of the American Academy of Political and Social Science* 524 (1): 143–55.

Iannaccone, L. R. 1992. Religious Markets and the Economics of Religion. *Social Compass* 39 (1): 123–31.

Ibrahim, M. 2017a. *Sensational Piety: Practices of Mediation in Christ Embassy and NASFAT*. Unpublished PhD thesis, University of Utrecht.

—— 2017b. Oral Transmission of the Sacred: Preaching in Christ Embassy and NASFAT in Abuja. *Journal of Religion in Africa* 47 (1): 108–31.

Idowu, E. B. 1973. *African Traditional Religion: A Definition*. London: SCM Press.

Ilesanmi, A. 2010. Urban Sustainability in the Context of Lagos Mega-City. *Journal of Geography and Regional Planning* 3 (10): 240–52.

Ilesanmi, S. O. 1997. *Religious Pluralism and the Nigerian State*. Athens: Ohio University Press.

Introvigne, M. 2004. Grail Movement. In *Encyclopedia of New Religious Movements*, ed. P. B. Clarke, 244–5. London and New York: Routledge.

Janson, M. 2014. *Islam, Youth, and Modernity in the Gambia: The Tablighi Jama'at*. Cambridge: Cambridge University Press for the International African Institute, London.

—— 2016a. 'How, for God's Sake, Can I Be a Good Muslim?' Gambian Youth in Search of a Moral Lifestyle. *Ethnography* 17 (1): 22–46.

—— 2016b. Unity through Diversity: A Case Study of Chrislam in Lagos. *Africa: Journal of the International African Institute* 86 (4): 646–72.

—— 2018. Modern Love in Lagos: Dating the Halal Way. In *Femmes d'Afrique et émancipation: Entre normes sociales contraignantes et nouveau possibles [Women of Africa and Emancipation: Between Binding Social Standards and New Possibilities]*, ed. M. Gomez-Perez, 241–74. Paris: Karthala.

—— 2020. Crossing Borders: The Case of NASFAT or 'Pentecostal Islam' in Southwest Nigeria. *Social Anthropology* 28 (2): 418–33.

Janson, M. and A. Akinleye. 2015. The Spiritual Highway: Religious World Making in Megacity Lagos (Nigeria). *Material Religion: The Journal of Objects, Art and Belief* 11 (4): 550–62.

Janson, M. and B. Meyer. 2016. Introduction: Towards a Framework for the Study of Christian–Muslim Encounters in Africa. *Africa: Journal of the International African Institute* 86 (4): 615–19.

Johnson, C. 2012. *Bricoleur* and *Bricolage*: From Metaphor to Universal Concept. *Paragraph* 35 (3): 355–72.

Jules-Rosette, B. 1989. The Sacred in African New Religions. In *The Changing Face of Religion*, eds. J. A. Beckford and T. Luckman, 147–62. London: Sage.

Kalu, O. U. 2004. Sharia and Islam in Nigerian Pentecostal Rhetoric, 1970–2003. *Pneuma* 26 (2): 242–61.

Kane, O. 2003. *Muslim Modernity in Postcolonial Nigeria: A Study of the Society for the Renewal of Innovation and Reinstatement of Tradition*. Leiden: Brill.

Keane, W. 2004. Language and Religion. In *A Companion to Linguistic Anthropology*, ed. A. Duranti, 431–48. Malden, MA: Blackwell Publishing.

—— 2007. *Christian Moderns: Freedom & Fetish in the Mission Encounter*. Berkeley: University of California Press.

Kenny, J. 1996. Sharīa and Christianity in Nigeria: Islam and a 'Secular' State. *Journal of Religion in Africa* 26 (4): 338–64.

Kirsch, T. G. 2004. Restaging the Will to Believe. Religious Pluralism, Anti-Syncretism, and the Problem of Belief. *American Anthropologist* 106 (4): 699–711.

2008. *Spirits and Letters: Reading, Writing and Charisma in African Christianity.* New York: Berghahn Books.

Knott, K. 2005. *The Location of Religion: A Spatial Analysis.* Sheffield: Equinox.

Koolhaas, R. 2001. Harvard Project on the City, Lagos. In *Mutations*, eds. R. Koolhaas, S. Boeri, S. Kwinter, N. Tazi, and H. U. Obrist, 650–720. Barcelona: Actar.

2002. Fragments of a Lecture on Lagos. In *Under Siege: Four African Cities: Freetown, Johannesburg, Kinshasa, Lagos. Documenta 11_Platform* 4, eds. O. Enwezor et al., 173–83. Ostfilderns-Ruit: Hatje Cantz Publishers.

Laguda, D.-O. 2010. 'Pentecostalism' and African Religious Movements in the 21st Century: A Case Study of Indigenous Faith of Africa, Ijo Orunmila. *Journal of Oriental and African Studies* 19: 191–205.

2015. African Religious Movements and Pentecostalism: The Model of Ijo-Orunmila, Ato. In *Contemporary Perspectives on Religions in Africa and the African Diaspora*, eds. I. S. Aderibigbe and C. M. Jones Medine, 49–59. Basingstoke: Palgrave Macmillan.

Laitin, D. D. 1986. *Hegemony and Culture: Politics and Religious Change among the Yoruba.* Chicago, IL: University of Chicago Press.

Lambek, M. 2008. Provincializing God? Provocations from an Anthropology of Religion. In *Religion: Beyond a Concept*, ed. H. de Vries, 120–38. New York: Fordham University Press.

Lambertz, P. 2018. *Seekers and Things: Spiritual Movements and Aesthetic Difference in Kinshasa.* New York and Oxford: Berghahn Books.

Langewiesche, K. 2011. Funerals and Religious Pluralism in Burkina Faso. In *Funerals in Africa: Explorations of a Social Phenomenon*, eds. M. Jindra and J. Noret, 130–53. New York and Oxford: Berghahn Books.

Lanz, S. 2013. Assembling Global Prayers in the City: An Attempt to Repopulate Urban Theory with Religion. In *Global Prayers: Contemporary Manifestations of the Religious in the City*, eds. J. Becker, K. Klingan, S. Lanz, and K. Wildner, 17–43. Zurich: Lars Müller Publishers.

Lanz, S. and M. Oosterbaan. 2016. Entrepreneurial Religion in the Age of Neoliberal Urbanism. *International Journal of Urban and Regional Research* 40 (3): 487–506.

Larkin, B. 2008a. *Signal and Noise: Media, Infrastructure, and Urban Culture in Nigeria.* Durham, NC: Duke University Press.

2008b. Ahmed Deedat and the Form of Islamic Evangelism. *Social Text* 26 (3): 101–21.

2016. Entangled Religions: Response to J. D. Y. Peel. *Africa: Journal of the International African Institute* 86 (4): 633–9.

Larkin, B. and B. Meyer. 2006. Pentecostalism, Islam and Culture: New Religious Movements in West Africa. In *Themes in West Africa's History*, ed. E. K. Akyeampong, 286–312. Oxford: James Currey.

Last, M. 1967. *The Sokoto Caliphate.* London: Longmans.

2007. Muslims and Christians in Nigeria: An Economy of Political Panic. *The Round Table: The Commonwealth Journal of International Affairs* 96 (392): 605–16.

2014. From Dissent to Dissidence: The Genesis and Development of Reformist Islamic Groups in Northern Nigeria. In *Sects & Social Disorder: Muslim Identities & Conflict in Northern Nigeria*, ed. A. R. Mustapha, 18–53. Oxford: James Currey.

Launay, R. 2004 [1992]. *Beyond the Stream: Islam and Society in a West African Town*. Long Grove, IL: Waveland Press.

Lentz, C. 2016. African Middle Classes: Lessons from Transnational Studies and a Research Agenda. In *The Rise of Africa's Middle Class*, ed. H. Melber, 17–53. London: Zed Books.

Leopold, A. M. and J. S. Jensen. 2004. General Introduction. In *Syncretism in Religion: A Reader*, eds. A. M. Leopold and J. S. Jensen, 2–13. New York: Routledge.

Lévi-Strauss, C. 1966. *The Savage Mind*. Oxford: Oxford University Press.

Liotta, P. H. and J. F. Miskel. 2012. *The Real Population Bomb: Megacities, Global Security & the Map of the Future*. Dulles, VA: Potomac.

Loimeier, R. 1997. *Islamic Reform and Political Change in Northern Nigeria*. Evanston, IL: Northwestern University Press.

2005. Is There Something Like 'Protestant Islam?' *Die Welt des Islams* 45 (2): 216–54.

2007. Nigeria: The Quest for a Viable Religious Option. In *Political Islam in West Africa: State–Society Relations Transformed*, ed. W. F. S. Miles, 43–72. Boulder, CO: Lynne Rienner Publishers.

2016. Why Do We Compare and What Can We Compare? The Comparison of Religions and Its Traps. Unpublished paper presented at the Summer School Christians and Muslims in Africa: Towards a Framework for the Study of Multi-Religious Settings, convened by B. Meyer, A. Sounaye, M. Janson, and K. Kresse, ZMO, Berlin, 14–20 July.

Louveau, F. 2012. *Un prophétisme japonais en Afrique de l'Ouest. Anthropologie religieuse de Sukyo Mahikari (Bénin, Côte d'Ivoire, Sénégal, France) [A Japanese Prophecy in West Africa. Religious Anthropology by Sukyo Mahikari (Benin, Côte d'Ivoire, Senegal, France)]*. Paris: Karthala.

Luhrmann, T. M. 2004. Metakinesis: How God Becomes Intimate in Contemporary U.S. Christianity. *American Ethnologist* 106 (3): 518–28.

2012. *When God Talks Back: Understanding the American Evangelical Relationship with God*. New York: Alfred A. Knopf.

Macamo, E. 2018. Urbane Scholarship: Studying Africa, Understanding the World. *Africa: Journal of the International African Institute* 88 (1): 1–10.

MacGaffey, W. 1983. *Modern Kongo Prophets: Religion in a Plural Society*. Bloomington: Indiana University Press.

Mahmood, S. 2005. *Politics of Piety: The Islamic Revival and the Feminist Subject*. Princeton, NJ: Princeton University Press.

Malinowski, B. 1948. *Magic, Science and Religion and Other Essays*. Boston, MA: Beacon Press.

Marcus, G. E. and D. Cushman. 1982. Ethnographies as Texts. *Annual Review of Anthropology* 11 (1): 25–69.

Marcus, G. E. and E. Saka. 2006. Assemblage. *Theory, Culture & Society* 23 (2–3): 101–9.

Marsden, M. 2005. *Living Islam: Muslim Religious Experience in Pakistan's North-West Frontier*. Cambridge: Cambridge University Press.

Marshall, R. 2009. *Political Spiritualities: The Pentecostal Revolution in Nigeria*. Chicago, IL: University of Chicago Press.

2014. 'Dealing with the Prince over Lagos': Pentecostal Arts of Citizenship. In *The Arts of Citizenship in African Cities: Infrastructures and Spaces of Belonging*, eds. M. Diouf and R. Fredericks, 91–114. New York: Palgrave Macmillan.

Marshall-Fratani, R. 1993. 'Power in the Name of Jesus': Social Transformation and Pentecostalism in Western Nigeria Revisited. In *Legitimacy and the State in Twentieth-Century Africa*, eds. T. Ranger and O. Vaughan, 213–46. Basingstoke: Macmillan.

Mary, A. 2005. Métissage and Bricolage in the Making of African Christian Identities. *Social Compass* 52 (3): 281–94.

Masquelier, A. 2001. *Prayer Has Spoiled Everything: Possession, Power, and Identity in an Islamic Town of Niger*. Durham, NC: Duke University Press.

2009. *Women and Islamic Revival in a West African Town*. Bloomington: Indiana University Press.

2019. *Fada: Boredom and Belonging in Niger*. Chicago, IL and London: University of Chicago Press.

Masuzawa, T. 2005. *The Invention of World Religions: Or, How European Universalism Was Preserved in the Language of Pluralism*. Chicago, IL: University of Chicago Press.

Matory, J. L. 2005. *Black Atlantic Religion: Tradition, Transnationalism, and Matriarchy in the Afro-Brazilian Candomblé*. Princeton, NJ: Princeton University Press.

Mbembe, A. 2016. Decolonizing the University: New Directions. *Arts and Humanities in Higher Education* 15 (1): 29–45.

Mbembe, A. and S. Nuttall. 2004. Writing the World from an African Metropolis. *Public Culture* 16 (3): 347–72.

Mbiti, J. S. 1969. *African Religions and Philosophy*. London: Heinemann.

McFarlane, C. and B. Anderson. 2011. Thinking with Assemblage. *Area* 43 (2): 162–4.

McGuire, M. B. 2008a. *Lived Religion: Faith and Practice in Everyday Life*. New York: Oxford University Press.

2008b. Toward a Sociology of Spirituality: Individual Religion in Social/Historical Context. In *The Centrality of Religion in Social Life. Essays in Honour of James A. Beckford*, ed. E. Barker, 215–32. Aldershot: Ashgate.

McIntosh, J. 2009. *The Edge of Islam: Power, Personhood, and Ethnoreligious Boundaries on the Kenya Coast*. Durham, NC: Duke University Press.

2019. Polyontologism: When 'Syncretism' Does Not Suffice. *Journal of Africana Religions* 7 (1): 112–20.

Meager, K. 2010. *Identity Economics: Social Networks & the Informal Economy in Nigeria*. Woodbridge: James Currey.

Melber, H. 2016. 'Somewhere above Poor but below Rich': Explorations into the Species of the African Middle Class(es). In *The Rise of Africa's Middle Class*, ed. H. Melber, 1–16. London: Zed Books.

Meyer, B. 1994. Beyond Syncretism. In *Syncretism/Anti-Syncretism: The Politics of Religious Synthesis*, eds. C. Stewart and R. Shaw, 45–68. London: Routledge.

—— 1998. 'Make a Complete Break with the Past'. Memory and Post-colonial Modernity in Ghanaian Pentecostalist Discourse. *Journal of Religion in Africa* 28 (3): 316–49.

—— 2004. Christianity in Africa: From African Independent to Pentecostal-Charismatic Churches. *Annual Review of Anthropology* 33: 447–74.

—— 2009. Introduction: From Imagined Communities to Aesthetic Formations: Religious Mediations, Sensational Forms, and Styles of Binding. In *Aesthetic Formations: Media, Religion, and the Senses*, ed. B. Meyer, 1–28. New York: Palgrave Macmillan.

—— 2012. Mediation and the Genesis of Presence: Towards a Material Approach to Religion. Inaugural Lecture, Utrecht University.

—— 2015. *Sensational Movies: Video, Vision, and Christianity in Ghana*. Oakland: University of California Press.

—— 2018. *Studying Religion in and from Africa*. Keynote lecture delivered at the joint Centre for African Studies and Centre for Religion and Public Life Research Seminar, University of Leeds, 25 January.

Miller, C. L. 1990. Orality through Literacy: Mande Verbal Art after the Letter. In *Theories of Africans: Francophone Literature and Anthropology in Africa*, ed. C. L. Miller, 68–113. Chicago, IL: University of Chicago Press.

Momoh, A. 2000. Youth Culture and Area Boys in Lagos. In *Identity Transformation and Identity Politics under Structural Adjustment in Nigeria*, ed. A. Jega, 181–203. Uppsala: Nordiska Afrikainstitutet, in collaboration with the Centre for Research and Documentation, Kano.

Morgan, D., ed. 2010. *Religion and Material Culture: The Matter of Belief*. London and New York: Routledge.

Mudimbe, V. W. 1988. *The Invention of Africa: Gnosis, Philosophy and the Order of Knowledge*. Bloomington: Indiana University Press.

Mustapha, A. R. 2014. Understanding *Boko Haram*. In *Sects & Social Disorder: Muslim Identities & Conflict in Northern Nigeria*, ed. A. R. Mustapha, 147–98. Oxford: James Currey.

Mwakimako, H. 2007. Christian–Muslim Relations in Kenya: A Catalogue of Events and Meanings. *Islam and Christian–Muslim Relations* 18 (2): 287–307.

Nas, P. J. M. and A. Samuels. 2006. *Hypercity: The Symbolic Side of Urbanism*. London: Kegan Paul.

Nolte, I. 2007. Ethnic Vigilantes and the State: The Oodua People's Congress in South-Western Nigeria. *International Relations* 21 (2): 217–35.

Nolte, I. and N. Danjibo and O. Abubakar. 2010. Religion, Politics and Governance in Nigeria. *Religions and Development Working Paper* No 39, published by the International Development Department of the University of Birmingham for the Department for International Development (DfID).

Nolte, I. and T. Akinjobi. 2017. Marrying Out: Gender and Religious Mediation in Interfaith Marriages. In *Beyond Religious Tolerance: Muslims, Christians, and Traditionalists in an African Town*, eds. I. Nolte, O. Ogen, and R. Jones, 207–26. Woodbridge: James Currey.

Nolte, I. and O. Ogen. 2017. Beyond Religious Tolerance: Muslims, Christians and Traditionalists in a Yoruba Town. In *Beyond Religious Tolerance: Muslims, Christians, and Traditionalists in an African Town*, eds. I. Nolte, O. Ogen, and R. Jones, 1–30. Woodbridge: James Currey.

Nuttall, S. 2009. *Entanglement: Literary and Cultural Reflections on Post-Apartheid*. Johannesburg: Wits University Press.

Obadare, E. 2006. Pentecostal Presidency? The Lagos-Ibadan 'Theocratic Class' and the Muslim 'Other' in Nigeria. *Review of African Political Economy* 33 (110): 655–78.

2016. The Muslim Response to the Pentecostal Surge in Nigeria: Prayer and the Rise of Charismatic Islam. *Journal of Religious and Political Practice* 2 (1): 75–91.

2018. *Pentecostal Republic: Religion and the Struggle for State Power in Nigeria*. London: Zed Books, in association with International African Institute, Royal African Society, and World Peace Foundation.

Ojo, M. A. 1988. The Contextual Significance of Charismatic Movements in Independent Nigeria. *Africa: Journal of the International African Institute* 58: 172–92.

Olupona, J. K. 2011. *City of 201 Gods: Ilé-Ifè in Time, Space, and the Imagination*. Berkeley: University of California Press.

2016. *Odù Imole*. Islamic Tradition in *Ifá* and the Yorùbá Religious Imagination. In *Ifá Divination, Knowledge, Power, and Performance*, eds. J. K. Olupona and R. O. Abiodun, 168–78. Bloomington: Indiana University Press.

Olupona, J. K. and T. Rey. 2008. Introduction. In *Orisa Devotion as World Religion: The Globalization of Yoruba Religious Culture*, eds. J. K. Olupona and T. Rey, 3–28. Madison: The University of Wisconsin Press.

Omezi, G. 2014. Nigerian Modernity and the City: Lagos 1960–1980. In *The Arts of Citizenship in African Cities: Infrastructures and Spaces of Belonging*, eds. M. Diouf and R. Fredericks, 277–95. New York: Palgrave Macmillan.

Onuoha, G. 2011. 'Exit' and 'Inclusion': The Changing Paradigm of Pentecostal Expression in the Nigerian Public Space. In *Topographies of Faith: Religion in the Urban Space*, eds. I. Becci, M. Burchardt, and J. Casanova, 207–25. Leiden: Brill.

Orsi, R. A. 2012. Introduction. In *The Cambridge Companion to Religious Studies*, ed. R. A. Orsi, 1–13. Cambridge: Cambridge University Press.

Osaghae, E. 1998. *Crippled Giant: Nigeria since Independence*. London: Hurst.

Ottenberg, S. 1984. Two New Religions, One Analytic Frame. *Cahiers d'Études Africaines* 24 (96): 437–54.

Oyeweso, S. 2017. Kingship and Religion: An Introduction to the History of Ede. In *Beyond Religious Tolerance: Muslims, Christians, and Traditionalists in an African Town*, eds. I. Nolte, O. Ogen, and R. Jones, 31–55. Woodbridge: James Currey.

Palmié, S. 2006. Creolization and Its Discontents. *Annual Review of Anthropology* 35: 433–56.

Parkin, D. 1970. Politics of Ritual Syncretism: Islam among the Non-Muslim Giriama of Kenya. *Africa: Journal of the International African Institute* 40 (3): 217–33.

Parrinder, G. E. 1954. *African Traditional Religion*. London: Hutchinson.

Peel, J. D. Y. 1968. *Aladura: A Religious Movement among the Yoruba*. London: Oxford University Press.

1978. *Ọlaju*: A Yoruba Concept of Development. *The Journal of Development Studies* 14 (2): 139–65.

1990. The Pastor and the *Babalawo*: The Encounter of Religions in Nineteenth-Century Yorubaland. *Africa: Journal of the International African Institute* 60 (3): 338–69.

2000. *Religious Encounter and the Making of the Yoruba*. Bloomington: Indiana University Press.

2011. Un siècle d'interactions entre islam et christianisme dans l'espace Yoruba [A Century of Interactions between Islam and Christianity in the Yoruba Space], translated by R. Botiveau. *Politique africaine* 3: 27–50.

2016a. *Christianity, Islam, and Orişa Religion: Three Traditions in Comparison and Interaction*. Oakland: University of California Press.

2016b. Similarity and Difference, Context and Tradition, in Contemporary Religious Movements in West Africa. *Africa: Journal of the International African Institute* 86 (4): 620–7.

Pieterse, E. 2011. Grasping the Unknowable: Coming to Grips with African Urbanisms. *Social Dynamics: A Journal of African Studies* 37 (1): 5–23.

Piot, C. 2010. *Nostalgia for the Future: West Africa after the Cold War*. Chicago, IL: University of Chicago Press.

Premawardhana, D. 2018. *Faith in Flux: Pentecostalism and Mobility in Rural Mozambique*. Philadelphia: University of Pennsylvania Press.

Probst, P. 2011. *Osogbo and the Art of Heritage*. Bloomington: Indiana University Press.

Ranger, T. 2002. African Traditional Religion. In *The World's Religions: The Study of Religion, Traditional and New Religion*, eds. S. Sutherland and P. Clarke, 106–14. London: Routledge.

Reichmuth, S. 1996. Education and the Growth of Religious Associations among Yoruba Muslims: The Ansar-Ud-Deen Society of Nigeria. *Journal of Religion in Africa* 26 (4): 365–405.

Riesebrodt, M. 2010. *The Promise of Salvation. A Theory of Religion*, translated by S. Rendall. Chicago, IL: University of Chicago Press.

Robbins, J. 2007. Continuity Thinking and the Problem of Christian Culture: Belief, Time, and the Anthropology of Christianity. *Current Anthropology* 48 (1): 5–38.

2013. Beyond the Suffering Subject: Toward an Anthropology of the Good. *Journal of the Royal Anthropological Institute* 19 (3): 447–62.

Robbins, T. 2001. Introduction: Alternative Religions, the State, and the Globe. *Nova Religio: The Journal of Alternative and Emergent Religions* 4 (2): 172–86.

Rohregger, B. 2009. 'Church Shopping' in Malawi: Acquiring Multiple Resources in Urban Christian Networks. In *Social Security in Religious Networks: Anthropological Perspectives on New Risks and Ambivalences*, eds. C. Leutloff-Grandits, A. Peleikis, and T. Thelen, 146–63. New York: Berghahn Books.

Rudnyckyj, D. 2010. *Spiritual Economies: Islam, Globalization, and the Afterlife of Development*. Ithaca, NY and London: Cornell University Press.

Ryan, P. J. 2006. In My End Is My Beginning: Muslim and Christian Traditions at Cross-Purposes in Contemporary Nigeria. In *Muslim–Christian Encounters in Africa*, ed. B. F. Soares, 187–220. Leiden: Brill.

Sanneh, L. O. 1975. The Christian–Muslim Encounter in Africa. In *African Challenge*, ed. K. Best, 101–10. Nairobi: Transafrica Publishers.

1989. *Translating the Message: The Missionary Impact on Culture*. Maryknoll, NY: Orbis Books.

Sanni, A. 2004. *Muslim Youth Prayer Movements: A Signpost to Islamic Pentecostalism in Nigeria?* Unpublished paper presented at the African Association for the Study of Religions Regional Conference, University of Legon, Ghana, 5–8 February.

2012. Conversion and Reversion in the Power Accession Narrative: Muslim Prayer Groups in Nigeria. *Journal of Oriental and African Studies* 21: 157–66.

Sassen, S. 2006. *Territory, Authority, Rights: From Medieval to Global Assemblages*. Princeton, NJ: Princeton University Press.

Schielke, S. and L. Debevec. 2012. Introduction. In *Ordinary Lives and Grand Schemes. An Anthropology of Everyday Religion*, eds. S. Schielke and L. Debevec, 1–16. New York: Berghahn Books.

Schneider, A. 2003. On 'Appropriation'. A Critical Reappraisal of the Concept and its Application in Global Art Practices. *Social Anthropology* 11 (2): 215–29.

Schulz, D. E. 2012. *Muslims and New Media in West Africa: Pathways to God*. Bloomington: Indiana University Press.

Shankar, S. 2014. *Who Shall Enter Paradise: Christian Origins in Muslim Northern Nigeria, ca. 1890–1975*. Athens: Ohio University Press.

Shaw, R. 1990. The Invention of 'African Traditional Religion'. *Religion* 20: 339–53.

Shaw, R. and C. Stewart. 1994. Introduction: Problematizing Syncretism. In *Syncretism/Anti-Syncretism: The Politics of Religious Synthesis*, eds. C. Stewart and R. Shaw, 1–26. London: Routledge.

Silverstein, M. and G. Urban, eds. 1996. *Natural Histories of Discourse*. Chicago, IL: University of Chicago Press.

Simone, A. 2004. *For the City Yet to Come: Changing Life in Four Cities*. Durham, NC: Duke University Press.

Smith, D. 2007. *A Culture of Corruption: Everyday Deception and Popular Discontent in Nigeria*. Princeton, NJ: Princeton University Press.

Smith, J. Z. 1998. Religion, Religions, Religious. In *Critical Terms for Religious Studies*, ed. M. C. Taylor, 269–84. Chicago, IL: University of Chicago Press.

Smith, W. C. 1962. *The Meaning and End of Religion*. New York: New America Library.

Soares, B. F. 2005. *Islam and the Prayer Economy: History and Authority in a Malian Town*. Edinburgh: Edinburgh University Press.

2006. Introduction: Muslim–Christian Encounters in Africa. In *Muslim–Christian Encounters in Africa*, ed. B. F. Soares, 1–16. Leiden: Brill.

2009. An Islamic Social Movement in Contemporary West Africa: NASFAT of Nigeria. In *Movers and Shakers: Social Movements in Africa*, eds. S. Ellis and I. van Kessel, 178–96. Leiden: Brill.

2016. Reflections on Muslim–Christian Encounters in West Africa. *Africa: Journal of the International African Institute* 86 (4): 673–97.

Spies, E. 2013. Coping with Religious Diversity: Incommensurability and Other Perspectives. In *A Companion to the Anthropology of Religion*, eds. J. Boddy and M. Lambek, 118–36. Chichester: Wiley-Blackwell.

2019. Being in Relation: A Critical Appraisal of Religious Diversity and Mission Encounter in Madagascar. *Journal of Africana Religions* 7 (1): 62–83.

Spronk, R. 2014. Exploring the Middle Classes in Nairobi: From Modes of Production to Modes of Sophistication. *African Studies Review* 57 (1): 93–114.

Stark, R. 1999. Atheism, Faith, and the Social Scientific Study of Religion. *Journal of Contemporary Religion* 14 (1): 41–62.

Stewart, C. 1999. Syncretism and Its Synonyms: Reflections on Cultural Mixture. *Diacritics* 29: 40–62.

Taiwo, O. 2008. Òrìṣà: A Prolegomenon to a Philosophy of Yorùbá Religion. In *Orisa Devotion as World Religion: The Globalization of Yoruba Religious Culture*, eds. J. K. Olupona and T. Rey, 84–105. Madison: University of Wisconsin Press.

Taylor, C. 2007. *A Secular Age*. Cambridge, MA: Harvard University Press.

Tayob, A. 2018. Decolonizing the Study of Religions: Muslim Intellectuals and the Enlightenment Project of Religious Studies. *Journal for the Study of Religion* 31 (2): 7–35.

Thurston, A. 2016 'The Disease is Unbelief': Boko Haram's Religious and Political Worldview. Analysis Paper 22. Washington, DC: Brookings Project on US Relations with the Islamic World.

Travisano, R. 1981. Alternation and Conversion as Qualitatively Different Transformations. In *Social Psychology through Symbolic Interaction*, eds. G. Stone and H. Faberman, 237–48. New York: Wiley.

Trovalla, E. and U. Trovalla. 2015. Infrastructure as a Divination Tool: Whispers from the Grids in a Nigerian City. *City* 19 (2–3): 332–43.

Turner, H. W. 1979. *Religious Innovation in Africa: Collected Essays on New Religious Movements*. Boston, MA: G. K. Hall.

Ukah, A. 2013. Redeeming Urban Spaces: The Ambivalences of Building a Pentecostal City in Lagos, Nigeria. In *Global Prayers: Contemporary Manifestations of the Religious in the City*, eds. J. Becker, K. Klingan, S. Lanz, and K. Wildner, 178–97. Berlin: Lars Müller Publishers.

2016. Building God's City: The Political Economy of Prayer Camps in Nigeria. *International Journal of Urban and Regional Research* 40 (3): 524–40.

Umar, M. S. 2001. Education and Islamic Trends in Northern Nigeria: 1970s–1990s. *Africa Today* 48 (2): 127–50.

van Dijk, R. 2013. Counselling and Pentecostal Modalities of Social Engineering of Relationships in Botswana. *Culture, Health and Sexuality* 15 (4): 509–22.

2015. After Pentecostalism? Exploring Intellectualism, Secularization and Guiding Sentiments in Africa. In *Multiple Secularities beyond the West:*

Religion and Modernity in the Global Age, eds. M. Burchardt, M. Wohlrab-Sahr, and M. Middell, 216–38. Boston, MA, Berlin, and Munich: De Gruyter.
van de Port, M. 2011. *Ecstatic Encounters: Bahian Candomblé and the Quest for the Really Real*. Amsterdam: Amsterdam University Press.
van der Veer, P. 2008. Spirituality in Modern Society. In *Religion: Beyond a Concept*, ed. H. de Vries, 789–97. New York: Fordham University Press.
2016. *The Value of Comparison*. Durham, NC: Duke University Press.
van Klinken, A. 2020. Studying Religion in the Pluriversity: Decolonial Perspectives. *Religion* 50 (1): 148–55.
Vásquez, M. A. 2011. *More than Belief. A Materialist Theory of Religion*. Oxford and New York: Oxford University Press.
Vaughan, O. 2016. *Religion and the Making of Nigeria*. Durham, NC: Duke University Press.
Venn, C. 2006. A Note on Assemblage. *Theory, Culture & Society* 23 (2–3): 107–8.
Vertovec, S. 2007. Super-Diversity and Its Implications. *Ethnic and Racial Studies* 29: 1024–54.
Vigh, H. 2009. Motion Squared: A Second Look at the Concept of Social Navigation. *Anthropological Theory* 9 (4): 419–38.
Wariboko, N. 2014. *Nigerian Pentecostalism*. Rochester, NY: University of Rochester Press.
Weber, M. 1930 [1905] *The Protestant Ethic and the Spirit of Capitalism*. London: George Allen and Unwin.
Werbner, R. 2018. Grassroots Ecumenism in Conflict – Introduction. *Journal of Southern African Studies* 44 (2): 201–19.
Wise, J. M. 2005. Assemblage. In *Gilles Deleuze: Key Concepts*, ed. C. J. Stivale, 77–87. Montreal: McGill-Queen's University Press.
Wuaku, A. K. 2013. *Hindu Gods in West Africa: Ghanaian Devotees of Shiva and Krishna*. Leiden: Brill.
Young, C. 2004. The End of the Postcolonial State in Africa? Reflections on Changing African Political Dynamics. *African Affairs* 103: 23–49.
Zink, J. 2012. 'Anglocostalism' in Nigeria: Neo-Pentecostalism and Obstacles to Anglican Unity. *Journal of Anglican Studies* 10 (2): 231–50.

Other Sources

N. A. *Eckankar: Ancient Wisdom for Today*. Minneapolis, MN: Eckankar.
Abd-Ru-Shin. 1990 [1926]. *In the Light of Truth: The Grail Message*. Stuttgart: Stiftung Gralsbotschaft.
Abdul-Ganiyu, M. 2006. *Timeless Wisdom for Modern Managers: Leadership Strategies of Prophet Muhammad*. Ibadan: Emgee Books.
Adichie, C. N. 2019. Still Becoming: At Home in Lagos with Chimamanda Ngozi Adichie, *Esquire*, 29 April, www.esquire.com/uk/culture/a27283913/still-becoming-at-home-in-lagos-withchimamanda-ngozi-adichie/.
African Development Bank. 2012. *Annual Development Effectiveness Review 2012. Growing African Economies Inclusively*. Tunis: African Development Bank.

Bello, M. A. 2007. *Meeting Heart Desires: A Concise Discourse on Faith and Spiritual Consultancy*. Lagos: Crucial Press.

2010a. *Conquering Your Enemy*. Lagos: Aliyy Education Foundation.

2010b. *Towards a Blissful Married Life: Reflections of an Islamicist*. Lagos: Aliyy Education Foundation.

Human Development Report. 2006. New York: UNDP.

Lane, D. 1978. *The Making of a Spiritual Movement: The Untold Story of Paul Twitchell and Eckankar*. Del Mar, CA: Del Mar Press.

NASFAT Society. 2005. *Code of Conduct*. Lagos.

2006. *Prayer Book*. Lagos.

2011. *Constitution*. Lagos.

Noko, E. J. 2016. *Economic Recession in Nigeria: Causes and Solutions*. http://educacinfo.com/economic-recession-nigeria/.

Nolen, S. 1999. Give them Jesus, but Hold the Theology. *Globe and Mail*, 2 January: A1, A6.

Olusina, O. 2012. Nigeria: The Long Road to Renewing Lagos–Ibadan Expressway, 29 January, https://allafrica.com/stories/201201301120.html.

Onuzo, C. 2017. *Welcome to Lagos*. London: Faber & Faber.

Packer, G. 2006. The Megacity: Decoding the Chaos of Lagos. *The New Yorker*, November: 62–75. www.newyorker.com/magazine/2006/11/13/the-megacity.

Population Census of Nigeria. 1963. Combined National Figures, Volume III. Lagos: Office of Statistics.

Shekoni, N. A. 2012. *Prayer Digest (Believer's Sword) … Ida Mumeen*. Series One and Two. Lagos.

Twitchell, P. 2013 [1970]. *Shariyat-Ki-Sugmad*. Books One & Two. Minneapolis, MN: Eckankar.

UNCHS. 1996. *An Urbanising World, Global Report on Human Settlements*. Nairobi: Oxford University Press.

UN-Habitat. 2010. *The State of African Cities 2010: Governance, Inequality and Urban Land Markets*. Nairobi: United Nations Human Settlements Habitat.

Yusuf, J. 2005. *Falsafatul-Ikhiwa* [The Philosophy of Brotherhood]. Lagos

Websites

www.cfr.org/nigeria/nigeria-securitytracker/p29483

www.citifmonline.com/2014/09/nigerias-superstar-men-of-god/

www.eckankar.org

www.facebook.com/ademola.ifabunmi?__tn__=%2CdK-R-R&eid=ARAZqkYQrAzFbX6BPdSNES0duNnUGOoj45pG7EWq_iDFlXnkLtrBHPgtfzH2Tw2CQ3FTTgebs2yx0A4m&fref=mentions

www.facebook.com/groups/297672903678845/

www.facebook.com/NASFAT.WORLDWIDE/

www.fltfilms.org.uk/

www.gallup-international.bg/en/Publications/2017/373-Religion-prevails-in-the-world

www.grail-message.com

www.grailnet.info/english/grailland.html

http://ifeoluwamission.org/
http://ifeoluwamission.org/press/ifeoluwa-heals-the-world-covid-19/?fbclid=
    IwAR1B4685HL3thP-gA1JnDcvo4v1sgWSxsEqngqj5_
    7ghzNMeua1XoQ2XrDM
www.imcnigeria.org
www.nasfat.org/
http://nasfat.org/acceptance-speech-by-president-niyi-yusuf-sunday-oct-20-
    2019/
www.news.bbc.co.uk/1/hi/world/africa/1802175.stm
www.pmnewsnigeria.com/2015/07/13/buhari-to-end-fg-sponsorship-of-
    pilgrimage/
www.twitter.com/hashtag/nasfat
www.vanguardngr.com/2017/04/lagos-raises-alarm-increasing-rate-suicide/
www.vanguardngr.com/2018/02/lagos-preservation-yoruba-language/
https://widerimage.reuters.com/photographer/akintunde-akinleye http://www.
    youtube.com/watch?v=6mWcjrMcTsg
https://yorubawunmi.webs.com/

Index

Note: Page numbers followed by n indicate a footnote with relevant number and those in italic indicate illustrations.

Titles in The Series

CPSIA information can be obtained
at www.ICGtesting.com
Printed in the USA
BVHW051942210223
658948BV00012B/192